WINDOWS OF THE IMAGINATION

DARRELL SCHWEITZER

COVER ART BY
DAN CAMPBELL

For Alex —
best wishes,
Darrell Schweitzer

Wildside Press
Berkeley Heights, NJ · 1999

WINDOWS OF THE IMAGINATION

Published by:

Wildside Press
PO Box 45
Gillette, NJ 07933-0045

ISBN: 1-880448-60-9

CONTENTS

INTRODUCTION

NOTES FROM NOTES FROM BEYOND THE FIELDS WE KNOW

Here's a collection of nonfiction pieces, published in magazines over the years, which I think you might enjoy. Perhaps I need say no more by way of introduction.

But I might mention further that I had an essay I was going to use, in a modified form, as an introduction. It was called "Notes from Beyond the Fields We Know," and was written for *Empire* about 1982 at the request of editor Joel Rosenberg. Joel asked me to explain what fantasy was all about and to present myself in that context, explaining what I'm all about as a fantasy writer. Only now, when I go back to reread that piece, I don't like it very much. Not only is it dated, with references which would seem opaque to the present-day reader, but I also find it narcissistic and self-serving.

No, this won't do. I never have been very good at autobiography.

So what we have here collected are expositions of ideas. They're things I find interesting or important, and hope you will too. While I hope you will find something to argue with in this book, there's nothing here which is intended to be offensive or which is even designed to smash all in its path and convert you to the One True Way.

Yet, I write this the afternoon after a woman stormed out of my writing class, almost in tears at the suggestion that "fantastic" experiences are culturally relative, and that a New Ager's paranormal experiences (which might involve finding one's spirit guide from Lost Atlantis) would not be the same as those of a nineteenth-century spiritualist (more likely the ghost of the late Aunt Millie), and neither would have much in common with the ancient Greek runner who saw and had a conversation with the god Pan on the road while bringing news of victory from Marathon to Athens. At issue was whether or not the character in the woman's story, which was set in a very different time and place, would have the same "experiences" a modern believer would.

"I've had lots of psychic experiences and I won't let you say I'm crazy!" she said on the way out, slamming the door behind her. (Actually, no one had made any such suggestion.)

I'm sure this lady would take deep offense at a couple of the pieces herein, particularly the first two.

Well, too bad. I don't apologize. Ideas bite sometimes. If you feel threatened by that sort of thing, read no further. You have been warned.

This whole book does, in a sense, accomplish what "Notes from Beyond the Fields We Know" set out to do. You should get some sense of who I am and what I write. I think of myself as primarily a fiction writer, a fantasy writer, who does other things on the side, although an objective examination of even my published work might suggest otherwise. Add up the numbers and I am a book-reviewer and critic and letter-writer and interviewer who writes fiction on the side, having published, at this count, thousands of nonfiction items, but a mere two hundred or so short stories and just three novels.

But most of my fiction—excepting a small number of science-fiction stories and, to date, two historical mysteries—is fantasy fiction, which, to me, means fiction which uses the factually-impossible for metaphorical or other artistic purposes. For me, the essence of fantasy is that it is made up. True-believers run into trouble at this point, as I explain at length in "The Necessity of Skepticism." The problem is that what may seem to you as *realism* is to me made-up, and if it can be made up one way, it can be turned around and made up another way. If you tell me a fantastic "true" yarn about an apparition you met aboard a UFO which revealed that Elvis killed the Kennedys, my response is, "I can do that too."

As my class exploded into a six-way argument, someone said, "Well, what about Nostradamus?" I responded, "Anyone can do that." I didn't have a chance to demonstrate, but here's a Quatrain in the Nostradamian tradition:

> The red bull and the white calf evade the eagle,
> Year six, seven, six, seven times three,
> While silence reins in the heavens.
> A great city shall be devoured.

This of course prophesies that London will be destroyed by Mad Cow Disease, or else that the Dodgers will return to Brooklyn. Either way, you read it here first. But of course the meaning will only be apparent *after* the event. Oracles have a way of screwing you like that.

Okay, sometimes I have a bad attitude. But it stems from my being a fantasy writer. I am someone who makes things up. It is my stock in trade. When someone comes to me with a fantastic anecdote, I look at it in a professional sense as pretty good, or not very imaginative, or just plain dull. I am in the position of James Randi watching Uri Geller do table-top parlor-tricks. *Yes*, Randi thinks. *I know how he does that. He's not even doing it very skillfully.*

So I am someone who makes things up. The essay "Notes from Beyond the Fields We Know," when it was not trying to rationalize away my lack of greater success or provide a potted history of literature from the fireside anecdotes of Og the Dawn Man up to the first stories of Darrell Schweitzer, did attempt to explore why we make things up and what we do with the material thus created. I had a juicy quote from Le Guin, from her seminal essay, "From Elfland to Poughkeepsie":

> ...its affinity is not with daydream, but with dream. It is a different approach to reality, an alternative technique for apprehending and coping with existence. It is not anti-rational, but para-rational; not realistic but surrealistic, super realistic, a heightening of reality. In Freud's terminology, it employs primary, not secondary process thinking. It employs archetypes, which, as Jung warned us, are dangerous things. Dragons are more dangerous, and a good deal commoner, than bears. Fantasy is nearer to poetry, to mysticism, and to insanity than naturalistic fiction is. It is a real wilderness, and those who go there should not feel too safe. Their guides, the writers of fantasy, should take their responsibilities seriously.

Always steal from the best. At least you demonstrate good taste. Le Guin has, of course, said it better than I ever could. "Not anti-rational," she says, and "nearer to mysticism." Well then, if I am to define who I am as a writer, I am someone who is intellectually in the *Skeptical Inquirer* camp, who knew and looked up to Isaac Asimov, an admirer of James Randi, Carl Sagan, and Sprague de Camp, who has devoted a good deal of his life to writing fantasy, and manages to do it without contradiction, without lapsing into belief.

I simply cannot manage the arrogance of the mystic, who says, "I possess special knowledge, which came to me by means other than reason or the senses, but which transcends the need for scientific proof." I can't do that. I have no special revelation. If I tell you that I believe that the Earth goes around the sun, and that I have personally checked,[1] I still don't ask you to take my word for it.

I have at times wondered whether or not writing fantasy contributes to the social malaise which Sagan describes in his last book, *The Demon-Haunted World*, whereby many Americans have simply set aside reason, have completely submerged themselves into magical thinking. We may one day find ourselves clutching our crystals as we freeze to death in the dark between food-riots, while the Japanese are colonizing Mars.

I'm not responsible for the Reality Impaired. My fiction is about something else. It do not find it inconsistent with reason in daily life, any more than I believe that Shakespeare had to believe in fairies to write *A Midsummer Night's Dream*. It's art, folks. Art takes the artist where it will. You might expect me to have become a hard-science fiction writer in the manner of Gregory Benford or Arthur C. Clarke, but it somehow didn't work out that way. My talents lay elsewhere. I could just as well be a rationalist and a pretty good abstract painter.

So here's the one good passage I'll quote from "Notes from Beyond the Fields We Know":

> ...keep your metaphysical speculations apart from day-to-day reality. A metaphor will not fix your car, nor will it clean up the atmosphere. I suspect that the intellectuals of late Roman times, for all their Neo-Platonisms, did not wait around for an archetypal, ideal litter to carry them to the neighbor's for dinner. They took an everyday one, borne by everyday bearers. At the same time, the ignorant looked for signs and omens, and they let such things run their lives. The difference is profound.

What I *am* suggesting is that we have become aware that the universe is vast, and not wholly and immediately comprehensible. Ignorance may be bliss, but it isn't very useful. In Classical times, as in the Middle Ages, or now, one finds three possible recourses: you can remain unaware. You can retreat into a belief system which provides all the answers in pre-digested form, thus precluding the need for further thought on the subject. Or you can go on thinking. This thinking may find literary expression in the special, figurative dreams we call fantasy, by which we are able to venture Beyond the Fields We Know.

So there. Enjoy the book. Watch for the sequel.

—Darrell Schweitzer
April 16, 1997

I.

THE NECESSITY OF SKEPTICISM

i.

My inspiration for this article comes from a variety of sources, but my first text for today's homily is taken from Martin Gardner's classic work, *Fads and Fallacies in the Name of Science*:

> ...As it is, psionics promises to be even funnier than dianetics or Ray Palmer's Shaver stories. It suggests how far from accurate is the stereotype of the science-fiction fan as a bright, well-informed, scientifically literate fellow. Judging by the number of [John W.] Campbell's readers who were impressed by this nonsense, the average fan may well be a chap in his teens, with a smattering of scientific knowledge mostly culled from science fiction, enormously gullible, with a strong bent toward occultism, no understanding of scientific method, and a basic insecurity for which he compensates by fantasies of scientific power.

Gardner wrote that in 1957 and it still hits home. I think that if he were writing it today, he might up the age of the average reader by a decade or so, and perhaps remove "scientific" from the last line, but otherwise the passage stands.

Onward. Cut to Balticon, 1988. I was on a panel there, entitled "Divination in Fantasy." I had asked to be on it and expected to add a touch of levity, since I had recently written a very silly article for *Twilight Zone* on "penniomancy," the occult art by which all Hidden Truths may be divined from the change you find on the street. (The meaning of life is forty-two, yes, about forty-two dollars a year.) I had written an even sillier and quite well-received story, "Pennies from Hell," for *TZ*'s companion, *Night Cry*. There is also a certain amount of prophecy and foretelling in my fiction, but usually more a matter of theolepsy—possession by the divine—than tea-leaf reading or whatever. So, I was ready to discourse.

But I found myself smack in the middle of the New Age, which of course is not new at all. New Age mysticism is no more than Stone Age mysticism, only it costs more. Your back-street palmist charges, what, fifteen dollars an hour? Shirley MacLaine charges *three hundred dollars an hour* to delve into your past lives, presumably telling the customer, "In your past life, before you came to see me, you were *much* wealthier..."

I was on a panel with a practicing diviner, a moderator who was certainly "soft" on this sort of thing, and an audience full of True Believers. I am sure I disappointed them. I hope I infuriated them.

I am not the best debater under these circumstances, but I tried. The problem was that no one else in the room had made any intellectual progress since around 2000 BC. The diviner spoke of the virtues of (yes!) tea-leaf reading and such things as Eskimo shamanism. Astrology was a science to her. There was no distinction between "mystical" and "rational" thought. Even for purposes of discussion the two could not be set up as opposites. I suggested that all you need for divination is *any form of seeming randomness*, to which you can assign any (suitably vague) meaning you like. You can imagine how far I got with that idea. And there was a woman just bursting to tell everyone about the novel she was writing about her past life as a priestess of (I think she said) Atlantis. This was certainly the audience for it...

This is one of the great Embarrassments of Science Fiction (and Fantasy), which Thomas Disch did not cover in his celebrated essay of that title.

I get the distinct feeling these days that rationalists are a minority in science-fiction fandom, possibly even among professional writers. I once saw an *Analog* writer give Tarot readings in all seriousness. I know a fan—a friend, someone I otherwise respect—who claims she can "prove by logic" that H. P. Lovecraft was writing Occult Truths which he received telepathically from "another dimension." The same lady was passing around what looked to me like a jade carving at a party. "Ooh, can you feel the *energy?*" she crooned. There was a lot of crooning in response. It never came to me, or I might not have been polite enough to avoid saying, "No I can't and neither do you. It's a piece of *rock.*"

Most people I know in fandom and out of it believe in (pick several) UFOs, telepathy, crisis apparitions, water-witching, faith-healing, assorted vaguely defined "occult powers" and "energies," ghosts, reincarnation, etc., etc., etc. Some of them half seriously believe in ouija-boards. I knew one person—again a friend, for whom I had an enormous amount of respect otherwise, a quite talented would-be science fiction writer—who spoke to a "spirit" on the ouija board regularly. I saw her do it once, in a trance, her eyes closed, the veins on her forehead bulging out, sweat running down her face, the pointer whirling around too fast for anyone else to know what it said. I think she had managed to tap into a part of her subconscious, as if she had temporarily called forth something like a secondary personality. But I am not an expert and can't tell you for sure. The experience *did* leave me with a powerful impression of the mind's awesome talent for self-deception.

Hugo Gernsback would have been appalled. Gone are the days when he could offer a "$10,000.00 spiritualism challenge" in one of his magazines and not get a deluge of angry letters.

It's not against any religion, as Tom Lehrer remarked on another subject entirely... I am not talking about religion at all here. If you believe in God or even Joseph Smith's version of American prehistory through faith, I have no right to dissuade you. That is your own business, and protected by the Constitution. It is only when you start claiming that these things are amenable to scientific proof that I will start to argue. I think someone should. Not many people do.

It's about time that we recognized the need for a little skepticism. This has gotten entirely out of hand. It can only be a kind of malaise when science-fiction and fantasy fans and writers no longer know what is real and what is made up. Since we are in the business of (or devote considerable time to the appreciation of) deliberately making things up, is it too much to suggest that absolutely unchallenged credulity is going to rot out the whole fabric of what we do?

ii.

I am a what those of the UFO faith call a "noisy negativist," that is to say, a skeptic. A skeptic is someone who demands that non-religious, fantastic claims be provable and that the burden of proof is on the claimant. Lots of people, particularly the insecure types Martin Gardner wrote of, find this attitude terribly offensive, bigoted, and narrow-minded. They are perfectly willing to have any number of occultists and mystics and obvious flim-flam artists make any number of fabulous claims, but if this is challenged, horrors! The arrogance of Established Science! *The Skeptical Inquirer* is held to be a nasty, "witch-hunting" journal published by Vested Interests who want to hide the truth.

Frankly, I think it is much *more* arrogant for an individual to claim to have intuited an unprovable truth, without methodical study of the external universe.

Real science requires humility. The whole of the Wisdom of the West is simply that reality is not a matter of human opinion. We were born into this world. We did not create it. The fossil record strongly suggests that it created us. (This does not preclude a creator God, who simply started the process.) Things are *true* or *not true*, but never both. If the answer doesn't seem as clear-cut as that, then you have asked the wrong question. But, during all the time mankind believed the Sun went around the Earth, the reverse continued to be true. Two hydrogens and one oxygen will always make a water molecule, whether you believe it or not. Reality, as someone put it, consists of the tumor you don't believe in killing you.

Wishing will not make it otherwise. Sorry. I am not responsible for this situation. We all dearly wish that we could be assured of survival beyond death, that we could have the marvelous power to send our thoughts through the air, that our loved ones would in fact love us so much that they come to us in spirit, for an instant as they die, just to say goodbye, or perhaps to impart some wisdom or give a warning.

But it may not be true, alas.

True/not true. On/off, like a switch. The universe works that way. The scientist is someone who goes out into that universe claiming no special knowledge, admitting he isn't responsible for this setup and doesn't even have the instruction manual, and *finds out what is there*. He must always be willing to change his views on the basis of new data or faulty interpretations of the old. Nobody believes in phlogiston anymore. Science can discard old notions. But occultism can't. So the only progress occultism has made over the past several millennia is reflected in Shirley MacLaine's $300-an-hour fees.

Let me give you a few of my skeptical positions. These are opinions, based on my layman's interpretations of the available evidence. A century hence, some of them may prove faulty. But I am demanding proof first.

1). I don't believe in psi of any kind—telepathy, telekinesis, PK, teleportation. I have gravest doubts about water-witching, which, if genuine, will probably have something to do with a hitherto unknown electrical sense. But I suspect that the reason that telepathy, for instance, is not amenable to laboratory conditions is simply that it *does not exist in nature*, that the mind does not have this capacity, and that all reported instances are faulty memory, wish-fulfillment, assorted tricks of perception, or lies.

On a panel recently (which I did not attend, but read about in the fanzine *FOSFAX*), a pro science-fiction writer asked why someone didn't do a genetic study for psi. I suggested (in the *FOSFAX* letter column) that the real reason is that there is no evidence that these powers exist. The *phenomenon* to be studied is that people claim to be telepathic. But since actual telepathy is not demonstrable the way, say, hemophilia is, it becomes very difficult to trace the genetics of telepathically-endowed people. You might as well try to find the gene for liars.

("Remarkably hard-headed, for a fantasy writer," Taras Wolansky commented, as if to say I was a Credit To My Race. Gee Mistah Wolansky, that's awfully white of you.)

2). While I take it as a given that there must be life elsewhere in the universe—although none elsewhere in the Solar System, it seems—the universe is an awfully big place. A spacefaring civilization 5,000 light years away, which ceased to exist 10,000 years ago, is *very close* on a cosmic scale of things. Even one in existence now, say, a thousand light years away, would have no reason to pick out our star as worthy of special notice.

In other words, I am completely unconvinced by UFO-logical visitations, whether they involved proctological operations on Whitley Strieber or not. (About which, more anon.) I have never seen a photograph or heard or read a testimony of a UFO witness which I have found the slightest bit believable. Most are based on obvious delusions or scientific ignorance. One thinks of George Adamski's photographs of clouds and forests on the far side of the moon. (Which caused me to formulate Schweitzer's Law of UFO Photography, which states that at a great distance, the photograph may be pretty good. But the quality of photography declines in proportion to the nearness of the saucer. If the UFO lands and an alien gets out, the photographer *always* forgets to take the lens cap off.)

As for physical evidence, it always conveniently disappears. I believe that we are in the position of Aztecs trying to prove the existence of Spaniards. An Aztec who sees a Spanish galleon at a distance may not be believed. But sooner or later those Spaniards are going to land. Evidence will start to pile up, strange footprints, campfires, the impressions of a rowboat dragged onto a beach. Well, perhaps they were faked, say the skeptical Aztecs. Perhaps they were. But the question will be settled when an incontestably alien artifact turns up, such as a Spanish sword or helmet or musket. Or a dead Spaniard. Or, better yet, a live one. By the time Cortéz reached Mexico City, no one seriously doubted the existence of Spaniards.

This will doubtless upset the UFOs-are-hostile believers, who say, "Yes, and by then it will be too late!" To which I can only reply, "That is because I am a card-carrying member of T.H.E.M., Technical Hierarchy of Earthly Manipulations. We are the guys in the black suits you read so much about. So watch it."

I argue with UFO-logist friends that if only they would admit that their belief is a *religion*, that these miraculous visitors are akin to angels, and that the whole belief-system works on *faith* which interprets the alleged evidence the way medieval Christians interpreted relics, then I would stop arguing with them. But no, the UFO believers I know are not the mystical types. They think they're being scientific. I think the evidence is pretty shoddy.

And if you don't think it's a matter of faith, go hear the noted UFO-logist Stanton Friedman lecture sometime. I found it a rather disturbing experience, to be in a whole auditorium filled with people who were *crazy* in this particular aspect. The Rev. Friedman spent the first ten minutes of his lecture reassuring his flock that it was *all right* to believe in UFOs, that most people already did, but were being silenced by the dread "laughter curtain" of "orthodox" scientists, who are themselves a minority in the scientific community, since the evidence is "overwhelming." He then went on about the Roswell Incident, the alleged saucer crash in the late '40s, which was of course hushed up by President Truman. A slideshow included supposed letters from Truman, which didn't impress me for the very obvious reason that all you had to do was get a piece of presidential stationery and write whatever you want, then trace Truman's signature. Or, better yet, in a three-page letter, let the first (letterhead) and last (signature) pages be genuine, match the typeface, and write whatever you want on page two.

But the congregation lapped it up. At the informal cheese-and-crackers party afterwards, I met a variety of contactees and sightees (or, to use a more appropriately religious term, Witnesses). At one point in the course of a conversation I made a Möbius Strip out of a piece of paper to show what it was, and someone immediately came over and asked in all seriousness, "Are you working on time-travel too?"

I would suggest, to get back to the point I raised earlier, that a lot of these people would have fit right in at a science fiction convention.

3). I have my doubts about the sasquatch, the yeti, and the Loch Ness monster. The ape-critters have the annoying habit of never appearing in the fossil records. They seem to have had no forebears in the more recent strata from which the evidence is relatively complete. More than that, they don't seem to just die in the woods every once in a while. No bodies have turned up. The Loch Ness monster(s) presumably would represent a breeding population of something which *not once* has ever washed up dead. And, if they're air-breathers and there are a lot of big creatures in the loch, they should be seen far more often than they are.

This is a strictly yes/no, real/not real sort of question. Either they exist or they don't. There is no conclusive way to prove that they don't, of course, but I won't believe that they do until one turns up in a case in the Smithsonian, rather like the giant squid that's on display in the entrance hall near the giant elephant. There it is, in a case, minus tentacles, but still impressively large. A century ago people didn't believe in giant squids, but then this specimen was found and preserved.

4). Spiritualism, channelling, life-after-death? Wish-fulfillment, involving our deepest emotional needs and cravings.

5). Okay, how *about* fortune-telling? Well, I do recite the mystical occult cantrip, *see a penny, pick it up, all the day you're one cent richer*, but, seriously, I should think that if the occult sages of yore were able to see the future, they wouldn't have ended their lives in such wretched muddles as did Cagliostro, Dr. John Dee, or Aleister Crowley. Sorry, folks. More wish-fulfillment and lots of financially motivated fraud. It's a game as old as mankind, and no more convincing now than it was two thousand years ago. I recall the comment of Cicero, who said he couldn't understand how two augurs could pass each other in the street without breaking up laughing. (Augurs were the official diviners of the Roman Republic, often wont to declaring the omens inauspicious and closing down senate sessions when things were going against the interests of the aristocratic class.)

6). The same goes for spirit-journeys, curses, witchcraft in the magical as opposed to religious sense, raising the dead, demonic possession, or summoning Cthulhu from sunken R'lyeh. Don't blame me. I didn't design this universe.

So, once we have established that a great deal of credulity is to be found among science-fiction folk, how does this affect science fiction and fantasy. Let's ignore science, ignore what people believe, and talk about the literature itself. How does credulity effect the stories that are written?

Adversely.

But first, to borrow a phrase from R. A. Lafferty, who injected a chapter of *The Fall of Rome* this way, a brief history of the world up to this point.

iii.

Science fiction has had a long and unhappy relationship with crackpottery, occultism, and pseudo-science. The present credulity is not unique. There were credophiles in every period of the field's history. In the earliest pulp magazines, a good deal of occultism was taken for granted as fact by the readers (if the letter columns are any indication): Atlantis, Mu, and Lemuria belief, particularly when derived from James Churchward, or even from Theosophy. Madame Blavatsky is underappreciated as an inspiration for early science fiction. Her influence on Edgar Rice Burroughs has been chronicled somewhat in an article entitled "John Carter, Sword of Theosophy," by Fritz Leiber.

When Charles Fort's *Lo!* was serialized in *Astounding Stories* in 1934 to much hoopla, very few readers seem to have expressed the opinion, in 1934 slang in what would have been printable by the standards of the time, of "Hey! This is horseshit!" Charles Fort compiled four volumes of odd newspaper clippings and hearsay, of which the best-known is *The Book of the Damned*. They make boring reading, not only because of Fort's hysterical and sometimes very muddled prose, but because one unsubstantiated report after another after another will not undermine your perception of reality. It will only make you appreciate the wisdom of L. Sprague de Camp's celebrated remark, "Should you chance to attend a catastrophe, you will not recognize it in the morning papers."

Science fiction writers of the first and second pulp generations mined Fort for story ideas, and produced at least one classic, *Sinister Barrier* by Eric Frank Russell, but more than anything else, a fondness for the works of Fort helped give Martin Gardner his impression of just how scientifically-literate most SF fans are.

Then in 1945 came the major blot on the family escutcheon, the Shaver Mystery, which from a literary point of view must be the most purely concentrated garbage ever published in a science fiction magazine. But nobody was judging it from a literary point of view, of course.

The scene was the once-proud *Amazing*. The magazine had been declining throughout the 1930s as its elderly editor T. O'Conor Sloane proved unable to adapt to changing times or even keep up to where he had been in 1929. By 1938, *Amazing*, and the editor, seemed to have developed a coat of utterly undisturbed dust. Then brash young Raymond Palmer took over. He introduced bang-bang pulp action stories by new writers and old. He even published a few good ones. For a while, the result must have been refreshing. You could *read* the magazine again, not just snore over it. But the stories were sensationalistic, semi-juvenile formula stuff, rather like what was appearing in *Thrilling Wonder* at the same time. (We are at about 1940. The Golden Age is in progress, but *only* in *Astounding*, which held a virtual monopoly on adult-level science fiction until the end of the decade. The other pulps went trashy-juvenile because they didn't even want to try to compete with John W. Campbell, Jr. in his prime. Probably a smart move.)

Palmer was the sort of editor who would do *anything* to increase circulation. He was enormously successful, and achieved the highest sales ever reached by a science-fiction magazine, about 150,000 copies per issue. He started well, commissioning new Mars and Venus stories by Edgar Rice Burroughs, and having them illustrated by the great Burroughs illustrator, J. Allen St. John. But then he overstepped himself. Howard Browne (Palmer's assistant and later successor) tells how it all started, in his memoir, "A Profit Without Honor" (*Amazing*, May 1984):

> I was at my desk sorting casually through letters from our readers. One specimen caught my attention: a six-page spewing of such egregious nonsense as I've ever run across. The article, written by Richard Shaver, mentioned, among other things, that he had positive proof that a crazed race of sub-humans numbering in the thousands were living in caverns

> throughout the world, that by means of "rays" they brought about practically all of Earth's problems, including but not limited to wars, earthquakes, floods, pestilences, and terminal dandruff. These creatures were called "deros" and, unless eliminated, would eventually destroy humanity... Included in this drivel were examples of the dero language, including the startling information that God spelled backwards was dog!

Indeed, the ancient deros (DEgenerative RObots) seemed to have spoken modern English, as anyone may see from page 71 of the March 1945 *Amazing*. Modern Roman letters stood for English words: A for Animal, B for Be (to exist), C for See, and so on. Thus any number of awesome revelations should be derived from any word. M stood for Man, N for Child. M-A-N becomes "Man, animal, child." How terribly profound. Palmer was supposedly astounded that this worked in any language he tried!

Browne saw Shaver's ravings for what they were, read a few passages aloud for general amusement, and pitched the whole thing in the wastebasket. But Palmer retrieved it and rebuked him: "You call yourself an editor?"

Thus the Shaver Mystery was born. The "letter," somewhat rewritten by Palmer, became a short novel, "I Remember Lemuria," and numerous other stories and novels followed, all of which purported to be *true*. It was classic paranoid stuff: *They* wouldn't allow this material into print except "disguised as fiction." Sinister things nearly prevented the appearance of the Shaver issues anyway.

The result sold like crazy. There was no UFO cult yet (Palmer had a great deal to do with its beginnings, as the founding editor of *Fate*), and Blavatsky's Atlantis/Lemuria stuff was all so far in the past or removed to other planes of existence. Here was something supposedly happening in the *present*. It touched a nerve. *Amazing* reached its peak in circulation. Letters poured in, some of them from clearly disturbed people, such as the correspondent who explained how a "daughter of Damballah" spoke through his wife and revealed that her brain was infected with worms (March 1948, p. 170-171). Palmer thanked the writer for this "actual experience" which corroborated Shaver's theories.

It has never been entirely clear how much of this was Shaver and how much was Palmer, or how much either believed, but from best evidence it would seem that Palmer did most of the writing at first, later training Shaver to be a barely adequate pulpster. (Shaver later sold a few non-"Mystery" stories to completely unrelated magazines in the early '50s. He even had one in the first issue of *If*. Long after there was any money to be made this way, Palmer went on publishing a money-loser of a magazine called *Hidden World*, which had a circulation of a mere 4000 and production values barely short of *National Geographic*. Why? Did he really believe it? Had he staked too much of his emotions and reputation on Shaver to ever back down? Or did he just realize that if he stopped doing this, no one would care about Ray Palmer anymore? He could hardly expect to be remembered as a great editor of science fiction.

Shaver seems to have been a mental patient, who was in an asylum during the period he later claimed to have done his "research" in the caves. A mystic I know remains convinced that something strange and interesting *did* happen inside Shaver's mind at this time. Palmer inadvertently revealed something close to the truth when the Mystery enjoyed an one-issue revival in *Fantastic* in 1958. At first, he assured us, he thought Shaver was a nut. After all, the guy claimed if he dropped his shoes loudly on the floor before going to bed at night, this would summon the cave folk! But then he (Palmer) overheard Shaver talking in his sleep one night, arguing in *four distinct voices*, about whether or not Palmer should be let in on the secret. Those were the cave people, Shaver explained the next morning...

Palmer left *Amazing* at the end of 1949 and Browne ditched the remaining Shaver material in inventory, "because it stank up the place," but the damage was done. Once more it was clear that quite a lot of science fiction readers were not quite sure what they were reading was actually fiction. The mainstream world noticed. The controversy was written up in national news magazines. One group of science-fiction fans proposed that the Shaver-dominated *Amazing* be banned from the mails on the grounds it was harmful to the mental health of the readers.

The family escutcheon got an even worse blot the following year when L. Ron Hubbard introduced "Dianetics" (later the supposed religion of Scientology, for tax purposes) to a gullible world in the pages of *Astounding*. There is no need to go into the history of Hubbard's activities in great detail. Martin Gardner's book gives a pretty good summary of the early part of the story, and Russell Miller's *Bare-Faced Messiah* tells it all in a manner one old-time Hubbard associate described as "too kind," but with general accuracy. The original Hubbard *Astounding* article reads like a mix of Shaver and Charles Fort, a breathless mass of illogic and unproven assumptions claiming to be rock-solid fact.

And lots of people believed, most notably the editor, John W. Campbell, Jr. This was far more embarrassing than the Shaver Mystery because *Amazing* was a trash magazine and no one took Ray Palmer seriously. But Campbell was still riding high on the Golden Age. He had single-handedly raised science fiction up out of the pulp morass. The stories he published were to become classics. His writers would still dominate the field in the 1980s. *Astounding* was, to the reader of the day, the *one* magazine which showed that science fiction could be real literature, for grown-ups.

How disappointing it must have been to discover that the Great Man was fully as gullible as Ray Palmer! Campbell was, for a couple years at least, completely bamboozled by Hubbard's frauds. He failed to recognize that Hubbard had out-Campbelled Campbell, taking the very story idea Campbell himself had once given to Robert Heinlein (a phony, pseudo-scientific religion for ulterior motives, the premise of *Sixth Column*) and applied it to real life.

When he got over that, Campbell developed new crackpot fixations, psionics, the Hieronymous Machine (about which Gardner has much to say), and especially the Dean Drive, an alleged anti-gravity device, an early version of which (as described to me by George Scithers, who heard about it from Willy Ley, who saw it) consisted of a metal frame, an electric motor, and a mechanized hammer mounted on the frame which struck the frame. Put this on the floor and it bounced around the room. The "nuclear physicist" John W. Campbell Jr. declared this to be "action without reaction," demonstrating a whole new principle of physics. A later version vibrated while the experimenter stood on that most precise of instruments, a bathroom scale, and seemed to lose weight as it defied gravity. Of course vested interests in the orthodox scientific community suppressed this breakthrough.

A third such lapse has occurred quite recently, in the person of Whitley Strieber, who, very much in the Shaver tradition, tells us how mysterious little men have visited him again and again, performing strange experiments and trying to get him to kick the chocolate habit. They offer, of course, vast and profound wisdom for mankind if only poor Whitley can figure out what is going on. For all this he offers no proof whatsoever. Again, it is hardly necessary to refute his claims in detail. I merely refer you to the two wonderful essays by Thomas M. Disch, first published in *The Nation* and later reprinted in *Interzone*, which demonstrate, among other things, how easy it is for just anyone to make these claims.

Strieber's *Communion* and its sequel have both been best-sellers. His approach is very Shaveresque throughout, a breathless account of fantastic events which are completely "true," only Strieber is a much better writer than Palmer and/or Shaver ever were. Before he went off the deep end, so to speak, he published some quite respectable novels such as *The Wolfen* and *Warday*, and he returns to acknowledged fiction every once in a while.

Now I do not know Whitley Strieber, and have only seen him in public a few times, mostly at NECons, an informal Rhode Island convention once described as "boys' summer camp for horror writers." I vividly remember him telling an audience in grueling detail how he barely escaped with his life one day on the University of Texas campus when Charles Whitman, the sniper, opened fire. Was he really there? Nowadays he isn't so sure. I am in no position to judge his character, but I will say that if Whitley Strieber told me he'd ridden on a bus in Manhattan, I wouldn't necessarily believe him. There are some people with reputations such that, if they say the sun rises in the east every morning, you'd better check.

The *Skeptical Inquirer* has not given Strieber as much coverage as you might expect, mostly because, without any evidence offered, there is nothing to refute. One writer did suggest that he has undergone a religious conversion and truly believes what he says.

It hardly matters whether Strieber is crazy, sincere, or a fraud out for the money. He has greatly contributed to the otherwise sagging UFO mythology by popularizing the "abductee phenomenon." Again, the phenomenon is not that people are abducted and have strange things stuck up their private parts (an alien preoccupation of late), but that they *report* such things. Strieber himself makes a valid point when he says "Scoffing at them is as ugly as laughing at rape victims. We do not know what is happening to these people, but whatever it is, it causes them to react as if they have discovered a great personal trauma."

Rape. Exactly. I suspect that the psychological mechanism at work here is similar to one which would cause a person to falsely report and even believe that they have been raped. A masochistic desire to be a victim. The craving for attention and sympathy. A hysterical, mental equivalent of hypochondria. Whatever, there are a *lot* of these people. Strieber has become a major force in the UFO faith. I recall seeing a newspaper story about his addressing a whole *convention* of abductees in Washington. The purpose of the gathering, the newspaper said, was mutual support, so that all these people who had similarly suffered could help one another live with the pain and terror of their experiences.

This is serious business. If Strieber is a fraud, he is grossly immoral. If he believes what he is doing, he is just as grossly disturbed. While we may enjoy the delicious wit of the Thomas M. Disch articles, abducteeism, ultimately, is no laughing matter.

Once more, in the tradition of Shaver/Palmer, Hubbard, John W. Campbell, and the thousands of readers who followed them, a science-fiction writer, a practitioner of the made-up fantastic, has lost the ability to distinguish between fantasy and reality.

iv.

It's enough to make one pause and wonder if continuing to write and publish fantastic literature isn't a bad thing. Are we perhaps harming society by supplying such notions to the mentally unbalanced? I am, after all, a spook-monger, a writer of fantasy and supernatural horror stories which lack even the pretense of realism that most science fiction displays. Much of my fiction is distinctly mystical, replete with gods, sorcery, and, yes, even divination. I am co-publisher of *Weird Tales* (now *Worlds of Fantasy & Horror*), which features stories that involve all manner of occult, supernatural, and a-rational goings-on. Even science-fiction writers must have wondered about this: is it harmful to write about psionics and visiting aliens because the stories will inspire the credophiles of this world? UFOlogy is nothing more than science-fictional imagery seeped down to the lowest intellectual level of society.

The answer comes from Alfred Hitchcock, who, after being told that a murderer committed his second murder after viewing *Psycho*, remarked, "Well what did he do before his first one, drink a glass of milk?"

In other words, the artist cannot be held responsible for what a deranged person makes of his art. Think of all the Renaissance masters you'd have to ban to prevent some lunatic from seeing the sado-masochistic possibilities in crucifixion scenes.

I got another answer at that Balticon, from the roomful of New Agers. Someone told me, "Oh the magic in your fiction isn't like the real thing." I found that very reassuring. Yes, *The Shattered Goddess* is fantasy. I made it up. I don't care if some neo-pagan tells me "the real Mother Goddess isn't like that." In fact I wish one would. I am rather disturbed by the possibility that there are people out there who think that the made-up part of my stories are real. I wrote a series of stories once about sorcery through self-mutilation.

It is, I think, enormously limiting and, yes, *damaging* for a writer to believe in the fantastic elements he or she writes about. Yes, there have been occult believers in the past who wrote good fantasy fiction, Algernon Blackwood and Arthur Machen among them. (Interestingly, Machen criticized Blackwood for being too credulous.) But, by and large, even they knew what they were making up.

Lovecraft pointed out that occultists seldom make good supernatural fiction writers because, if they take the phenomenon for granted, they won't give it sufficient buildup to make it convincing.

Or, to put it another way, a writer of any sort of fantastic fiction *needs to be skeptical* so that story decisions will be made on *artistic* rather than doctrinaire grounds.

Let me given you an example. At another convention I was invited to a meeting of professional writers, in the course of which a shared-world fantasy anthology was to be cooked up. J____, the editor and chief creative mind behind it all, explained the premise of the series in very vague terms, something about, if I remember correctly after several years, long-buried occult powers (possibly Old Gods) manifesting themselves in the modern world. At this point E____, now a well-known fantasy novelist and a good friend, joined me in what writers normally do in these sessions. We batted the ideas around. "Well, why don't you do it like this...? No, switch this to this, and it'll all be different—"

J____ screamed at us. We would have to be serious, she said. We would have to get the magic *right*, to do *research* and find out how it *really works*. She was quite upset. I found it entirely impossible to take her seriously. The anthology never got off the ground. If it had, I would have had to have bowed out.

It was only later that I fully understood what had happened. J____ is a serious occultist and adherent of numerous of pseudo-scientific beliefs. What was, to her, part of the *realistic background* of the proposed book was, to the rest of us, part of the *imaginary premise*. She *believed* this stuff and became angry when E____ and I seemed unwilling to do our homework and get all the "facts" right. Had she said, "This anthology will be based on such-and-such system of belief," that would have been fine, albeit a little limiting.

For E____ and myself, how the magic worked, where the occult powers came from, and the like were artistic matters. We could manipulate them to the demands of the story. J____, for doctrinal reasons, couldn't. She was unable to see the difference. Unless she could find enough like-minded people who also happened to be professional writers, she had no hope of ever filling her anthology. Possibly that's why it never came out.

And now a word about self-mutilation. It is precisely because I don't believe in sorcery that I am able to write about it effectively. I have published three stories, "The Story of a Dadar," "The Diminishing Man," and "Holy Fire," about two brother sorcerers locked in a more-than-deadly feud. They keep sending *dadars* against one another, semi-living projections which can dwell in society for years as seeming human beings before coming awake to their actual, malign missions. But to animate each of these, the sorcerer must contribute a part of his own flesh, a bigger piece for the more powerful or longer-lasting *dadar*. As they go on, mutilating themselves, substituting artificial or alien tissue to make up for the missing parts, both brothers become grotesquely transformed, until they are hardly human anymore, and can barely remember why they are fighting.

Somewhere there is an occultist saying, "No! No! It isn't like that at all!"

Of course. I made it up. There are no such things as *dadars*. But I think the image is a good metaphor for senseless, all-consuming hatred.

Fantasy and science-fiction writers make things up. They do it consciously. The reader knows it, too, there being a contract between writer and reader best stated in antiquity by Lucian of Samosata:

> I write of things which I have neither seen nor suffered nor learned from another, things which are not and never could have been, and therefore my readers should by no means believe them.

Fantasy fiction, as opposed to mythology or religious scripture, could not even come into existence until readers understood that. Fantasy is a *deliberate* act of the imagination for specific artistic, rather than doctrinaire purposes. Sure enough, fantasy as we know it didn't appear until about Lucian's time (second century AD), when a sufficiently skeptical audience was able to recognize—and enjoy—the imagination of Lucian or of Lucius Apuleius. As the Dark Ages descended, fantasy became myth again. I would guess that the original audience of *Beowulf* had a very different experience from sophisticated Romans reading *A True History* or *The Golden Ass*.

The story which is avowedly made up entertains, or instructs, or even (I think it is C. S. Lewis's phrase) forms an *addition to life*. It takes us where we have not been. It can be *true* in a very deep sense (as Le Guin has described) without being *factual*. I hope that the stories about the self-mutilating sorcerers contain some truth about the destructiveness of hatred. But they are not factual. No such magic exists. If you want to get your enemy, don't start by chopping your fingers off.

Lay persons often wonder if science-fiction writers get their ideas from UFO-logy and similar pseudo-science. A few writers did get some from Charles Fort, that is true, but as a rule, I suspect they do not. In fact it seems to be a rule that once an idea has trickled down to the *Weekly World News* level, it is too hackneyed for any but the most sophisticated or satirical use. There are exceptions, of course. Garfield Reeves-Stevens has published a pretty good novel, *Nighteyes* (Doubleday Foundation, 1989) based on the Strieber-type contactee mythos, a fact the blurb-writers were not shy about pointing out. But science-fiction's best answer to flying saucerdom came with Avram Davidson's "The Grantha Sighting" (*F&SF*, April 1958), in which a flying saucer lands in a rustic family's yard. (For some reason aliens always seem to land in rural Appalachia.) The space creatures get out, picnic on the lawn, change the baby's diaper, and leave. But before long reporters descend on the witnesses and force the story into the accepted pattern, complete with a warning against the arms race and a secret message which may not be revealed to the public. Even in 1958, UFOs were too trite for serious science-fictional use. And as for, say, the Bermuda Triangle, that was done best by William Hope Hodgson (*The Boats of the "Glen Carrig"*, etc.) in the first years of this century.

I certainly don't find UFO-logy or serious occultism very inspiring. My main objection is not that I disbelieve it, but that I can *do better*. The folk imagination is seldom as sophisticated as the deliberate, literary imagination. Rumors, pseudo-science paperbacks, and supermarket tabloids tend to rehash the same few elements again and again. (You know, the ultimate *National Enquirer* headline: LIZ RECEIVES PSYCHIC MESSAGE FROM DICK ABOARD A UFO: REVEALS NEW MIRACLE DIET.) There is a paucity of imagination there. The material is aimed at the most unsophisticated, uneducated, and probably unimaginative reader out there.

The skeptical writer can take what he wants from those sources, but then deliberately build something far richer, far more entertaining, far more meaningful. He can make forceful, convincing speculations, or psychologically valid metaphors. He remains in control of his material.

But if we lose our skepticism, if we can no longer tell what is real and what is made up, we lose control. We cease to imagine and create, but subsist on (second-rate) Received Wisdom.

That is precisely where the danger of credulity lies.

A Few Words About My Brief Career As a Medium

To be fair, I had an occult experience once. It went like this: at a fan party at Linda Bushyager's house, someone got out a ouija board. An only slightly serious "séance" ensued. At first, I was not invited in, because of my known Bad Attitude, which disturbs the spirits. But the spirits weren't being very cooperative anyway, and the pointer kept producing meaningless strings of five or six consonants in a row.

So I offered to join, and was allowed to. I soon proved to be the only competent medium present. I demanded that the spirit name itself, and at once the pointer spelled out:

M—O—E

I had contacted Moe Howard of the Three Stooges!

I asked Moe about his old buddies, Larry first, and got:

C—H—O—W—D—E—R

As in "chowderhead," one of Moe's kinder epithets for Larry. In the hereafter he must have forgotten how to spell "porcupine."

I then asked about Curley:

V—I—C—T—I—M

A victim of *coi*cumstance!

At this point narrow-minded skeptics ruined my séance. Much laughter ensued. My protestations of innocence were not believed, even though *another supernatural event occurred!* Convulsed with laughter, I proceeded to do the "Curley shoulder-spin" right there on Linda's living-room rug! Normally I am not agile enough to perform such a feat. Unquestionably, I had been momentarily possessed by the spirit of Curley. This was the only documented case of *Stoogeolepsy* known to science.

I came away from the experience shaken, but enlightened. I had pierced the Veil of the Beyond and come away with an awesome secret, a reliable method of getting coherent answers each and every time one uses a ouija board.

You *push the pointer.*

II.

THE COST OF CREDULITY

(1992)

Why debunk pseudo-science? It's a pretty futile undertaking, certainly. People will continue to believe in astrology, UFOs, psychic powers, Atlantis, or whatever because it pleases them to do so. Rationality has little to do with it. It's not hard to learn enough real astronomy and anthropology to understand that astrology is no more "real" than any other form of divination—entrail-reading, for example.

But a lot of people would rather ignore the facts and go on playing with their brightly-colored toys. Why not just let them? Not everyone has to relentlessly seek the truth. So what if some people chose to opt out?

A good friend of mine once took me rather passionately to task for making light of other people's beliefs, for robbing people of comfort in a world which provides too little comfort. Actually, all I'd done was suggest that, since New Age magic crystals are nothing but placebos, it might be better to get the believers to accept mass-produced, artificially grown crystals, which would "heal" or yield "energy" just as well as ones taken from caves. Since these magical properties don't actually exist, the New Agers will never know the difference, and a lot of beautiful cavern formations won't have to be defaced. Everybody is happy. No loss of comfort there.

And if the Asian pharmaceutical market were suddenly flooded with fake rhino-horn, which would have no more or less healing powers than the genuine article, wouldn't that be a good way to save the rhinoceros from extinction?

But my friend's whole point was that it's terribly arrogant of me to decide which of my neighbors beliefs are nonsense and which are not.

Certainly it would be no more than refined cruelty to descend upon an elderly man who is near to death and convince him that his lifelong religious beliefs are hogwash, that there is no hope of the hereafter, that all the sacrifices made to prepare for the afterlife have wasted a good deal of *this* life, etc. Let's not. Whatever we believe, that other person has a right to believe something too. And I'm sure that a lot of atheists, as they near the end, envy the religionists in their certainty, which can be tremendously comforting, *even if it is an illusion.* The whole Catch-22, of course, is that you must not *know* that it is an illusion. So it can be cruel to pop the bubble.

But aside from such extreme cases, my only answer can be that it's a dirty job but someone has to do it.

The physical universe is no respecter of human illusions. As someone succinctly put it, reality is the tumor you don't believe in killing you. So if the New Ager is using his crystals to cure what would *now* be operable cancer, but which will kill him in a year if left untreated, somebody had better pop his bubble as soon as possible, out of kindness, friendship, and social responsibility.

Some things just don't work. More importantly, they don't work merely because we wish they would. Magical cures are the most obvious example. Years ago, I read heard about a science-fiction fan who had cancer but had gone off his treatment and removed himself to a Laetrile clinic in Mexico. *Oh God*, I thought. *He's going to die right on schedule.*

And he did. While "orthodox" cancer cures may have a low success rate, ground-up peach-pits have *no* success rate.

Am I my brother's keeper? Well, when he's covered himself with gasoline and started playing with matches, yes, I am. Who decides what is *right* in such a situation? Ultimately, the universe does. No opinion poll is taken. But in the immediate situation of the guy with matches, I decide. If this be arrogance, let us make the best of it. I would hope that someone else would do the same for me, and that when I had recovered my sanity to the point I no longer wanted to immolate myself, I would be suitably grateful.

Someone has to decide. I support, for instance, the right of the government to step in and overrule parents who endanger their children's lives by depriving them of medical treatment for pseudo-scientific or religious reasons. We had a case like that in Philadelphia recently. A fundamentalist Christian sect refused to allow their children to be vaccinated against (I think it was) measles. An epidemic started. Several children died. The city forcibly vaccinated the rest.

I also think of a colleague's elderly relative who suffered from, as I've often put it when telling this story, "a bad case of glaucoma and Christian Science." She had become totally blind, but refused to believe it, since the central tenet of Christian Science is that all physical ailments are illusions brought on by sin and a lack of faith. It was no illusion that she stumbled into things. Since her life was not immediately in danger, and she was an adult, I suppose you could say she had chosen to go blind, and should be left alone.

Indeed, this is no laughing matter. It raises the most serious ethical and philosophical questions.

The core of it is this: false beliefs can hurt you. Surely, then, the humane thing to do in most cases is to try to remove the source of the hurt. If someone lives in terror of demons, or is bankrupted and made miserable by an urge to have "engrams" erased so the "operative thetan" is freed of earthly influences, wouldn't it be a kindness to convince the victim that there are no demons, engrams, or thetans? Think of all the suffering that was caused by witchcraft hysteria in the fifteenth and sixteenth centuries. Wouldn't it be the greatest kindness of all of go back in time and somehow convince those people that there was no black magic, that the power they lived in abject dread of couldn't hurt them?

While rationality may sometimes remove comfort, as often it *provides* comfort by setting us free from fear.

Ah, but the believers have a *right* to believe in Devil-inspired witches, don't they? Yes, under the U.S. Constitution, which protects freedom of religion, they certainly do. What they *don't* have a right to do is burn them, as some of today's "Satanic cult experts" would probably like to.

Who knows? The time-traveller might also have managed to prevent the Thirty Years War, which was surely the most extensive and goriest outburst of Reformation-era religious frenzy.

Illusion may be fun, but it can cost you: in terms of grief, terror, sickness, death, or just a lot of money. There are dozens of cults and pseudo-scientific movements in our society primarily devoted, despite claims to the contrary, to relieving the gullible of large amounts of cash as quickly as possible. Unreality-addiction can be as expensive—and destructive—as drug addiction.

Sometimes strong-arm tactics may be necessary, even those described in Ted Patrick's *Let Our Children Go!* (with Tom Dulack; E. P. Dutton, 1976, Ballantine Books, 1977). Patrick is the man who added "deprogramming" to the language. I am not sure what he's doing these days, but in the '70s he made a sensation rescuing the victims of brainwash cults, the Children of God, the Moonies, and the Hare Krishnas especially, not to mention a former engineer from Brooklyn who called himself Brother Julius and claimed to be Christ.

Yet again, no laughing matter. It is life and death. Patrick had only the greatest compassion for the victims.

Most science-fictionists ridicule flying saucer believers, but at the core of this particular delusion there is something quite unfunny, which is, simply, a lot of pain. David M. Jacobs's *Secret Life: First-hand Accounts of UFO Abductions* (Simon & Schuster, 1992, 336 p.) is a believer's book, by and for the faithful. It has undeniable value as a primary document in the study of the folklore on the subject. We can only wish that someone had written a similar one three or four centuries ago, interviewing victims of the quite similar fairy-abduction phenomenon.

Certainly Jacobs's opus will provide very little inspiration for the science fiction, since, for the science-fiction writer, reading a UFO book is rather like an auto-designer's tour of a junkyard. All around him are used, banged-up, and obsolete parts which are *totally familiar*. It is through the cultural influence of science fiction that this particular belief-system has taken on technological, rather than supernatural, imagery and language. I might further add that SF writers know more science than Jacobs (a Ph.D. of history at Temple University) apparently does. His biology is especially weak if he fails to question how extraterrestrials could interbreed with humans. As Carl Sagan remarked, Mr. Spock's mom would have had better luck with a petunia than with Sarek.

The *phenomenon* to be studied is not that flying saucers are grabbing people by the dozens and performing vaguely sexual or proctological experiments on them, but that people *believe* this is happening. The more scientifically minded might want to also check out David Hufford's *The Terror That Comes in the Night* (University of Pennsylvania Press, 1982), which is "an experience-centered study of supernatural assault traditions," and goes into the psychology and physiology of the virtually universal "night hag experience"—sleep paralysis—which I, at least, think has a good deal to do with UFO and fairy abductions.

In either case, abduction-belief causes a great deal of pain. If this is a new cult, the beginnings of a new religion, it is the saddest, the most pathetic faith to come along in quite some time. Abduction-belief offers *only* agony and humiliation, without the attractions of salvation or immortality characteristic of mystery-cults of the past. The victims suffer fully as much as rape victims do. They report being treated like laboratory animals by extraterrestrials who care no more for human desires and dignities than human experimenters do for their rats. In the abduction mythos, as it has now emerged, Earth people are mere *things*, part of some inscrutable alien breeding program.

The victims' lives are shattered. They struggle to understand what has happened to them. They will cling to any available solution which might help them get over what they have been through. Since the sociology of this belief takes them outside the bounds of conventional psychiatry, they tend to cluster together in support groups, attempting to heal one another or to be healed by writers of books like this one, or Whitley Strieber's *Communion*. I once read a newspaper account of an abductee therapy-session/convention at which Mr. Strieber was guest of honor. It sounded like he was well on his way to becoming a clergyman in the new sect.

I can't say what is going on there. Perhaps Strieber is a compassionate man, who actually tries to help these people. But since he is, by his own account, himself a victim, he seems unable to take the final step: to assault the belief itself, to provide healing by convincing these people that what they think happened, didn't.

Again, I think it is compassionate to free people from the fear generated by their own illusions. I think many UFO-abductees need the services of a skilled deprogrammer. Ted Patrick has his own agenda (it wouldn't be fair in this context not to mention that Patrick is a strict Christian who might be accused to trying to beat out the competition), but someone else, using similar techniques, might do a lot of good.

Otherwise, I'm sure you all can see how vulnerable these victims would be to exploitation by the unscrupulous.

Let me offer a scenario, some of which, I admit, sounds an awful lot like the plot of Kate Wilhelm's excellent 1970 novel, *Let the Fire Fall*. Quite possibly science fiction helps protect us from this sort of thing, by reminding us over and over that it is the stuff of fiction, that people like Kate Wilhelm or Darrell Schweitzer can make it up.

Here goes: combine a ruthless brainwash cult with sophisticated mass-media promotion and bargain-basement faith-healing, then employ a defrocked stage magician on the order of Uri Geller to do a few sleight-of-hand tricks and pretend to be psychic. He is the persona to be promoted—though probably not the real *leader* of the operation. Next, add a sprinkling of UFO-abduction/contactee mythology, and what do you get?

You get a potentially large-scale religious cult, created in utter cynicism, based on the premise that the psychically-empowered preacher *is a space alien*, here to "save" us from all manner of menaces, including, by no coincidence, the other aliens who take people aboard flying saucers and do awful things to them.

Most of these elements are already present among various charlatans and cults already. I'm just combining them in a (slightly) original fashion. We've already seen dozens of UFO-based religious cults, even some of the "sell all your goods and wait to be taken away before the world ends" variety, but these seldom convince more than a couple dozen suckers, who, inevitably, are let down when the rescuing saucer fails to show up. You could rationalize the no-shows as a failure in interplanetary communications, since the leaders of such a sect merely claim to be contactees who have received their instructions from the aliens.

That's the one crucial difference. This time, the front-man claims to be an actual extraterrestrial. He need not wear fake antennae or Spock-ears. The public doesn't seem to grasp the concept that a creature which is the product of an entirely different evolutionary system would be *profoundly* different. (My own opinion is that if we ever found an E.T. which even walks on two legs and has two arms and binocular vision, that will be an *eerie* coincidence, worthy of a lot of research.)

Never mind. Say he's assumed human form for our sake, and that only the initiates into the sect may behold his true form, which is too ravishingly awesome for plain folks to bear. Even that may be an unnecessary frill. Keep it simple. So this guy's a space-alien. He "proves" it by doing the stage-magician's tricks the way Uri Geller does, clumsily by the standards of the professional magician, never well enough to earn more than contempt from The Amazing Randi and *The Skeptical Inquirer*. Don't worry about that. The rubes will eat it up. No amount of debunking will stop the preacher from space.

The space preacher is also a faith-healer, using standard faith-healing techniques, asking audience to help him "focus energy" to cure the afflicted, not merely suffering UFO-abductees, but *any* afflicted. This has the additional strength of enabling the believers to believe that they are *participating* in these great works.

The space preacher's assistants will be glad to sell you genuine alien crystals which will help you focus and develop your personal "psychic" energy. But only use as directed. Remember that He, and these artifacts, are the products of a higher civilization than our own.

And I think our E.T. has something of the "psychic surgeon" about him. Magically, without surgery, he removes "tumors" which only a vile skeptic could allege may have begun life in a hen house.

There is a sense of urgency. Conspiracies abound and the apocalypse is at hand. What kind of apocalypse? That hardly matters. Nuclear war is the tried-and-true standby, or it might be AIDS, which everybody "knows" started in a C.I.A. laboratory somewhere and may be unstoppable.

The government and the C.I.A. are out to silence the Space Savior because he is a "threat" to them. Scientific "orthodoxy" refuses to acknowledge him because scientists, too, are dupes of the bad guys. Cult-leaders will be smart enough not to name a specific date for the End, but something bad is going to happen very soon, unless it can be prevented by the outer-space savior, unless you, friends, send all the money you can to help him in his good works; and after you've done that you should move into a believer community, cut off all ties with unbelievers, and devote your every waking moment to working for the Cause of preventing nuclear war, rescuing UFO-abductees, stopping pollution, saving the whales, eliminating corrupt government officials, "curing" homosexuals, diverting a huge asteroid which is about to collide with the Earth, raising every human being to a higher and more enlightened plain where their own inner powers may be revealed...all Before It Is Too Late.

Sounds crazy, doesn't it?

Somehow, I'm not laughing. This will mean pain, fear, bigotry, ruined lives, and considerable financial expense.

That's the cost of credulity.

Darrell Schweitzer

1997 Update

When this was written, long before the Heaven's Gate Cult suicides, it was *almost* funny...

III.

THE LAYERCAKE OF HISTORY

OR, TIME TRAVELING ON THE VIA DEL CORSO

This isn't an exercise in What I Did On My Summer Vacation, nor is it a travel column, but I'm going to tell you about Italy. Stay with me. It gets quite science-fictional, if you keep your eyes open. Keeping your eyes open is very much the key. How can we read and write of strange futures and alien planets if we cannot first appreciate the strangeness of other parts of our own globe?

On August 20, 1990, I flew to Rome. I was on my very round-about way to the World Science Fiction Convention, Confiction, to be held in The Hague, Netherlands, a week later. Everybody I knew who was going planned to "do" Europe somehow, before or after the con. I was the only one who started in Italy. Fascination with the ancient Roman Empire drew me there, inevitably. I'm by no means a genuine historical scholar, much less a Latinist; but I knew what I wanted to see and I knew enough to understand what I was seeing. Therefore, *Roma Mater*.

I've travelled extensively in the U.S., but I had never been overseas before. I don't speak Italian. My attempts to master a few phrasebook sentences proved useless. (I could ask a few questions but never understand the answers. Fortunately, tour guides speak English. Street vendors and shopkeepers speak Tourist.)

There I was, suddenly plunked down alone in an authentically foreign country. The first of many details: *That woman in front of me*, I thought while standing in line at the currency exchange, *looks like Mussolini's daughter*. She had his face, that distinct, bulldog look. Romans do not look like most Italian-Americans, whose ancestors came from the South, Naples or Sicily. Italian-Americans tend to have oily complexions and the men are rather hairy. A Roman type, if there is such a thing, is strong-featured with heavy, prominent cheekbones and jaw, thick lips, and relatively hairless, olive skin.

But then there was Max, the tour guide who got into an animated discussion about Italian music with an American lady on the trip to the Naples and Pompeii. They were pulling out tapes, playing this and that back, when *bam!*—surprise! The Italian had never heard of

Pavarotti. Max was a Roman who could have been Irish, pale, slender, with curly red hair.

Advice to the traveller: never *quite* trust your impressions. (I forgot to mention that Mussolini was born in Predappio, which is closer to Ravenna than to Rome.)

But I'm getting ahead of myself. Da Vinci Airport is out in the country. I saw only a couple of large, tile-roofed farmhouses from the air on the way in, and the bus went on through miles of gray and brown, empty land that looked rather like northern California at the same time of year. One minute, rusticity, then turn in the road and, as some writer of antiquity noted, you come upon Rome quite suddenly. It is a city almost without suburbs.

I had never been here before, but within seconds I suddenly knew where I was. I spotted the façade of the church of St. Paul Outside the Walls (desecrated by the Arabs in the eighth century or thereabouts, partially burnt in the nineteenth; but the mosaics inside are fifth century, in what was to become early Byzantine style), the pyramid of Caius Cestius (a contemporary of Caesar who got so rich by using his political office to line his toga that he wanted to be buried with the magnificence of a pharaoh) and the medieval fortifications incorporating it, the Flavian Amphitheater (Colosseum), the Palatine ruins, the Arch of Constantine...all this just glimpsed on the way to the bus depot. It was a *very* strange feeling, so much *familiar*...doubtless ancestral memories from my Gothic and Vandal forebears, who, while they did not help build Rome, certainly helped sack it. I only failed to recognize the later stuff, anything built after the fifth century.

The first thing I did upon arriving was buy a guidebook with a good map. I discovered that I could reach my hotel with a two-stop subway ride, which cost the equivalent of seventy cents. (A cab ride the same distance, I later learned, cost 45,000 lira, or forty-five *dollars*.) Next, I bought a can of soda and a bottle of mineral water, the latter reserved for such things as brushing teeth. (It turns out you *can* drink Roman water, even out of the public drinking fountains. This tip will save the traveller fifteen dollars a day. The water comes from the Aqueduct of Nero, I was told.)

The next thing I did was smack a Gypsy kid with the soda can.

Another sudden jolt: bystanders scolded the *child*. I was in a country where at least one ethnic prejudice is completely acceptable. In detail which would result in anti-defamation suits in the United States, official guides, hotel personnel, bus-drivers, everyone, will tell you that Gypsy children (migrants, who begin in what was then Yugoslavia and work their way seasonally across southern Europe) are taught to steal as soon as they can walk—for the same reason that American drug-pushers use children. They can't be prosecuted as long as they're minors. The Italians will point them out to you. You see unaccompanied children anywhere there is a crowd, reaching, tugging, probing. So, in Italy, everybody hates Gypsies intensely. Rumor has it the cops shoot one occasionally, and no one else much cares.

The Liberal in me wonders if all those juvenile pickpockets were in fact Gypsies, and not just poor Italians. Either way, the tourist has to be on constant guard. But frankly, an eight-year-old Gypsy is a lot easier to evade than an adult, gun-toting Philadelphian or New Yorker. The rule is simply that you must see the Gypsies first. If they approach you, hold onto your bags and say *"No!"* Be particularly wary of any kid carrying a sign or newspaper (he'll hold it up to distract you and work under it). If one tries to touch you, hit him.

Rome in August is virtually empty of Romans, who are on vacation at the seashore. The climate is hot mid-nineties in the afternoons—but comfortably dry. In late summer the grass in the parks has turned brown. Gray dust swirls in the Forum.

I explored the city on foot, eating very little since food was fantastically expensive, drinking a lot of fluids, walking eight or nine hours a day. By the time I got to The Hague, friends said I looked thinner. "The Special Italian Weight-Loss Program," I said.

People often stopped me to ask directions, *in English*, and often I could help them. (Always English. The number of, say, Swedish-speaking Dutchmen or Italian-speaking Japanese, much less Swedish/Dutch/Japanese-speaking Italians, is probably slight. But everyone has English as a second language. "Piazza Navona? Well, you go down the Via Del Corso and hang a right at the Column of Marcus Aurelius, then left down the next side-street to the Pantheon, then right again...")

I began to notice the sort of texture and *detail* you just cannot find in an American city. This is where we get science-fictional. The purpose of my Italian excursion was nothing less than time-travel. Rome today is as New York will be in three thousand years, genuinely ancient, so that wherever you go there are not only remnants of the past, but remnants of one past era's reflections on another.

Think of it as the layercake of history. One epoch piles onto the next and the people routinely sweep up the crumbs, mixing them further.

My hotel was on the Via Sestina. There was a Bernini fountain (early seventeenth-century) at the subway stop. Three blocks the other way, and the street opened out onto the Spanish Steps (eighteenth-century), named after the then all-important Spanish embassy. (But the eras and cultures mix. At night the steps are covered with young tourists, Americans and Germans, listening to Oriental musicians perform American rock-and-roll.) At the top, a Renaissance church: not one of the famous ones, but it does have a Raphael fresco. Go a couple blocks and turn right, pass through the ancient-cum-medieval city walls and you come to the lovely Renaissance Borghese Gardens, which widen into a magnificent park (the Pincio) built by Napoléon Bonaparte, where you can find the ancient Egyptian obelisk the Emperor Hadrian (second-century) erected to his boy-lover, Antinoüs. One of the most scenic of all Roman vistas is a sunset view from the heights of the Pincio over the Piazza del Populo, which contains yet another obelisk. (Roman sunsets are noisy. In the evening the streets fill with Italian teenagers on motorbikes.)

There are apparently more obelisks in Rome than remain in Egypt. They were the rage for centuries, looted by the various triumvirs and emperors, or perhaps handed out as political prizes, like the "Cleopatra's needle" in New York's Central Park, which the Khedive of Egypt sent in the 1880s as a token of his esteem. (What else to do with a slightly used obelisk?) Initially they decorated the Circus Maximus, then were moved anywhere and everywhere at the whim of succeeding centuries. My favorite bit of trans-temporal tackiness may be found just behind Hadrian's celebrated and perfectly-preserved Pantheon (itself facing a row of fast-food concessions): a seventeenth-century marble elephant (Bernini again) with a hieroglyphic-covered obelisk on its back and a papal cross on top, the whole mess now a traffic obstacle for tiny Italian automobiles.

Papal inscriptions are everywhere. The popes claim some of the old imperial titles, including "Pater Patriae" (Father of the Fatherland) and most notably "Pontifex Maximus" (chief priest), which the emperors relinquished in the fourth century and which actually dates back to the Etruscans. The current pope, by the way, uses exactly the same monumental calligraphy (with a distinctive descending flourish on the "Q") as Augustus Caesar, whose autobiography is inscribed on the side of his rather tumble-down temple. (The tomb of Augustus is in a vacant lot adjoining. It looks very much like an enormous layer-cake, round, overgrown with weeds. The sign on the chain blocking the entrance says "S.P.Q.R." Down in the trench around this tomb was the only place I encountered the once-numerous feral cats of Rome.)

They don't call it the Eternal City for nothing. The architectural styles haven't changed much since the classical times, and may be categorized variously as Massive, Grandiose, and Overwhelming. The ancient buildings, even in ruin, are *huge*. You could have parked three Zeppelins side-by-side in the Basilica of Maxentius. Imagine how awesome it must have been to my barbaric, Visigothic ancestors.

Even the decidedly twentieth-century McDonald's on the Esquiline Hill near the Spanish Steps is enormous: a complex like a small shopping mall, with tiled floors, potted plants, and fake classical statuary in the corners. I dubbed it the McDonald's of the Caesars.

Not to be outdone by mere pagans, the Renaissance popes built churches you could land small planes in. And they did it tastefully. For all St. Peter's might double over as a Space Shuttle hangar, it is one of the most beautiful buildings in the world. As I first entered, about seven o'clock in the evening as sunlight streamed through the dome at a forty-five degree angle, and stepped into a majestic vastness that seemed to swallow all echoes, my first thought was, *All those indulgences were worth it. The money was well spent.*

The saint himself resides in the basement, in a golden box about three feet by four feet, having diminished somewhat over the centuries. (Indeed, a bit of his skull has been across town these sixteen hundred years, in St. John of the Lateran.) Peter's comparatively modest shrine, amid the tombs of the popes, is surely the very heart of the Christian world, the Catholic Kaaba. The power of the place is undeniable. I genuflected before St. Pete.

Everywhere, a mixture, stirred with a many-centuried spoon: on the way back from St. Peter's, I explored a side street and found part of the old imperial aqueduct system with its arches filled in and medieval battlements added. Medieval buildings, as a rule, are still in use, not regarded as worth noting as monuments.

Walk from St. Peter's to the Tiber, turn left, and before long you reach the Castel Sant' Angelo, the tomb of the previously-mentioned second-century Hadrian, used as a fortress when Count Belisarius's Byzantine army was besieged there in the 530s. The Byzantines broke most of the Hadrian's decorative statuary over the heads of more of my barbaric ancestors. For centuries, the place was a refuge for beleaguered popes. Cagliostro, the L. Ron Hubbard of the eighteenth century, died in its dungeons. An angel appeared atop the castle in 590 in answer to Pope Gregory's prayer for relief from a plague. The angelic statue commemorating the miracle is of a much later date.

Layer upon layer: Ancient, Medieval, Renaissance, Baroque, occasional modern, all jumbled together. One of the few twentieth-century buildings I entered was a bookstore, in search of a copy of *Alle Morte della Dea*, by that noted Italian fantasy author, Darrell Schweitzer, published by Mondadori.

It's impossible to *dig* anywhere in Rome without hitting an archaeological relic, which makes subway-expansion difficult. Once I glanced down a hole at what looked like a construction site and saw an ancient archway, a storey below modern street level. It was the Porta Octavia, named either after the sister of Augustus or the unfortunate first wife of Nero. I'm not sure which.

There are limits, though. You won't find anything from the era of the Roman kings, or the Etruscan period, outside of the (excellent) museums. Very few of the ancient buildings predate Julius Caesar.

Imperial-era construction is distinguished by the tiny bricks, about the size of large candy bars. These remained uniform wherever the Romans went. You can see some of them in a fragment of the Roman wall near the Tower of London.

Cross the Tiber in front of the Castel Sant' Angelo on a bridge dating from the time of Julius Caesar, but lined with statues by students of Michaelangelo. We see Renaissance imitations of the ancient, modern imitations of Renaissance, and the inevitable plaques of Pope Sixtus the Fifth.

Sixtus must rank as the greatest graffiti artist of all time. He put his name *everywhere*. The Arch of Titus, erected in the first century AD to celebrate the conquest of Jerusalem has, on one side, what you'd expect: thanks from the incredibly grateful senate and people to the divine emperors Vespasian and Titus, etc. etc. But in a rare moment of modesty, the ancients left the back *blank*. Since the sixteenth century, it has borne an inscription, fully as massive as the original one, saying, in effect, "HI! SIXTUS WAS HERE."

But some relics are less enthusiastically displayed. Across the street from the Forum of Augustus there is a bronze statue of the old boy, obviously once intended for a much higher pedestal since the upper body is larger than the legs. The inscription on the base reads, discreetly, "Anno XI a Fascibus Renovatus."

That would be about 1933, by my count. It was the only open reference to Fascism I saw. Guides will show you Mussolini's balcony, from which he made his speeches, but it's not marked. (Overlooking a quite small plaza near the Arch of Severus. With the right camera angle, it would be easy to make the place look as packed as a Nuremberg rally.) The real survivors of the Fascist regime are the manhole covers, which aren't marked "City Water Works," but, consistent with Il Duce's neo-imperial pretensions, "S.P.Q.R."—*Senatus et Populusque Romanus*—the proud slogan once borne on the standards of the legions. Never mind that Rome doesn't even have a senate anymore. That Fascism should be commemorated this way—on the sewers—is one of history's little jokes.

I don't see this kind of multi-centuried detail in science fiction, particularly in American science fiction, probably because most American SF writers have never really *looked* at a city as old as Rome. The movie *Blade Runner* actually caught the effect better than most novels, but the layercake there was only about three centuries deep.

Let's think of it this way: it's the year Four Thousand. The colony worlds are like the twentieth-century United States. Their histories are only a couple hundred years old. Anything older is imported. Some of the buildings are imitations of older styles, but they are only imitations, like pseudo-medieval American churches.

Meanwhile, back on Earth, the city of New York has been continuously inhabited for over twenty-three centuries. The inhabitants themselves may surprise you, since most off-world colonists originally came from Japan. New Yorkers are either extremely dark, or else very pale, with long noses.

The city is a fascinating hodgepodge:

In the ancient district of Manhattan, we can behold the still impressive ruins of the Empire State Building, but also the even more impressive, meticulously-preserved neo-Deco Burger King Building, built around 2700, which now houses the complete JFK Airport (moved from its original site in 2743), plus the galaxy's largest collection of baseball cards. There are many picturesque legends relating to the statue of the giant ape at the top, which dates from about 2950.

The World Trade Center was mistaken for a tuning fork and destroyed during the Denebian occupation of the late thirty-second century. Little remains of it but two, square, grassy fields. The Denebian slime-creatures themselves are long gone, but the ubiquitous pedestals they installed still lead to jokes about Denebian anatomy and sexual habits. Some of them were converted into fireplugs in succeeding centuries.

The tourist should not miss the quaint nineteenth-, twentieth-, and twenty-first-century structures in the outlying district of Brooklyn, which never suffered the ravages of urban renewal or extraterrestrial invasion. (Pre-nineteenth-century structures are extremely rare, though the collection of the many-times rebuilt Metropolitan Museum contains artifacts dating as far back as the Dutch period, when the city was called New Amsterdam.) There you can also see the remains of the ancient elevated train lines (many filled in with other materials and made into the "longhouses" of the Native American Ancestral Movement of the 2050s). The most ancient buildings are made of a characteristic material known (for reasons unclear to modern scholars) as *brownstone*. Other nineteenth- and twentieth-century bricks are equally distinctive.

Since the institution of the Robotic Church in 2216, New York has been the residence of the Grand Robot of Earth, whose palace stands atop the rocky northern tip of Manhattan, and whose emblematic "spare parts" may be seen affixed to anything and everything, including many buildings long predating the era of Roboticism. Perhaps the most amusingly absurd is "Cleopatra's Pit Stop" in Central Park: an ancient Egyptian obelisk atop a titanium-alloy Volkswagen Bus (by Zarg O'Connor, the thirty-third-century Neo-Warholist), topped with the outstretched hand of Grand Robot ZX41.38, who renovated much of New York after the departure of the Denebians.

Of course contemporary New Yorkers take all this for granted. New York evenings are continually punctuated by the *pop-pop-pop* of local teenagers teleporting from building to building in their immemorial adolescent rituals.

Beware of telekinetic pickpockets.

The one writer who captured the sense of the layering of history and time, better than any generic science-fiction practitioner, was Mark Twain. He didn't do it in a science-fiction story either, but in charming, little-known essay called "A Memorable Midnight Experience," written in 1872 and collected in *Europe and Elsewhere*.

Twain visited Westminster Abbey. Much of what he saw, I saw when I was there the week after the worldcon, but *he* paused before an inscription reading, "Wm. West, toome shower, 1698." In other words, graffiti left by a seventeenth-century tour guide (tomb shower).

Writes Twain:

> This was a sort of revelation to me. I had been wandering through the Abbey, never imagining but that its shows were created only for us—the people of the nineteenth century. But here was a man (become a show himself now, and a curiosity) to whom all these things were sights and wonders a hundred and seventy-five years ago.... Charles II's tomb was the newest and latest novelty he had; and he was doubtless present at the funeral. Three hundred years before his time some ancestor of his, perchance, used to point out the ancient marvels, in the immemorial way and say: "This, gentlemen, is the tomb of his late Majesty Edward the Third—and I wish I could see him alive and hearty again, as I saw him twenty years ago; yonder is the tomb of Sebert the Saxon king—he has been lying there well on to eight hundred years they say." And three hundred years before *this* party, Westminster was still a show, and Edward the Confessor's grave was a novelty of some thirty years' standing—but old "Sebert" was hoary and ancient still, and people who spoke of Alfred the Great as a comparatively recent man pondered over Sebert's grave and tried to take in all the tremendous meaning of it when the "toome shower" said, "This man has lain here well nigh five hundred years."

Twain looks to the future:

> And some day a curiously clad company may arrive here in a balloon ship from some remote corner of the globe, and as they follow the verger among the monuments they may hear him say: "This is the tomb of Victoria the Good Queen; battered and uncouth as it looks, it was a wonder of magnificence—but twelve hundred years work a great deal of damage to these things."

Having visited that curious, ancient New York with its Robotic palace, fragmentary Empire State Building, and thirty-second-century Denebian fireplugs, the interstellar tourist returning to Earth may seek out Westminster Abbey and see the same things Twain saw, or go to Rome and see what I did—only there will be more layers by then. The meaning and perspective of everything will have changed—as it changes endlessly.

IV.

MY CAREER AS A HACK WRITER

I've got unpublished novels. Doesn't everybody? John Brunner had a whole drawer full of aborted novels. C. J. Cherryh once described how she wrote a novel a year for twenty years before selling any. That would be a closet full. After she became a professional, she managed to sell a couple that lay toward the top of the heap, possibly as far down as Novel #18, but I'd guess the rest will remain there.

So what else is new?

Well, I haven't made huge amount of money in my career so far, but I consider myself fortunate in many ways. I've sold over a hundred stories to places like *Twilight Zone* and *Fear* and Thomas Monteleone's *Borderlands* anthology. I've been translated into German, French, Italian, Dutch, Norwegian, and even Hebrew. All my fiction books are in print. It is true there are only four of them—*The Shattered Goddess*, *We Are All Legends*, *Tom O'Bedlam's Night Out*, and *The White Isle*—and that one, in a library reprint edition, only sold thirty-five copies last year, but there they are. As I write, my name is on the cover of the current issue of *Amazing*. I am sure there are people in writing workshops out there who would all but kill to get as far as I have. One murder later they'd discover that most of the slope is still before them, but never mind...

The point is that my unpublished novels are *hack* novels. They were written to order, for the express purpose of making money. They didn't work out. Should anyone grumble, "Schweitzer is a lousy hack writer," I can only nod in agreement. Readers profess to like my other stuff, but my *hack* writing has never reached a readership and probably won't.

Let me explain. There are two novels in question. One is called *Conan the Deliverer* ("Oh, he's become a midwife?" someone asked. "No," I replied. "More like a milkman.") And the other is *The Masks of Atlantis*, and was written, ferchristsake, to go with a *calendar*. Argh.

I sold the Conan novel on a proposal, in the approved fashion. It was accepted. I started writing. I received one-third of the advance on signing a contract, and another third on turning in the completed manuscript. At this point, the editor sent the manuscript back asking for specific revisions. I made them. Possibly because the publisher's right hand was not watching what the left was doing, I received the final third of the advance. *Then* the editor informed me that he was not going to publish this book. There it stands. I did the work. I got paid. The editor exercised his judgment, as was his job to do. I only wonder why, if he didn't like it, he didn't kill the project earlier.

A couple years earlier I made an appalling blunder. I wrote an entire 120,000-word novel for *free*. Oh, yes, I was supposed to get huge amounts of money, and the prospect of such money looked genuinely plausible. The book was to be a "collaboration" with a certain prominent artist, whose previous such "collaboration" made bestseller lists. Everybody was completely honest and above-board, explaining that this was a speculative venture. I was not in any way defrauded or deceived. It really wasn't a collaboration, though, because aside from some photographs of paintings I was supposed to link the book to, and a couple very vague discussions, I had no input at all from my "collaborator." I wrote it all myself.

But what I learned from this is that a book on the bestseller list doesn't necessarily make money. Those lists are a function of *orders*. The problem with the artist's previous bestseller was that it got a huge number of *returns*, and was, in fact, a disaster. The tie-in calendar to the Atlantis book appeared, but the artist's agent never managed to sell the book itself. Again, they treated me entirely fairly, and agreed to turn all rights to the book over to me at the end of 1990, nine years after the project had begun.

So, if I change the names and rewrite it a bit until you don't recognize any scenes from the calendar I have...a very long, pretty bad novel. It's lifeless. It rambles. It nakedly recycles large portions of *The Shattered Goddess*, which I had written just before beginning *The Masks of Atlantis*.

Why? Was it because I was a cynical hack and did a half-assed job? I don't think so. I gave it my best shot, but just *couldn't* make the story live. The reason for this bears some examining.

The Conan book isn't very good either. Oh, it has its moments. I particularly like the one in which Conan and a Stygian prince, in the manner of the characters in Gene Wolfe's *The Citadel of the Autarch*, have a storytelling session and swap creation myths. There is certainly some striking and scary imagery, and a *lot* about Robert E. Howard's mythical pseudo-Egyptian land of Stygia that you didn't know before. This was to be the definitive Stygian novel.

But it didn't work. The character of Conan is a muscle-bound *hole* in the story with nobody there to fill it. He spends a great deal of time looking at the scenery between swordfights. On a deeper level, he has nothing to *do* in the story. The plot—a quest into the Stygian land of the dead—really does not require him. The genuine protagonist is a sympathetically-depicted Stygian prince. (Howard's Stygians tended to be the bad guys.) Conan comes along as extra baggage.

I cannot say that the editor was wrong in refusing to publish this. It certainly would have been a *very strange* Conan novel, not at all like the others in the series, and it probably would not have pleased its intended audience.

What was lacking was that hoariest of artistic intangibles, *inspiration*. The book wasn't *mine*, any more than the Atlantis novel was mine. It was what I suppose I could call *externally motivated*. It hadn't come out of any need I had to write that story. It had instead been generated to fulfill a contract. Had there been no deal, I would not have written it. I can't think of a purer description of hack-writing than that. Next time you go to write a story, ask yourself the following question: if I had all the money I ever needed, and did not have to work in any way, and *would not be paid for this story*, would I still want to write it?

I thought I was going to have some fun with it though. I thought I was going to give good value. But when I actually came to do it, I froze up. The story wasn't *felt*. It was contrived. There were, certainly, additional problems, notably that Conan as he has now evolved in the continuing Tor Books series bears little relationship to the Robert E. Howard creation. He is not allowed to change or grow or feel real, human moods. He has become a static, one-dimensional pulp character like Doc Savage or the later Tarzan. Of course, I had no business claiming to be a purist while engaged in such a project, but it probably was a mistake for me to have gone back and reread all the Howard Conan stories and tried to emulate *Howard*, rather than the later Conan writers. The result doesn't read like Howard anyway, but like Darrell Schweitzer telling a sort of Conan story. Certainly the series hasn't evolved the way the Arthurian mythos has, so that there are hundreds of different voices telling the same story. Therefore, denied the possibility of doing any "internals," I stuck to externals. The book is all surfaces.

The Atlantis book is even worse, filled with ludicrous incongruities such as mastodons and dinosaurs existing at the same time, a fur-bikinied heroine carrying a huge broadsword through the jungle while the hero dresses like Buck Rogers and totes a raygun. At times I not-so-subtly parodied this, as in the restaurant scene—I think of it as an ancient Atlantean Denny's—where there's a whole tyrannosaurus turning on a spit in the middle of the room. A dino-bar! But—Gawd!—there was even a Cute Furry Critter in there, I kid you not, for the benefit of the stuffed toy concessions! I had little feel for these characters or the images depicted in the artist's paintings. So I tried to contrive a plot which would somehow wrap itself around all the prefabricated stuff and keep on going. This was going to be a coffee-table book, and my job was to fill in the words between the pretty pictures.

I did too. The artist and his agent were pleased with what I produced. But they couldn't sell it, so possibly the editors they submitted it to could tell the difference. I am sure that if I ever rewrite this book into something publishable, I will dispense with every one of those images, with the cute critter, the—excuse me, but I can't help it—broad with the broadsword, the dinosaurs, the mastodons, and all the rest. There were snatches of creative stuff in places where the book got the farthest from what it was supposed to be, and possibly I can salvage some of that.

Colleagues and fans warned me at the time that this was a Really Bad Idea, that it would ruin my reputation and wreck my career. I countered that I didn't expect anyone to take it any more seriously than, say, Joe Haldeman's *Attar the Merman* novels or George Alec Effinger's *Planet of the Apes* novelizations. The Conan book I didn't expect to be taken any more seriously than a *Star Trek* novel. There has been a recognized tradition of serious writers doing this sort of thing on the sly, at least as far back as Theodore Sturgeon's novelization of *Voyage to the Bottom of the Sea*. I regarded these jobs as wholly apart from my regular writing, as if, for the money, I'd taken time off to paint a house or deliver pizza. I was certain that I would never mix the two.

Quite possibly, my sheer inability to do this sort of thing saved me from a dire fate. Far better writers than I have *not* always been able to keep the self-generated and externally-generated writing apart. You get hooked. You find yourself economically dependent on novelizations or sharecropping in someone else's universe or ghosting, and before long your own career vanishes. We can all think of several promising novelists who got swallowed up this way. Many of them are still around, writing novels "in the universe of" somebody VERY FAMOUS.

I can't claim moral superiority to the people who do this sort of thing, even the ones who destroy themselves this way. I *can't do it*. It's as if I hired myself out to deliver pizza and discovered I didn't know how to drive. I learned the important lesson that there are two kinds of writers in this world: creative ones and verbal technicians. The verbal technician is, archetypically, a TV writer, though nowadays as TV marketing and production techniques invade print-fiction, he might be working on series novels for a packager.

The verbal technician has very real skills. He has to deliver the goods or the boss will have to find someone else who can. *Who* does the job in the end hardly matters, any more than it matters which writer wrote a particular TV episode, as long as that episode is up to stuff. The verbal technician has to be able to write *anything* to a certain level of competence. Let's say a producer or packager has sold a series to a network or a publisher. Now it's time to hire writers to write the episodes. But the whole appeal of fiction—or film—the secret of audience enjoyment and consequently what makes the paying customer pay, is *emotion*. The story has to be exciting, funny, sad, or something. It can't just lie there.

You know what they say: *be sincere whether you mean it or not. Once you've got that down, you can fake anything*.

There are some writers who have both talents. Haldeman and Effinger obviously aren't hacks. They can write their own, unique fiction and both have found a wide audience. But they also had the ability to type out *Attar* or *Planet of the Apes* novels and produce whatever it is that consumers of that particular kind of literary cheese-doodle find nourishing. That is precisely the skill which I find I don't have. As Walter Brennan used to say on some TV western or other, *No brag, just fact*. That's why I never made it as a hack writer and why my hack productions were not even good enough to be published by the standards of such things. The ability to contrive, to put something you didn't create into an acceptable package, is quite different from reaching into your own subconscious and coming up with material which, to you at least, makes a thrilling or funny or sad story, then writing with such conviction that you can touch the emotions of others.

Ever notice that the work of verbal technicians doesn't *really* move you? Well, not very much. Some of it's *okay*, rather like adequate cafeteria food as opposed to fine cuisine, but we're not likely to get a *More Than Human* or a *Childhood's End* or a *Lord of the Rings* from novelizations or packaged series or Darrell Schweitzer writing Conan novels. My inability is a matter of degree. I can't do it *at all*, but I'm not sure anybody else out there can fully fake sincerity either. Sure, Robert Silverberg, Randall Garrett, and Harlan Ellison did it on a monthly basis for *Amazing* back in the '50s when that magazine was staff-written and the stories were concocted to match already-existing covers, artwork, and even titles.

Silverberg, in an interview I did with him back in 1975 (see *Amazing*) described it this way:

> ...I had considerable contempt for those mass-produced factory magazines, and this of course involved some schizophrenia for me when I started writing for them. I simply separated my head from my fingertips, and...produce $500 worth of junk a month. But...by the time I was twenty-eight or so I had outgrown that very dangerous and destructive division of the soul, and had decided; in fact I had no choice but to decide; to write only the kind of fiction I would want to read.

He goes on to describe how, after the collapse of the SF magazine market in the late '50s, he drifted into other things, and rediscovered his self-respect when he found himself a well-regarded popular science writer. Only after that was he able to come back and write *Nightwings* and *Downward to the Earth* and *Dying Inside*.

Aside from the certain competence of the verbal technician, those assembly-line stories for *Amazing* had little to offer. Go look in issues from about 1955 and see for yourself. Maybe you'll come away understanding why packaged series novels are never as good as individual works by the same writers, why all the subsequent Conan novelists can't even *touch* what Robert E. Howard was doing. Or maybe you have to have been there, and tried it, and gagged. I'm like someone who tried beer because everybody was drinking it, then found I *didn't like* it, couldn't keep it down, and so never became a drunkard. Sometimes circumstance favors you, even if you don't know it at the time.

Hack-writers can't overcome the fact that what they're writing is not theirs. Deep inside, such writers have nothing to say except, "Give me more money." The most successful ones, who can make a lifelong career that way are, I suspect, people who never had anything to say *at all*, and who never would have become writers in the first place if they'd found some better source of income.

Sure, the writer has to eat. Sure, the smart writer is going to sell his or her story to the best-paying magazine or to the publisher who gives the largest advance, but there is a vast and profound difference between marketing what you have created and filling in what someone else has commissioned. It's the difference between poetry and occasional verse.

But sometimes what the writer needs, far more than hack contracts, is an honest job.

1997 Update

John Brunner died in 1995. He never sold out and remained a real writer until the end.

My hack-writing career remains as moribund as ever, for all I have done a small amount of what I might call "stunt writing." I have contributed stories to commissioned anthologies, where the editor sets out a series of guidelines and the writers write stories to match.

These can be fun if you don't take them too seriously. I am able to do this sort of writing sometimes, if I have sufficient enthusiasm for the material and some modicum of something to say about it. While I do not recommend myself for, say, *Alternate Historical Vampire Cat Erotica*, I was pleased to get into Marvin Kaye's *The Resurrected Holmes* (St. Martin's Press, 1996), the premise of which was that the unwritten cases alluded to by Dr. Watson were farmed out to other writers after his death, circa 1930. So I got to write "The Adventure of the Grice-Pattersons in the Isle of Uffa" in the manner of Lord Dunsany, as a Jorkens story. Such writing is almost a kind of parody, but sometimes the sheer outrageousness of the premise recommends it, at least in shorter lengths.

There was a stirring of interest in *Conan the Deliverer* when the editorship of the Conan series changed a couple years ago, particularly since this manuscript was already finished, turned in, and paid for. But the new editor agreed with his precedessor. I suspect that is the end of that. If I ever become as famous as Lovecraft, maybe it'll be published by Necronomicon Press long after I'm dead. More likely, trees will be spared.

But the time spent writing Conan was not entirely wasted. Most of the novel is set in Howard's land of Stygia, which is the Hyborean Age equivalent of Pharonic Egypt. In the course writing this, I immersed myself in the lore and history of ancient Egypt. On the rebound, I wrote the novella "To Become a Sorcerer," which, while it bears no discernable relationship to *Conan the Deliverer*, does make much use of pseudo-Egyptian imagery. This was later expanded into the novel, *The Mask of the Sorcerer*, which was published in England in 1995 to some acclaim.

To be safe, I made a point of not rereading *Conan the Deliverer* while writing *The Mask of the Sorcerer* and anything I could remember from the Conan book, I left out. I still haven't reread it. Memory fades. The one link between the two is in the names, which I cribbed out of William Kelly Simpson's *The Literature of Ancient Egypt* (Yale, 1972). In the Conan book, there is a prince named Sekenre. In *The Mask of the Sorcerer* and several subsequent stories, this is the name of the eternally-adolescent, multiple-personality sorcerer who often narrates. The two have nothing in common, save that for both, the name is actually a typo. The properly transliterated Egyptian spelling is "Sekenere," with an extra "e."

I also haven't reread *The Masks of Atlantis*, and am making a point not to as I write a new Atlantis novel, presently entitled *The Thief of Memories*. My new Atlantis will be very short on rayguns and dinosaur-on-a-spit, and long on eldritch sorcery and dead (or missing) gods. An agent I once had said of the first Atlantis project, "Maybe you'll just have to walk away from that one." He turned out to be right. I haven't looked back.

V.

THE LANDS THAT CLEARLY PERTAIN TO FAERY

THE ELUSIVE BASICS OF FANTASY

1. The World of the Imagination, and How We Arrived There

A lot of people want to go to Elfland these days, so many that you would think someone would build a superhighway. But the road to Elfland is more difficult to reach than that: the way is tangled, passing through a dark wood, and there are dangers along the route. There are no signs to mark the way. You have to get there by reading books which fall into the broad and ill-defined category of Fantasy.

In the broadest sense, all fiction is fantasy, since it deals with things which are not true; in a slightly narrower one, a fantasy story is any containing elements which are fantastic or impossible. *Impossible to whom?* you may well ask. If Shakespeare believed in fairies, does that mean *A Midsummer Night's Dream* is an example of realism? What about ghost stories in societies that believe in ghosts, including our own?

When we speak of Fantasy in today's publishing world, we have to be more specific. We arrive at a description, if not a definition, by the following route: a fantasy story is one based on a premise which the author considers to be made up. It is a departure from observed reality. True, but by this definition Kafka's *The Metamorphosis*, Tolkien's *The Lord of the Rings*, and the movie *Splash* are all fantasy. Indeed, they are, but they otherwise have little in common. When we are talking about a fantasy *genre*, only *The Lord of the Rings* is a relevant example.

The epic or heroic fantasy, of which *The Lord of the Rings* is the premier example, is descended from the world's great myths and epics, and more directly from medieval romance. The first modern writer of such fiction, William Morris (1834-1896), wrote lush, leisurely novels in archaic, pseudo-Malory prose, dealing with pure heroes wandering across beautiful, completely imaginary landscapes vaguely resembling medieval Europe, replete with enchanted isles, haunted castles, magic wells, and the like. His *The Well at the World's End* (1896) is a long quest novel, which set the pattern for much that followed. Foremost among his successors were E. R. Eddison (1882-1945), whose *The Worm Ouroboros* (1922) is a chivalrous adventure, told in thunderously good Elizabethan prose, set on a Mercury quite unlike any planet known to astronomy; and Lord Dunsany (1878-1957) who wrote fantasy as if it were lyric poetry. In Dunsany's *The King of Elfland's Daughter* (1924), the hero is sent on a quest with instructions to "go from here eastwards and pass the fields we know, till you see the lands that clearly pertain to Faery; and cross their boundary, which is made of twilight, and come to that palace that is only told of in song."

Dunsany dominated the field for a good half century, but then J. R. R. Tolkien arrived. After the publication of *The Lord of the Rings* (1954-1956), nothing was ever the same again. Tolkien wrote of that dream place, which Dunsany called Elfland, but in exhaustive detail, complete with maps, charts, genealogies, and historical and linguistic appendices. Readers were fascinated. When Tolkien came out in paperback in 1965, he was almost immediately a bestseller, and this spurred publishers to seek more books which would appeal to the same audience. The result was the Ballantine Adult Fantasy Series, beginning in 1969, ably edited by Lin Carter, which included the first paperback printings of Morris, Dunsany, Eddison, and many others, plus occasional new works, some of which are now regarded as classics. It is impossible to overestimate the importance of the paperback editions of Tolkien and the Ballantine series. They demonstrated the strengths and appeals of fantasy, to readers, writers, and publishers. As a direct result, what was once esoterica for the connoisseur has become an extremely successful form of popular literature, published by virtually every paperback house in existence. Dozens of fantasy books appear every month, most of which may be described, at least in a general sense, as Tolkienesque. This sort of fantasy, which we might call the imaginary-scene or imaginary-world fantasy, may have antecedents going back decades, even centuries, but it has existed as a publishing category for less than twenty years. It is a new genre.

Fantasy writer L. Sprague de Camp has suggested that fantasy became popular as part of a reaction against all those "mainstream" novels about snivelling little wimps suffering in grey, tedious, modern settings. There has always been an appeal in stories of heroic figures, straightforward action, clear moral values, magic, wonder, and not an IRS agent in sight. Further, Tolkien demonstrated the appeal of the imaginary world so realistically detailed that the reader can immerse himself into it completely. A fantasy world, like Tolkien's Middle Earth, is someplace we would like to be, or at least visit. But since it does not exist, it can only be visited through books. Readers like to visit again and again, hence the popularity of the fantasy series.

Or, to go back to the Dunsany and Morris model, a fantasy can be a kind of clear and vivid dream, either filled with meaning or existing for its own sake, like an Oriental landscape painting.

Tolkien showed that the reader delights in details. The more imaginary lore, the better. Once the reader has accepted the world of the story, he may well want to know the histories of the chief countries in that world, or the lives of the kings who ruled two thousand years before the main action of the novel. He will also want to know the lay of the land, the geography of imaginary rivers, mountains, forests, cities, and possibly even a haunted stretch, suitably marked *Here There Be Monsters*. Tolkien may not have been the first fantasy writer to include a map (Morris was, in *The Sundering Flood*, 1897), but Tolkien started the current fashion for them.

2. Write Like a Native

The most basic rules for writing fantasy are the same as for any fiction. The prose must be competent, so that descriptions describe, dialogue sounds like people talking, and the narrative gets the story across, rather than making the reader stop and notice how beautifully or (artificially) you are writing. The plot has to make sense and come to a resolution. The characters have to develop. There has to be some overall point to the action.

But there are many elements of fantasy which are *not* the same as ordinary fiction. For instance, the matter of the imaginary setting. How do you communicate a *whole world* to the reader at the beginning, so he will be able to follow the action?

You do *not* do it with a long lecture at the front, or with a barrage of maps, genealogical tables, capsule histories, and the like, which the reader may dig through with fascination later on, but which will not get him hooked. Tolkien, significantly, put all such secondary material in *The Lord of the Rings* at the end of Volume Three. First, he told the story.

You do *not* try to cram all the information into the narrative itself, particularly with an opening paragraph like this:

> Gorglock, forty-seventh prince of the half-elvish line, stood on the battlements of the castle of Fnork in the Vale of the Grey Lord's Doom. He stared out into the distance, remembering how, in ancient times, far beyond the Many-Toothed Mountains, by the shore of the River Yig, which divides Upper Thongor from Lower Jongor, the first of the elvish lords battled the Dark One for forty days and nights... [And so, on, and so on, for several hundred words.] Now,

> for the first time in untold eons, something stirred out there in the misty forest. Gorglock drew his sword.

Start small. Begin with something which is commonplace to the people of your imaginary world, but which is strange to the reader. Start, perhaps, with some *process*, which is a regular part of the characters' lives. T. H. White is particularly adept at this in *Once and Future King*:

> On Mondays, Wednesdays, and Fridays it was Court Hand and Summulae Logicales, while the rest of the week it was the Organon, Repetition, and Astrology. The governess was always getting muddled with her astrolabe, and when she got especially muddled she would take it out on the Wart by rapping his knuckles. She did not rap Kay's knuckles, because when Kay grew older he would be Sir Kay, the master of the estate.

Thus, with a few words we are drawn into White's Arthurian world. The relationships between some of the characters are deftly drawn, and, for all that nothing out of the ordinary has happened yet, we know that we are not in the world we see outside the window.

Sometimes the smallness of the beginning can be physical confinement. Tolkien begins *The Lord of the Rings* in the little village of the hobbits, and only gradually, as the characters begin their travels, does he show us the broad world of Middle Earth. In my own novel, *The Shattered Goddess*, I took this a step further: the protagonist is first seen as a child raised in secret in a small suite of rooms. Every time he is taken anywhere, new and vast vistas open up. He is a stranger in the world himself, and must learn everything, as does the reader.

A successful imaginary world is largely a matter of viewpoint. Characters may be divided up into two categories, native-born and intruders. The native-born character lives there, in Middle Earth or wherever, and knows nothing else. Therefore everything he sees, says, or thinks will be in terms of that world. He has no other perspective. The trick for you, as a writer, is to write as if you too were native-born. Thus, if everyone in the world believes implicitly in omens, the character might say, "I saw a black swan, and I was afraid, because I knew that someone was going to die." He would not say, "I saw a black swan, which my people believed to be a sign of bad luck." Further, if his world has elves in it, he would never stop to explain what an elf is. He would merely accept its presence. The story must contain nothing, either in first person narration or third, which is beyond the experience of the characters. The imaginary world has to speak with its own unique voice, no matter how the story is otherwise told. If it does not, the illusion will be broken, and the reader will no longer be immersed in the story.

When some of the characters are visitors, the viewpoint shifts radically. This is the technique of Mark Twain in *A Connecticut Yankee in King Arthur's Court*. Twain sends a contemporary man into the world of King Arthur, not the historical world of post-Roman Britain either, but the completely imaginary Arthurian milieu of knights and chivalry, as decribed in Malory's *Le Morte d'Arthur*.

Twain's Sir Boss is an outsider, and the book is written from an outsider's viewpoint. Anachronistic language and imagery are not only acceptable, but often quite effective. In Twain's case, the contrasts between the nineteenth century and the imaginary sixth century were being exploited for satirical purposes. The more clashes, the better.

If you are narrating the events as seen by a visitor from the real, contemporary world, perhaps magically transported Elsewhere, it can be quite effective to say that a dragon came roaring out of a cave like a New York subway train out of a dark tunnel.

But if all the characters are native-born, this only breaks the spell, since no one could plausibly know what subways are. The reader hears the *author* talking, and this is as much an interruption as if the playwright came on stage in the middle of Act Three to explain something.

This sort of perspective shift isn't unique to fantasy. One of the best exercises for any fantasy writer is simply reading books produced by other cultures, particularly cultures far removed in time. Read something like *The Lives of the Twelve Caesars* by Suetonius, or the *Histories* of Herodotus. Pay special attention to the details, the little bits of daily living which the author takes for granted, but which are strange to the twentieth-century American reader. Suetonius, for example, is obsessed with portents and supernatural manifestations, and lives in a world closely tied to the Fates, where the events in a man's life are preordained, but hidden, and the truth may sometimes be discovered a little bit at a time. And yet there is no moral direction. He doesn't take the gods very seriously. So there are many Mysteries, without any order. His is a very different outlook from that of a scientific rationalist. The fantasy writer must do more than merely copy this. Instead, *make up* something which is as all-pervasive in your fantasy world.

3. A Few Magic Words About Magic

Fantasy novels and stories almost inevitably contain magic, either performed by magic-users or inherent in the world the characters find themselves in. Magic, in the broadest sense, means any supernatural force, such as might pervade an enchanted forest, but more specifically, it is the use of the supernatural by the magic-user to manipulate or change the world around him. Beyond that, you may make magic function any way you wish. The important thing is that *you* know how it works, at least for story purposes. You cannot, of course, *really* explain how to cast a spell which will make someone sleep for a hundred years, and it would be tedious to go on through pages and pages of occult jargon faking it.

But, you might find it convenient to have magic obey the laws of *sympathy* and *contagion*, as L. Sprague de Camp and Fletcher Pratt once suggested in a story called, appropriately enough, "The Mathematics of Magic." Or, as in Ursula Le Guin's *A Wizard of Earthsea*, magic may be an arcane discipline based on the discovery of the secret names of things, for which one goes to a special wizards' university. In Dunsany, magic is often metaphorical. It makes aesthetic sense, and the rest follows. In some of my own fiction, magic is a shamanistic experience, a matter of trances and visions.

The important thing is to be consistent, and not change the rules halfway through the story, just to get your hero out of a pinch. Thus, if you have established that the hero's broomstick only flies when rubbed with feathers (this is the de Camp/Pratt law of contagion: a part has the characteristics of the whole; a few feathers make something fly like a bird), it will not to to have him save himself by going into a mystical trance and floating ineffably away, when no feathers are available. There must be limitations. *If anything can happen, no one cares what does.* If your hero cannot get into danger because he always develops a new magical skill in the nick of time, his adventures will be a dull series of arbitrary wonders, without any possibility of suspense or narrative tension.

In *The Well of the Unicorn* (1948) Fletcher Pratt came up with a particularly effective idea. His magician hero gets sick every time he uses magic. He is exhausted and helpless for a while afterwards. This puts severe limits on what he can do, and so it is possible for him to get in danger, or even to fail.

A system of magic can either be made up entirely or borrowed from folklore and anthropology (Pratt & de Camp's derives largely from Sir James Frazer's *The Golden Bough*). Even if you are making yours up, it is still a good idea to familiarize yourself with a few *real* magical belief systems, so you can see how they work and what the believers expect of them.

4. Don't Forget the Real World

Most fantasy worlds tend to be at a low level of technology, pre-industrial, pre-gunpowder at least. For all a fantasy novel may be filled with magic, enchanted lands, elves, visitations of imagined gods, and other wonders, it is also going to contain real-world elements.

Thus, you must understand why it is impossible to ride a horse fifty miles a day at a full gallop, or why no one swings a fifty-pound sword, or why it is necessary, in a feudal society, that the peasants outnumber the kings and knights by a very large margin. If your characters go for a sea voyage, you need to have some idea of how sailing ships work. (If you don't know very much about sailing, make your viewpoint character a passenger, not a sailor.) You may even be able to use nautical details to plot advantage: a character delayed at a key moment because of contrary winds, and perhaps making a great sacrifice to gain a favorable wind by magic.

On one level, a fantasy novel requires all the research of a historical novel. You may make up the actual history, but you still have to make an unfamiliar milieu believable, even as a historical novelist does.

It is mostly a matter of common sense and careful observation. I once picked out three random fantasy novels in order to review them, and was astonished to find the same blunder in two of them: characters on foot in enemy territory, wishing to conceal themselves, making camp around a *huge bonfire*. However elaborately the magic may have been worked out, those books just didn't convince.

5. Prithee, Sirrah, Avoid Archaism

Several of the early, classic writers mentioned earlier wrote in deliberately archaic prose. William Morris mimicked the style of *Le Morte d'Arthur*. E. R. Eddison, amazingly, wrote brilliantly effective, genuine sixteenth-century English. His style compares well with the very best Tudor writers. Lord Dunsany wrote a strange, unique English derived from the King James Bible and from Irish daily speech. But all of these writers were eccentric geniuses, and, as fantasy has become more of a commercial category aimed at a broad audience, rather than at a small literary elite, thickly archaic prose has been been much frowned upon. Many readers find even the best of it tough going. Many editors will reject such writing out of hand.

Also, unless *you* happen to be another of those rare, genuine, eccentric geniuses, your attempts at archaic prose are more likely to come out sounding like dialogue from a certain infamous Hollywood medieval epic: "Withersoever thou goest, there also I goest."

Or, as Ursula Le Guin put it, a medieval version of Tonto.

Writers instinctively use archaic language in fantasy because they want the effect of distancing. The events, images, and personages in the tale are to be stately, beautiful, and remote. If a High Lord of Elfland says, "Wow, man, that magic is really far-out," the reader laughs, and the illusion the author has been striving for is lost.

But the secret of success is not strange syntax and exotic vocabulary. It is more a matter of image and idiom. If the High Lord of

Elfland says, "Your magic is powerful and strange, and I am amazed," the illusion will hold.

Write plainly and clearly, but, to make your magical world suitably enchanted and remote, concentrate on strange imagery, on the unique outlook of the hero, and on the other real content of the story. If you have genuine enchantment to present, you can present it plainly, as Tolkien did. By way of style, it is merely necessary to avoid *anachronistic* words and phrases. No one in a Bronze Age world can compare something to radar or pay for his lodging in dollars and cents. No lord of Elfland talks in 1997 street slang.

6. The Joy of Fantasy

If fantasy is done right, it provides a very special pleasure, for both the reader and the writer. If treated with serious ambition, it can touch the emotions more deeply than any other kind of writing. It can touch on profound truths, in the way that the great myths did in ages past.

Or, it can be just a game, giving its own unique amusement. It is fun for everyone to wander through imaginary constructs of magic kingdoms, perhaps to untangle oneself from the web-like complications of an elaborately-imagined magic system. Fantasy can work as satire, as fable, as tragedy, as light adventure reading, or sometimes, in a really great work, like *The Once and Future King*, as all of these things together.

Fantasy is still very much in demand. All you have to do is imagine a fantasy world and a story to go with it, then sit down and write that story to its completion, and you, too, can find your way to Elfland.

VI.

UTTERING THE P-WORD

OR, THE RETURN OF THE FACTORY SYSTEM

Have you noticed? We've got a new "bad word" in science fiction, a label which instantly and irrevocably hurls the labelled into the Outer Darkness to wail and gnash dentures. Right out of the lexicon that gave us "Imperialist," "Pinko," "McCarthyism," "Racist," "Sexist," "Politically Correct," "New Wave," "Old Wave," "Roger Elwood"...

The other day I was writing some ad copy for Owlswick Press, which is George Scithers's personal imprint. I proposed to describe the superb physical appearance of the recent Avram Davidson omnibus, *The Adventures of Doctor Eszterhazy*, which, since I didn't work on it, I can objectively tell you is as fine a specimen of book-design as this field has ever seen: elegantly laid out, with just the right selections of body type and titles, handsome little illos used as running heads (a different one for each story), superb production values the likes of which you seldom see from anyone other than Donald M. Grant, a very effective, full-color dustjacket by George Barr—in short, a great *package*, as I was about to phrase it.

"You'd better not use the word 'package,'" George said, pointing out that a *packaged book* now has very negative connotations.

I had uttered the P-word. Packaging. The public recoils. Possibly we should put a safety banner diagonally across the front: CONTAINS NO CYCLAMATES... err... A REAL BOOK. NOT PACKAGED.

A rather interesting state of affairs. You don't have to look very far to see the evidence. Customers are increasingly wary of anything they think is a "packaged" book these days, and with good reason.

Packaging isn't, *per se*, the subject of any controversy. No one objects to packagers acting as a freelance editorial team to get science fiction in the front door of publishers who have no science fiction editorial staff, and all the handsomely designed collections of stories by famous authors are a blessing to us all. Leiber's *The Ghost Light*, which was put together by one of the leading packagers, Byron Preiss

Productions, is something every fan should have in his collection. And we might commend Preiss Productions for some of their anthologies too. *The Planets* and its companions are attractive, interesting books.

But I have an acquaintance, H____, who is so lacking in common tact that he *says* what other people are just thinking. Sometimes this is refreshing. H____ puts it bluntly, "I won't buy any book that's packaged."

I don't think he's alone, or even extraordinary. "Packaging" *has* become a dirty word in science fiction of late. And we all know why. It's because packagers have some nasty habits.

The core of the matter is what is variously called *sharecropping* or *franchise* publishing: the mass-production of novels exploiting a famous name or a pre-existing series concept. Or, as one writer formerly involved and since recovered puckishly calls them, "McBooks." The literary equivalent of McDonald's hamburgers.

What we're witnessing is a wholesale return to the factory system of science fiction writing and publishing.

There's nothing immoral about this, as long as the product is labelled correctly. Various popular writers of the last century, the elder Dumas for example, had apprentices write parts of their novels, or possibly whole books based on an outline. Sir Walter Scott's friends allegedly joked with him, "Have you read your latest novel yet?"

In the pulp era there was what was called a "house name," a pseudonym used by all the anonymous writers of that particular product. Many of the one-character "hero pulps"—*Doc Savage*, *The Shadow*, *Captain Future*—were especially prone to it, the difference with the last named being that if the Captain Future novel bore the Edmond Hamilton byline, it was definitely by Edmond Hamilton. (About whom, more later.) If it was by Brett Sterling, the house name, it could be Hamilton or anyone else.

Amazing Stories was a pure factory system for three or four wasted years in the middle '50s. Robert Silverberg described it when I interviewed him in the January 1976 *Amazing*:

> I was asked...to contribute 50,000 words of fiction a month, in assorted lengths, anything from short stories to novelets, and I would receive a penny a word for this.... Now the publisher of *Amazing* didn't care what his 50,000 words of stuff were as long as they looked like science fiction, had a robot in them here and there, the hero triumphed, and there was a lot of dialogue.... This kind of publishing serves no human need that I know except for the publisher's need to get his product on the newstands once a month and the writer's need to pay his rent.... The climate of publishing then did not encourage a writer

> to stretch himself, to expand himself, especially a young writer. It was very seductive to be told, "Hey, come in and write some junk and I'll pay you enough to keep you eating".... I was led to make the worst of myself. The editors played to my weakest points, my own weaknesses in character...

Amazing was virtually a closed shop in those days. The artwork was done *before* the stories. Once a month the editor and his crew of hacks would meet, decide who wrote what story around which illustration—this is why there are titles, but no bylines on the covers of *Amazing* circa 1955—and an issue would be filled. Indeed, this sort of activity served no purpose at all save paying the rent of some writers who, once they broke free of this entrapment, happened to become famous, people like Silverberg, Harlan Ellison, and Randall Garrett. But the actual content of the magazine between about 1954 and 1958 is wholly negligible. (Happily, *Amazing* got a new editor in 1958, and, under the auspices of Cele Goldsmith Lalli, went on to what many consider its golden age.)

Arguably, the first purveyor of McBooks was Roger Elwood, a now virtually forgotten figure who cut a muddy swath through the field in the early '70s. Like a packager, Elwood approached publishers who had no science fiction department and promised the goods. He sold something like *eighty* anthologies of original science fiction in three years. For a while there, his books constituted full half of the *entire market* for short fiction, but it was a mass-produced, shoddy, bottom half. No Elwood-published story ever won a Hugo or Nebula, and to my knowledge only one, Philip José Farmer's "After King Kong Fell," ever made the final ballot. Economically, Elwood was a disaster. The readers decided, "If this is what SF anthologies are like, I'm going fishing." The anthology market was destroyed for at least a decade.

Then Elwood packaged his Laser Books line. He proposed to the publisher of Harlequin Romances a science-fiction line aimed at the husbands of the ladies who read Harlequins. He would provide the books. He would provide the art. Desktop publishing had not been invented yet, so he could hardly have provided the typesetting.

Lasers would be standard product, all about the same length, all with (admittedly attractive but eventually monotonous) covers by Frank Kelly Freas. The result was another disaster. Laser became the watchword for mediocrity. It was only much later that we discovered that a couple of the writers, particularly K. W. Jeter and Tim Powers, had real talent. They might have been noticed earlier if they hadn't been Laser authors.

What is wrong with packaging? I invite the readers of this essay to go read some packaged novels or anthologies, and see. Don't let me discourage you. Make up your own mind.

But if you're someone who can hear the world "Literature" without reaching for your revolver, I think what you'll find most packaged fiction to be like television in prose: told at a certain competence, but uninspired, hardly innovative or dangerous or startling. McBooks are the ultimate expression of the Age of the Yuppie: conformist, safe, predictable.

Dare I suggest that this is not the way to produce great science fiction? Writers should aim for *great* every single time they put words to paper, because we always fall short of our ideals. If we don't aim for great, we'll seldom hit good.

The inherent, irreparable weakness of the whole packaging scheme is simply this: the *packager* creates a proposal for a book or series, sells it, then *commissions text to be written* from whichever member of the packager's stable expresses interest or is available just then.

That's it. *The inspiration for the story is not coming from the author.* The author is merely someone hired to write what the packager has managed to sell. (Which is not the same as "work for hire." Contract terms are irrelevant to this discussion. We're talking literature here. Put that gun away.) If one author doesn't work out, the packager gets someone else to write that book. It won't matter in the end *who* does it. The packager is in the position of the story-editor of a TV series, handing out the series "bible" to a parade of screenwriters who then try to produce episodes within set parameters.

This is not how *More Than Human* or *The Martian Chronicles* or *The Caves of Steel* were written, or how they ever could have been written. Those books don't have credits like a TV show: produced by so-and-so, conceived by so-and-so, edited by so-and-so. They just have authors. Good fiction grows out of an author's own unique, intensely personal vision. It is expressed in that author's own equally unique voice. The whole point of Sturgeon or Bradbury or Asimov is that they are like *no other writers*. If you want that particular vision, you must get the genuine article, not a pastiche written by whoever the packager managed to hire. You can't get that individual voice on an assembly line.

Packaged novels are like occasional verse as opposed to real poetry. They are command performances. Not even Shakespeare could do his best under such circumstances. Queen Elizabeth said she wanted to see Sir John Falstaff in love, so, by God, she got a play in which Falstaff fell in love, but *The Merry Wives of Windsor* was hardly the Bard in top form.

Now before I seem Mr. High And Mighty, let me admit I've tried to dip into this particular hog-trough myself. I did it for the money. I wrote a Conan the Barbarian novel, which you will probably never get to see. (The gory details were related in "My Career as a Hack Writer.") But I took an old-fashioned attitude toward this sort of thing and jokingly called it "My *Attar the Merman* book," in reference to a couple of hack novels Joe Haldeman did in a hungry season, which no one was ever expected to take seriously. I thought I could keep this as entirely apart from my "real" writing, as if I had been hired to paint a house. It was to be a sideline. Of course I tried to give good value, as any honest craftsman would.

It didn't work out. Part of the problem was that I am a Robert E. Howard enthusiast, and tried to copy Howard's Conan, rather than what the series has evolved into. If you're going to do this sort of writing, you *have* to follow company policy. No excuses.

It wasn't a very good Howard pastiche either. More of the problem was that I was too far along in my career. I already had an individual voice, and I didn't sound like generic Conan.

But the main difficulty was that my heart wasn't in it. The story didn't express anything *I* particularly needed to express in fiction. I wasn't allowed to put some honest emotion into *my* vision of Conan, the way T. H. White put his own feelings into his version of King Arthur. So I froze up. My Conan was a muscle-bound cut-out with nothing to do in most of the novel except look at bizarre landscapes and get in a fight every twenty pages. The only real creativity went into those landscapes and some of the minor characters. Had this book been published in the Conan series, it certainly would not have performed like all the others. The editor was perfectly correct to squelch it.

The lesson I learned from that is that there are writers and there are verbal technicians. Writers write their own stuff. Verbal technicians can be called in to do any job. These are very different talents. Some people have both. I don't. But if I can only have one, I'm glad I'm a writer.

Let's get back to the immediate subject:

Friend H____ refuses to buy any book he even *suspects* is packaged. He is also very cynical (and he is *definitely* not alone) about the sort of collaborative series in which a FAMOUS NAME appears in large letters on the cover, with a lesser light in smaller letters beneath it. Sure, there have been great collaborations—in our field, Pohl and Kornbluth come immediately to mind—but finding a true collaborator, someone you're genuinely *sympatico* with, is like marriage. For most of us it happens only once in a lifetime, if that. H____ observes that in these series the name of the lesser-known writer changes *with every volume*. "I only buy those if I'm interested in the *minor* work of the *junior* writer," he explains. Which is to say, seldom.

This is unfair. It's clear that these books are honestly labelled, and that both writers did at least some of the writing, but it's TV-writing again. The senior writer works on the episodes with each junior writer, until the scripts have a uniform consistency. This hardly encourages sincere artistic expression. It is a job for a verbal technician, not a creative writer. Don't look for any award-winners here. The 1980s and '90s are going to be remembered for Dan Simmons's *Hyperion* and for William Gibson's *Neuromancer* and Gene Wolfe's *The Book of the New Sun*, not for prose-TV series novels. Those will be dust in a few years, like the factory-system *Amazing*. The collaborative inflations of some of the biggest bylines in our field will only be of interest to bibliographers.

I think that this sort of thing—serial collaborations with all comers, franchise novels like *Asimov's Robot City*, *Arthur C. Clarke's Venus Prime*, *Philip José Farmer's Dungeon*, and the rest—should simply be stopped. The authors whose names are being franchised should have enough guts to call a halt. They don't need the money. Such practices don't, contrary to myth, "give young writers a chance to break in." Instead, franchise writing actively hurts young writers, seducing them as Silverberg and the rest were seduced in the '50s, as the Laser Books writers were seduced in the '70s, delaying their emergence as recognized, individual talents, possibly preventing it altogether. A mid-list writer can get buried this way. Fans of William F. Wu's unique Chinese-American fantasy may have wondered what has become of Mr. Wu of late. He made a big splash with "Wong's Lost And Found Emporium" in *Amazing*, then published two novels (one packaged by Byron Preiss, coincidentally, in a line of juveniles for Walker), but why is there no William F. Wu section in your friendly neighborhood bookstore? Because you'll find Wu's last several books in the "A" section, under another, much more famous name.

Again I can only point out that the greats of the past—even the mediocrities of the past—didn't require this sort of apprentice system. Ray Bradbury didn't have to write scads of *Captain Future* before turning to the work that made him famous. He went right at writing Ray Bradbury stories, mediocre ones at first, then better, then *The Martian Chronicles*. As for Edmond Hamilton, who did most of *Captain Future*, he was an old, established pro, one of the pioneers of SF; but after a few years of such obvious hackwork, *nobody ever took him seriously again*. He wrote fine material late in his career, but his reputation never recovered.

It gets worse: friend H____, who is prone to snap judgments, now seriously doubts some bylines. Whenever he sees a book by an author who has been involved in franchise-publishing, or whose books even *look* franchised, he doesn't quite believe the book is by who the cover says it is by. He is less willing to pick up what may turn out to be a very minor, heartless work by someone else.

I am sure this is unfair in 99% of all cases, but I do not think H____ is alone in this perception, and public perception doesn't have to be *correct* to influence reality. Book-packagers may soon painfully learn what any politician already knows. If the public *thinks* you're lying, nothing you can say will ever prove otherwise. The famous by-lines involved are being slowly degraded. The names are appearing on books less than those authors' best, that hardly read like the authors' work at all. In every buyer's mind, there will always be that lingering doubt.

If packagers are going to fill in for editors, they should *act* like editors. They have a certain responsibility beyond the immediate, bottom line of sales. They should encourage writers to produce more than standard, look-alike products. Television, after all, is a vast wasteland, and a television mentality can turn book-publishing into a wasteland too. All of us—writers, editors, critics, fans, buyers—should be trying to combat this tendency, not encourage it.

Actually the most devastating, scathing critique on such practices I've ever seen was inadvertently written by one of the packagers himself. For abstruse, Machiavellian reasons, I'm going to be vague here, not mention any names, and let you hunt up the reference, but here is what the fellow said:

> Let's admit it—we all read packaged books as children and enjoyed them. Who here didn't read *Tom Swift*? *The Hardy Boys*? *Nancy Drew*? Or any of the other quality series?
>
> There's no reason those same high standards can't apply to series books packaged in the science fiction field.

Somehow I think that writers capable of artistry should aspire to something higher than *The Hardy Boys*. This is not what we want for science fiction.

VII.

WHY HORROR FICTION?

Why horror fiction? Lots of people want to know. They stare at us aficionados as if we had three heads and fangs—and of course if we *did*, that would be horror fiction.

Well, it's *neat*. That's why. Ask any ten-year-old why he likes scary stories, monster-movies, or, for all it may bode ill for the future of our culture, slasher films, and you'll get an answer like that, very basic, very elementary, explaining everything and nothing.

The usual objections from Regular Folks are that stories of ghouls and graves are *morbid* or *unpleasant* or even *sadistic*, since they contain descriptions of people in physically, mentally, or spiritually *painful* situations. And we're supposed to *enjoy* this? We must be a bunch of sickos, right?

But *all* fiction involves situations we wouldn't want to experience ourselves, even the fluffiest situation comedy with its betrayals, embarrassments, pies-in-the-face, and dirty tricks. You and I would prefer a quiet evening at home, or maybe some sight-seeing, but that would make a dull story. A story needs excitement, and excitement is more fun to read about than live through. The characters in *Moby Dick* are not having a good time, and Sam Spade does not enjoy *The Maltese Falcon* after Miles Archer is shot. And, to take an example from a recent television comedy, I doubt Homer Simpson much enjoyed getting lost in the woods without his clothes, being mistaken for Bigfoot, and made a fool of in front of his family and neighbors.

One thinks of Valentine Michael Smith's attempt to "grok" Earthly humor: "It hurts," he said.

As someone in *The Lord of the Rings*, either Frodo or Samwise, commented, adventures, which make glorious stories when you relate them later, are "just trouble." Ninety percent of most plots can be boiled down to pain and situations leading up to pain. Indeed, at writing workshops it is commonplace to define the protagonist of the story in terms of "Who hurts?"

So, given that horror fiction, like all others, partakes of pain and trouble, and not necessarily to an inordinate degree, what makes it different from other types of storytelling?

Horror is not quite as elusive as science fiction, for which there are as many definitions as definers. Most modern practioners will agree that it's a matter of *mood*, not of specific content. A story can be horrific without being supernatural or even fantastic, as much of Edgar Allan Poe readily demonstrates. In the simplest sense, a horror story is one that scares us.

We *like* to be scared. Trust me. We do. This is the whole secret of storytelling, any sort of storytelling. *You* would not want to journey through the Mines of Moria or up to the top of Mount Doom, but wasn't Tolkien's description of Sam and Frodo's "trouble" *enjoyable?* Come on. Admit it.

Let me qualify further. "Horror" has been so degraded as a label for violence-pornography movies that the general public thinks that the point of horror fiction (or films) is to be as gross as possible. To which I reply, in the words of (was it M. R. James?), that the idea is to make the hair stand on end, not the gorge rise. If your immediate impulse is to reach for the air-sickness bag, that wasn't a horror story.... And as far as films go, arguably there have been *no* real horror films in a long while. Certainly less than one a year for the past twenty years. I have to grasp to come up with any at all...*Rosemary's Baby*, *The Lady in White*, *Fanny and Alexander*, *Night of the Living Dead*—and, and—? Not many. Huge amounts of gorge-risers, lots of kill-porn, but proper horror films? Very few indeed.

Horror does not require huge amounts of gore, still-steaming viscera, and an motivationless maniac with a knife. In fact, it seldom flourishes under such conditions.

A contemporary, very distinguished horror writer, Thomas Ligotti, suggests in his book *Songs of a Dead Dreamer* (Carroll & Graf, 1990) that ultimately the tale of terror seeks to be "magic, timeless, and profound."

I would add that such a story deals with dark and, yes, terrifying elements which *fascinate* and *attract* in exactly equal proportion to how much they frighten or repel. If the contents of the story are merely ugly, the reader can so easily put the book down. There has to be something more. Quite often, in the hands of a master such as Arthur Machen, Robert W. Chambers, or Shirley Jackson, a horror story will strike a note of unearthly beauty at precisely the same moment it strikes terror. So we keep on reading.

The horror is not so much physical pain, or even death, but the *inexplicable*. The menace is an abnormality, an intrusion into our everyday existence, which by all the rules we hold near and dear, *should not be*. But there it is. That is the horror of it.

This is so even in such an overtly physical story as Stephen King's "The Raft." In it, several teenagers go back to their summertime vacation site in October for one last dip in the lake. Alas, the lake is now inhabited by a nameless, shapeless, black blot which traps them on a raft and eats them one after another, even dragging a victim bodily through an inch-wide crack between the boards, mashing him to a pulp in the process. But the story is about how the characters face death, what they (or the reader) learn from the experience. Mere descriptions of people being eaten or terrorized won't do. The point to "The Raft" becomes clear at the end, when the last survivor lets slip his one authentic chance at escape. Just as someone near and dear to our hero is dying hideously, he *could* get away, if only he were so heartless as to abandon her and strike out for shore while the monster is occupied. But he can't, and as the story ends, the opportunity is gone. *That* is the horror, that if only he could have found that brutality within himself, he might have made it. Life is not fair. The monster is implacable. The whole situation is a violation—physical, scientific, moral—of the way we think the universe ought to work. But, the story is telling us, the universe never asked our opinion.

H. P. Lovecraft considered horror to be a matter of man against the unknown universe. In his seminal *Supernatural Horror in Literature* he wrote:

> The true weird tale has something more than secret murder, bloody bones, or a sheeted form clanking chains according to rule. A certain atmosphere of breathless and unexplainable dread of outer, unknown forces must be present; and there must be a hint, expressed with a seriousness and portentousness becoming its subject, of that most terrible conception of the human brain—a malign and particular suspension or defeat of those fixed laws of Nature which are our only safeguard against the assaults of chaos and the daemons of unplumbed space.

In other words, the horror story gives us a glimpse of something beyond knowledge and experience. Only in a horror story can we explore the other side of death—what it would mean if the dead returned, or if we could continue to exist, neither dead nor alive, as a vampire. The horror is not so much the physical depredations the monster may inflict, but the *implication* of the monster being there at all. One more bucket of blood here or there hardly matters, but a convincing sense of unreality, of our conceptual universe coming apart at the seams—that's terrifying.

Even when it's being overtly bloody, the horror story should be subtle, and of course it is not necessary to be bloody. To my mind the best horror novel of recent years was Jonathan Carroll's *The Land of Laughs* (Viking Press, 1980), which I like to describe (half-jokingly, but only half) as "what would have happened if Philip K. Dick and Franz Kafka had collaborated to write L. Frank Baum." There's scarcely a drop of blood in it. Our hero, an admirer of the works of the great (and imaginary) children's author, Marshall France, meets a like-minded heroine and journeys to the midwestern town where France lived his whole, rather short life. After some resistance, he is accepted by the townspeople and France's daughter as the correct person to write the definitive biography of the late, great author. To this point, halfway through the novel, we have a warm, lovely, often slyly funny story about people who love books and strive for art. But the storyline darkens. It seems that the real purpose of this biography is to bring France back to life, literally, after which point the townspeople (some of whom may be characters imagined by France) plan to murder the biographer and go on forever in a solipsistic dream. The first real stab of horror comes, not when somebody gets disembowelled as they would in the initial five minutes of a *Friday the 13th* movie, but, more than halfway through, when *a dog begins to speak*. Unreality has begun its invasion. From that point, it never lets up. The hero slides into fantasy, possibly into madness as well, and in the end he has fled to Europe, possibly accompanied by his own dead father (a famous movie star) busily killing off agents of Marshall France's reality as they continue to appear. He is trapped. There is no end to this, no way he can return to his normal life. *That's* horror.

For all its quirks and specialized tropes, the horror story is like any other in the end. It has to have a point, a *theme*. It is more complicated than a child in a mask jumping out from behind a tree shouting "Boo!"

(Now if it were an *adult* in the mask shouting "Boo!" you might have a horror story, about the appalling circumstances which have caused this abnormality. Imagine it, a deft mixture of pathos and savagery, as the grown man shouts "Boo!" at first, but then when this isn't enough finds that he must genuinely become a monster, because somehow his twisted psyche demands that there be monsters.)

It has to be *about something*. But, however abstruse its concepts, such a tale must work on the *emotions* of the reader. If we can define the horror story at all, it is in terms of a specific emotional impact.

The true horror story requires a sense of evil, not in necessarily in a theological sense; but the menaces must be truly menacing, life-destroying, and antithetical to happiness. Where this evil comes from varies with the times. When Shakespeare wrote *Macbeth*, evil could plausibly come from the Devil, though the Bard was too shrewd an observer of human nature to ignore the fact that the Devil did no more than fan the fires of Macbeth's ambitions. In Poe's time, evil came from within the mind. In Bram Stoker's, it could be an infection, something from far away which polluted the familiar world and irreparably changed innocent people, as Dracula changed Lucy, into something quite different and terrifying. (It would be quite easy to make a case for *Dracula* as an allegory of Victorian perceptions of syphilis.) In Lovecraft's time, as Einstein and Hubble suddenly revealed a vast and chaotic universe, evil came from outer space, threatening to erase the insignificant flyspeck of mankind without so much as a shrug of a tentacle. Today, a surprising number of horror stories are about the loss of identity. *The Invasion of the Body Snatchers* is only the most obvious example. We have seen the horrors of totalitarian movements, mind-control cults, and the painful anonymity of life in our cities. Evil can erase us as individuals.

And the horror story must have characters we care about. This is Stephen King's great strength. His monsters, by and large, are second-rate, strictly off-the-shelf. But he writes so well about suburban teenagers, small town folks, fathers who love their children, broken families trying to cling together, that when a vampire or dripping, slobbering *Thing* intrudes, we are caught up emotionally. We are alarmed, scared. He's got us. Clive Barker, on the other hand, is far more inventive, but sometimes suffers from the "lunchmeat syndrome." That is, his characters seem to exist only to be sliced. It's hard to care.

Otherwise, the rules of the horror story are like those of any other sort of fiction: coherence, clean prose, logical consistency, a climax which somehow resolves (or at least alters) the conflict. It's all basic storytelling stuff, which has been with us ever since one of our Paleolithic ancestors got tired of telling about last week's mammoth hunt and started spinning a yarn about the three-headed, ravenous, shambling monstrosity which bites your head off in the dark, but is so subtle that it may have already slipped past you, the audience, and already be waiting *inside* the cave when you get sleepy and retire to your bearskins....

Boo.

Happy Halloween.

VIII.

INTIMATE HORROR

Cards on the table first: this is, to some extent, a reply to S. T. Joshi's "Weird Fiction and Ordinary People" in *Necrofile* #6, with which I must respectfully differ on some points.

And it is also an exercise in literary theorizing, and I have the traditional fiction-writer's suspicion of literary theorizing. Theory, most of the time, is of little interest to the working writer. It is best left to professors and pretentious twenty-year-old wanna-be's. If it is to be of any use at all, theory must be retrospective and descriptive. It tells us where, artistically, we've been, and maybe even explains how fiction already written works, but literary theory, quite unlike scientific theory, cannot predict where we're *going*. Stories to be written in the future are going to come out of someone's imagination. They will surprise even the author, and, in the act of surprising, they will gain their validity.

What the fiction writer *doesn't* do is come up with (or adhere to) theory first, then write stories to match.

Let me suggest that Lovecraft was able to elucidate his quite complicated aesthetic of cosmic horror because he discovered it in his own fiction. The stories came first, then the theory. This is the normal order of things. Not surprisingly, when any writer, be he Poe or Hemingway or Tolkien or Raymond Chandler, turns to theory, he tends to explain the workings of the short story or the novel in terms of what he's already been doing. Poe's aesthetic explains Poe. Hemingway, of course, held that the realistic, almost reportorial novel of the sort he wrote was the highest form of art. He was interested in honest depictions of life, written cleanly. Tolkien wanted to *add to* life. Chandler had quite different ideas, closer to Hemingway's, but more given to invention, to contriving plots.

Sometimes, if we're lucky, a writer's theory applies to more than his own work. It is still an exercise in historical description—not a formula for how new stories should be written—but it may explain what a lot of writers have been doing, rather than just one.

So, inevitably, I am going to describe what I do. The validity of what follows, let me suggest, stems from the fact that I'm not the only one who does it.

I think we all agree that the first appeal of a horror story is emotional. It's scary. This is a *feeling*. We know if it's there or not, well before we consider matters of form or idea or theme. No matter how elegantly written, a horror story which does not scare cannot be accounted a success.

There is more than one way to scare the reader.

Lovecraft's method, the method of Cosmic Horror, is to do it by intellectual implication. Sure, the heroes sometimes face personal danger or the prospect of physical pain, but the horror stems from the realization that we, Mankind, are as insignificant as ants or dust-motes in a vast and uncaring universe, that our comforting laws of "reality" are at best a local effect and do not apply on a larger scale. Therefore the horror isn't a matter of *monsters* (which in Lovecraft too often resemble spoiled seafood) but of what that monster's presence *means*. From this Lovecraft derives a powerful *emotional* effect, the familiar "fright" of horror fiction.

The opposite of Lovecraftian Cosmic Horror is what we might call intimate, or personal horror. It is certainly far older than that scene in *Hamlet* in which the ghost announces himself to be the spirit of Hamlet's father, come to make shocking revelations. In Lovecraftian horror, it would have been enough for there to have *been* a ghost, any ghost; but Hamlet's ghost is unique, and for him alone to deal with.

Arthur Machen caught the sense of personal horror in "The Children of the Pool," when the protagonist hears malevolent fairy voices enumerating his own sins. Shirley Jackson certainly has it all the way through *The Haunting of Hill House*. These particular manifestations are not an all-purpose, generic haunting, but very personal indeed.

Not to put myself on the same plane with Lovecraft or Machen or Jackson (or Shakespeare)...but, this is what I write. Retrospectively, I find myself a practitioner of intimate, rather than cosmic horror. My recent collection, *Transients*, is filled with examples. There's a story called "Peeling It Off" about a man who, in a moment of rage, peels off his ex-wife's face because he knows that underneath the surface of our physical reality—behind our faces—there are other people waiting to emerge. As a child he saw his grandfather commit a strange form of suicide this way, peeling his own face off, becoming someone else, walking out of the house into a world in which grandfather no longer existed. But not quite. A few times, once dramatically in adolescence, our hero thought he glimpsed some trace of Grandpa emerging in other people: a gesture, the way someone moves, an old man seen in a park whom the boy is certain *is* his grandfather, until the old man looks up and proves to be a stranger. Now, as an adult, having disposed of his ex in this fashion, my protagonist is haunted by similar details all the time: the way one woman wears her hair, a ring, old love letters found in his files at work where they couldn't possibly have been left, etc.

Of course, these are guilt manifestations. One could argue that intimate horror is an older form than cosmic horror, that it implies a moral order of creation, and at its most extreme it becomes solipsistic, like Robert A. Heinlein's "They," in which the entire universe proves to be a vast hoax designed to deceive one man. Well, maybe so, but the moral order is not the essence. The horror, as in "Peeling It Off," comes from a kind of "impossible" manifestation which says, "This is for you. All your secrets aren't secrets anymore."

Imagine a Lovecraftian scenario: an ancient mummy of a possibly pre-human creature is unearthed in the ruins of R'lyeh. What could be more shocking than the idea that this creature might *return to life*, filled with awesome memories of an unimaginable past, and possibly with an agenda of its own?

How about this? The archaeologist opens the tomb, pries the lid off the mummy-case, and the shrivelled corpse within flicks its eyes open and says, *I know you. I have been waiting for you all this time.*

Personal horror. Someday I may write a story about an archaeologist who, digging up the ancient past, accumulates detail upon detail of his *own* life. I haven't figured it all out yet. I'd like to avoid a rationale as trite as reincarnation, but I like the basic image of the man in the trench beneath the hot sun, patiently brushing dirt away from the remains of artifacts, gradually coming to realize that all this is *familiar*.

Which brings us to the subject raised in the Joshi essay, of characterization. I will stick to my contention that *all* stories, even Lovecraft's, are about people. Whether the characters are human beings, dogs, sentient crystals, brains in bottles, or insecto-fungoid monstrosities from Beyond, stories are inevitably about people. They relate to the reader through emotions, and since both the author and the reader are human, that means human experience and human emotion. If it were possible to write a story from a truly non-human viewpoint, encompassing truly non-human ideas and experiences, no human reader, even S. T. Joshi, would be able to understand it.

While detailed banalities are not to be confused with characterization, let me suggest that most stories benefit from having recognizable individuals in them, about whom the reader cares. We are concerned about the fate of the correspondent Akeley in "The Whisperer in Darkness," even as Wilmarth is. The story derives much of its suspense this way. "The Dunwich Horror" comes closer to lacking any sympathetic characters, but who will deny that Wilbur Whateley, and even his mother Lavinia, are memorable creations? And probably the reason that *The Case of Charles Dexter Ward* works better than *At the Mountains of Madness* for at least some readers is that in the former we have the sympathetic figure of young Ward, whose fascination with the unknown we share, and concern for whom motivates Dr. Willet to expose the evil Joseph Curwen. Once he finds out that Curwen has in fact murdered and impersonated Ward, Willet's quest becomes driven by moral outrage.

At the Mountains of Madness, without any differentiated characters—without any attempt to make the horror *personal*—is more of a museum tour than a story.

In other words, even Lovecraft needs what often narrow or vestigial characterization his stories contain. Lack of further character development is often a serious failing indeed. He never once managed to convincingly motivate a Cthulhu cultist. How much stronger might "The Dunwich Horror" have been if Lovecraft had been willing to explore *why* Wizard Whateley and Lavinia did what they did, and what their experience must have been like? The story has the potential for being all the more horrific by being poignant: did the—admittedly small—human part of Wilbur Whateley ever exert itself? Were there ever flashes of a human relationship between parents and son, something which, inevitably, must have perished as the non-human aspect grew stronger?

This kind of emotional complexity Lovecraft merely ignores. I am not sure that was such a good idea.

If intimate horror is the opposite of cosmic horror, let me violate my own stated premise for an moment. Let me predict, from theory, a kind of story which perhaps has not yet been written: combine the two. It should be possible to write an honestly-felt story about a real, distinct individual, who has a full emotional life in relation to other individuals, coming to personal terms with some aspect of a vast an impersonal (or malign) cosmos.

Actually, I think some writers have already done this. So I'm not violating my premise after all. Retrospectively, T. E. D. Klein's work comes immediately to mind. And some of Fritz Leiber's. Some of Machen's and de la Mare's.

Fiction, after all, conveys the experience of human beings. At least for the human beings involved, the goings-on, however cosmic their implications, cannot help but be intimate, personal, and emotionally immediate.

IX.

HORROR BEYOND NEW JERSEY

Searchers after horror haunt strange, far places, Lovecraft told us in the opening paragraph of "The Picture in the House," the catacombs of Ptolemais, the carven mausolea of the nightmare countries, forgotten cities in Asia, and, in general, locales far more exotic than New Jersey.

Not that you can't find horror in New Jersey. Jules de Grandin, Seabury Quinn's psychic sleuth, discovered more spooks per square foot of pavement in Harrisonville, New Jersey, than anywhere else on Earth. F. Paul Wilson has written of horror in New Jersey too—and he's even been able to make it *scary*, something which Quinn, after ninety-two tries at the de Grandin series, never managed. But possibly for some, the Pine Barrens are a strange, far place.

Lovecraft's point in "The Picture in the House" was that you *don't* have to seek out horror at the remote ends of space and time, because you can find it in your own back yard, in his case, rural New England.

Stephen King has told us how Richard Matheson's *I Am Legend* came as a revelation: vampires didn't have to haunt crumbling castles in remote Transylvania. They can be waiting for you in your local supermarket.

I don't deny it. Both Lovecraft and King have written effectively of things which might be lurking right outside the door, right now, in the parking lot. Such fiction has a built-in advantage. The reader doesn't have to make much of an imaginative leap to accept the reality of the setting or the characters—who act and think like people we know—and the author can put all his verisimilitude-stretching into the monsters.

But, not so fast. Let's not write off Transylvanian castles just yet. Most people agree that the strongest chapters of Stoker's *Dracula* are the first four, which take place in Transylvania, in Stoker's day an almost unreachably remote recess well beyond the regular tourist routes. Dracula seemed utterly believable there because he was *at home*. He was a—I hesitate to use the word "natural"—product of this environment.

So there are still terrors in those crumbling castles yet.

DARRELL SCHWEITZER

At a recent convention I was on one of those *Is Horror Really Dead?* panels. You know the type. Four or five of our colleagues get up behind a table at a loss to explain why, if horror is really dead, we keep having these panels year in and year out.

Inevitably, such panels turn to marketing. (There's a theory that *all* convention panels, on whatever ostensible topic, are ultimately about marketing.) I brought up the idea that within the commercial genres there is a sharp and unnecessary distinction on the basis of *setting* alone, which goes something like this:

> Imagine a hideously intimate story about a man who comes back from the grave, is delighted and amazed at his seeming reprieve from death, and hurries home to his wife and kids. But, somehow, no one will acknowledge that he is there. His wife does *not* greet him, nor does she actually look away, though he knows by her reactions that he's not invisible, that she can see him, but she too is inexplicably denying his presence. One of his children pipes up, "Look! It's Daddy!" But the mother firmly tells the child, no, Daddy is dead and not coming back. That night, the husband tries to crawl into bed with his wife, perhaps to make love. She moans softly, not out of passion, he soon realizes, but because she is sick with horror, muffling her screams with her hand in her mouth, biting so hard that she bleeds.

If you set that story in Moorestown, New Jersey, it would be obviously classified as horror and published accordingly.

But if you set it in Babylon three thousand years ago, or in lost Atlantis or Hyperborea *forty* thousand years ago, or in a completely imaginary world—if you set it in Middle Earth—no matter how frightening it might be, it would still be classified as *fantasy*, not horror, and would not be welcome in *Cemetery Dance* or *Shadows*.

At this point one of my fellow panelists, a Respected Novelist, whose masterful, quietly terrifying books are sometimes set in New Jersey, broke in.

"That's because Atlantis isn't *real*," he said. "Nobody is going to believe horror in such a setting. You gotta have something real to start with."

We will overlook the point that Babylon three thousand years ago was just as real as Camden today. Let's talk about imaginary settings.

I brought up the counter-example of Clark Ashton Smith, who set some of the most ghastly horror tales ever written in, you guessed it, Atlantis, Hyperborea, and most especially Zothique, the Earth's foundering last continent, at the end of time.

"Clark Ashton Smith wouldn't be able to sell a word today," the Respected Novelist said.

I beg to differ. He most certainly would. He would be able to sell to me, and would have been a regular in the Terminus *Weird Tales* and in its successor, *Worlds of Fantasy & Horror.* I think he would also have been a regular in Stephen Jones and David Sutton's *Fantasy Tales*, and in the small-press generally. He wouldn't have had a place in the commercial paperback world, or not much of one. Category-obsessed publishers would not have known what label to put on his books. He might well have become an underground cult author, like Thomas Ligotti, but he would never have made the bestseller list with seven-hundred-page paperbacks with double-layered black covers, raised silver type, and a single drop of blood in the see-through.

There is no reason that what we call "fantasy" can't also contain what we call "horror." Fantasy worlds don't have to be solely limited to bucolic forest scenes with cute elves. Tolkien achieved memorable horror in the Mines of Moria. Some of the best horror scenes ever written occur in Mervyn Peake's *Gormenghast* Trilogy: the part where Lord Sepulchrave goes mad and thinks himself an owl, only to be devoured by owls soon after, or Titus's long descent into the crushing tunnels beneath Gormenghast castle—guaranteed to make a claustrophobe out of anyone.

Lord Dunsany hits a fine note of horror—so admired by Lovecraft—in his play *The Gods of the Mountain.* The scene is set in one of Dunsany's fantastic Oriental lands. A band of beggars enter a city, and, by sly tricks, convince the townsfolk that they are gods, those same stone gods who are normally seen as carven idols atop a nearby mountain. It's supposed to be a miracle that the gods have taken human form and sanctified the city with their presence. Flattered, the citizens load up the "gods" with gifts—and the impostors think they have it made.

But then grovelling worshipers come to beseech them to *remain* in human form, because they are so terrifying when lumbering about as animate stone. *Rock should not walk in the evening*, someone says.

You've figured out what happens next. *The Gods of the Mountain* ultimately falls on its face as drama—or it is reported to have fallen; I've never seen it performed—because Dunsany then brings the vengeful stone gods *on stage*, shortchanging the expectations built up in the audience's mind from those terrifying reports that the gods are now *gone* from their traditional perch atop the mountain.

But it reads well. There is real horror here. *Rock should not walk in the evening*, in New Jersey certainly, or in what Dunsany calls "The East."

There are two kinds of horror, in terms of setting. In one, the horrific element is an *intrusion* into our safe and domestic world. Horror arises, as Lovecraft told us, from the violation of natural law. The façade of rationality we've built up comes tumbling down. Most modern horror fiction works this way. We might call it horror's default configuration.

The other kind confronts the monsters on their home turf. Dracula was just as scary back in Transylvania, tossing peasant babies to his vampire brides for midnight snacks. Jonathan Harker had ventured into a *realm* of horror, where such things are only to be expected. While Stoker manages to have his cake and eat it too—writing *both* kinds of horror in the same book—it would have been possible to set the entire novel in Transylvania.

Or in Dunsany's East. Or in Lost Atlantis. Or, as Clark Ashton Smith might have, on the planet Saturn.

Rock walking in the evening in New Jersey would have to be a matter of someone bringing a magical statue to Hoboken and having it come to life on them. Frankly, I find this sort of happening more convincing in the East, particularly when it is a matter of offended gods. Those stories in which the skeptic learns to his dismay that the native tribal fetish from the South Seas works just as well in Vineland have always impressed me as a bit hokey. There are times when the horror works more effectively in an exotic setting than not.

Clark Ashton Smith was hardly alone. Before him, there was Stoker, and before him Rider Haggard, who produced memorable shivers in the Caves of Kor, in Darkest Africa, in his novel *She*. Before him, there was a century of Gothic novels. In Smith's own day, Robert E. Howard, C. L. Moore, and quite a few others placed horror in fantastic or remote settings, including other planets. Remember that "Shambleau," one of the all-time horror classics, takes place on Mars.

Today, Tanith Lee continues the tradition superbly, which is probably why we publish her so much in *Weird Tales*—which is now *Worlds of Fantasy & Horror*. I write such stories myself. I won't deny that one of my reasons for editing the variously-named Terminus fantasy magazine is to keep fantastic horror alive in a time when the horror field (if our slush pile is any indication) seems to be more a matter of sex, serial killers, and post-Splatterpunk slice-and-dice.

Let me tell you how the story of the husband who returned from the grave ends. I wrote it. It is called "Going to the Mountain." I sold it to Tappan King for *Twilight Zone*, and it was scheduled for, but ultimately bumped out of, the final issue. It has since been published elsewhere.

The story doesn't take place in New Jersey, but in a country I can jokingly describe (not in the story) as Hellenistic Peru, far up in the mountains of an unnamed continent, near the source of the Great River, which is the river of the gods, reputed to flow out of the gaping crocodile mouth of Surat-Temad, who lies in the mud and darkness at the center of the universe.

Our hero has been summoned by his beloved uncle, a high priest, to be a sacrifice to the gods. He is buried alive, high among the cloudy peaks. *Nothing happens*. That is the unnatural strangeness of it. The eagle-headed messenger of Death is supposed to come and fetch our hero, but he doesn't. Eventually the man crawls out of his grave and returns to his walled, mountain-top village. Everybody shuns him, as if he were invisible, because his presence is an incomprehensible blasphemy. Possibly, after a while, they *cannot* see him. He flees from his wife's bed and turns to the uncle, who will not hear his complaints, or speak a word of comfort, but insists on playing a chess-like game, which is a form of divination. The nephew tries to grab the uncle by the arm, and his hand *passes right through*, as if the uncle were made of smoke. The two of them are not part of the same world anymore.

Eventually the hero must return to his grave and be buried again. Only then does Death's messenger come to him, not to carry him off, but to inform him that he is to become an oracle, neither dead nor alive, a go-between through whom the gods speak. His former life cannot be recovered.

This would not be believable in New Jersey. It is not the sort of story my colleague the Respected Novelist would ever write, or, I suspect, ever read, but it *is* a horror story, about violations of the most intimate norms, and the loss of everything that makes us who we are. There is little more horrifying than that, either in New Jersey or in Hellenistic Peru.

Such norms make the story real. In Middle Earth as in Atlantic City, husbands love their wives and children. People fear death. The erasure of identity is perhaps the ultimate horror.

It's a platitude of writer's advice that if you can make your characters real, all else follows—but it's still true.

But, could I have set that story in New Jersey?

Yes, I suppose so. A great deal of it would have been of necessity quite different. Better to say that I could have written another story, set in New Jersey, from the same opening premise.

But the New Jersey story could not have partaken of its mythic material directly. No eagle-headed Death messengers, no subsuming of a human being into the larger, supernatural order of things. The world of the Great River is a young one. The gods are still awakening in the mud at the river's edge. Creation is not yet complete. All the resonances of this, mythic, metaphorical, or whatever, are beyond our reach in New Jersey.

If we don't *have* to seek horror in the mausolea of the nightmare countries, let's not overlook the fact that we still *can*. There is horror to be found in remote, even imaginary places. With all due respect to my native state, horror is not of New Jersey, but of the soul.

X.

THE LIMITS OF CRAZINESS

"I don't think we should workshop this story at all," my friend the Doctor said. "It's pure child-pornography."

"It's a bit late for that," I said. "Everybody in this room has read it."

The scene was the writing workshop I conduct at Philcon (Philadelphia Science Fiction Conference) every year. I was not the only pro present. The plan has always been that we have a Panel of Experts, usually about five other writers, including some of the most distinguished names in the field (Hal Clement and James Morrow are frequent participants), who read and pass judgment on stories submitted by amateurs. Such as time permits, everybody else gets to have a say too, so the setup is a mix of teacher-student and everybody-equal. But I was clearly in charge. I am the one who introduces stories, calls on people to speak, and imposes a strict time-discipline so we can get the whole business over with in our two-hour time slot.

And now, I was on a spot. My friend the Doctor is an M.D. who works with the mentally ill, more, I gather, as a kind of paralegal advocate than a physician; but she is someone who has witnessed human extremes. She is not easily rattled. This manuscript had done it.

To describe it briefly, the piece was the opening of a novel. It was moderately well-written, a vaguely Delanyesque space opera, but without much genuine science-fiction content. If there were fresh ideas and concepts, we never got that far. What we did get was a graphic, grueling scene, which, if I recall correctly, occupied about ten pages of the total twenty, describing the anal rape of a pre-adolescent boy. It seemed sadistic. I did not see the artistic validity in it. Nor, apparently, did anyone else, as things turned out.

As a hook, it certainly got our attention. There's no denying that.

However.

Maybe this wasn't the right thing to do, but at one point I made light of it by remarking, "Ah, the tale of epic buggery." To those who attended that workshop, it's been the Epic Buggery story every since.

First, an aside: what is the morality of discussing in print the content of an unpublished manuscript? Well, if this had been a classroom situation—I teach a nightschool course in fiction-writing, so I am often in classroom situations—I would definitely not be going into such detail. Had this been strictly a teacher-student thing—I also teach through the mail, for Writer's Digest School—I wouldn't even be writing this article. But the circumstances were *public*. The author had presented copies of the manuscript to be read by anyone who happened to show up. Any member of Philcon (and there were about two thousand that year) could have come in, picked up a copy, and read it. You didn't even have to apply in advance for this workshop. No secret handshakes, oaths of silence, etc. It was as public as if the author had read that scene to the assembled multitudes. So my conscience is clear. But notice how I avoid identifying the author.

I was still on a spot. To make life interesting (in the sense of the old Chinese curse about "interesting times"), the author was a highly-regarded student of one of my Panel of Experts (neither Clement nor Morrow, but a fine novelist whose works you have enjoyed). Said Expert had probably seen some of this manuscript, or at least knew that the author wrote this sort of thing. Gulp.

What did I do? I went through it quickly, telling the author in no uncertain terms that I did not think this manuscript could ever be published in the science-fiction field, not in a million years; nor would any editorial reader in his/her right mind read much further after that opening. Were the buggery scene in chapter forty-seven, I think there would still be a problem, particularly if, as I got the impression, the rest of the book maintained similar...ah...sensibilities.

We got through it, rather nervously, in about five minutes. There was no debate. The Panel of Experts agreed with me. Most of the rest of the workshop kept silent. No screaming fits. No accusations of censorship, moral degeneracy, or anything like that. Strictly as the conductor of the workshop, I think, I handled it rather well. I got us out of a tight spot very smoothly.

Which, of course, does not actually deal with any of the quite complicated questions raised by the situation. That's why, considerably later, I am writing this essay.

Second aside: the issue of child pornography in this case is a red herring. I personally believe that child-pornography should incur legal penalties. Does this make me pro-censorship? No. It's not a censorship issue. Kiddie-porn, the sort that gets people arrested, is always photographic: stills, photo-magazines, films, etc. It should be viewed as *evidence of crime*. After all, if a murderer kills someone, then takes pictures of the corpse, or even records the whole bloody deed on videocassette, that's evidence. It doesn't matter if the murderer sells it, gives it way, or keeps it hidden.

Similarly, photos of children being tortured or raped is evidence of child-abuse, which is, in every state in the Union, a crime. However, the Epic Buggery Story was all *text*. The author hadn't molested any ten-year-old boys to produce it. So, no crime was committed.

That's precisely why this incident raises so many sticky questions.

I have since become casually friendly with the author of the Buggery Story. We talk pleasantly at conventions. The author asked me a question recently which won't go away. As I result, I am writing this article.

I was discoursing on the common enough conflict between what is observably *commercial* and what the writer feels he or she must write. I am not one of the world's more commercial writers myself. (Indeed, my income-tax returns will prove it.) I write something resembling modern-scene horror, sort of *Twilight Zone*-type fiction, but not nearly as bloody or graphic as much contemporary horror. Stories of this type sell, I admit, rather easily. You can find them in *Fear*, in Thomas Monteleone's *Borderlands*, Gary Raisor's *Obsessions*, Graham Masterton's *Scare Care*, etc. But I haven't managed a novel in this mode, something which, for me at least, would be the obvious commercial step.

I also write what may be loosely called non-generic fantasy, not really sword-and-sorcery, definitely not Tolkienesque, never trilogies (and rarely novels), and not at all Nice and Reassuring, as so much imaginary-world fantasy seems to be. Frequently my stuff is morbid and grim and downbeat, which is acceptable enough in Horror (and some of my horror is funny), but something of a no-no in Fantasy. I have all the marketing problems Clark Ashton Smith would have were he writing today. I am definitely skewed sideways to the rapidly-shrinking fantasy short-fiction market. My chief outlets for this sort of thing are *Pulphouse*, *Marion Zimmer Bradley's Fantasy Magazine* (where I have been allowed to get away with things which completely belie that magazine's image), *Weird Tales* (in which case my colleagues have to agree to buy the story; I don't get a vote), and *Weirdbook*. So far I have been able to sell everything, but I'm walking right on the edge of the Precipice of the Unpublishable. When I started out, fifteen years ago, there were dozens of fantasy small-press magazines, many paying respectable amounts. (Today's small press is all horror and pays about a quarter of what it did in 1975.) So, I cannot afford multiple rejections. I haven't got multiple markets.

Joel Rosenberg told me once that I have no right to complain. "You're like someone who says, 'This hurts!'" he said, waving his hand. "Well, stop doing it then!" He held his hand still.

Joel missed the point. I don't mean to complain. I'm just being realistic about my prospects. My only answer can be, Joel (shaking my hand), that's all I do. The alternative is to stop writing. I'll take my chances. Thanks.

I'm presently working on a novel, but not a modern-scene horror novel. It's a fantasy, very obsessed with death and the hereafter, complete with a decidedly morbid invented mythology, *and* it's told in the first-person from the point of view of a young man who happens to be a multiple-personality because he is possessed by the spirits of his sorcerer father (whom he murdered, though he was manipulated into doing so) and everybody his father ever murdered (lots). The plot does involve a Quest, but it's entirely internal, not for the Magic Can-opener of Elfland, but for identity and reconciliation. If Arthur Machen could write "the *Robinson Crusoe* of the soul" in *The Hill of Dreams*, I guess I'm writing the *Huckleberry Finn* of the soul.

This is not one of the most obviously commercial projects I could embark on, but I'm doing it, because it is the only novel I have to write just now. Some of my colleagues consider it complete lunacy. I admit I let them influence me, but all they managed to do was prevent me from writing any novels at all for several years. So, my first real novel in ten years, the first since *The Shattered Goddess*. As they say in the westerns, a man's gotta do what a man's gotta do.

Tim Powers explained the Meaning of Life to me during another of those late-night convention gabfests. "You have to believe in your own craziness," he said. "You have to believe that it will find its way into the market and reach an appreciative audience." I paraphrase, but that's the gist of what he said. Tim, you will observe, does not write generic pseudo-Tolkienesque quest trilogies, nor does he fill sharecropped pages in someone else's pre-packaged universe. He writes books which are uniquely his own, which did not exist before he set them to paper, as opposed to, say, the late Lin Carter, who spent his career writing pale imitations of books that already *did* exist, and, to my mind, accomplished absolutely nothing as a writer. Maybe Carter simply had nothing to offer, in which case he was merely a typist; but I don't believe that. I think Carter had some spark of creativity early on, but he carefully and deliberately snuffed it out. Now we'll never know. We do know about Tim Powers. He believes in his own craziness and has followed his individual vision with skill and determination to a fortunate result.

In the writing game, you're gambling everything, all or nothing, and money is ultimately not the issue. You take a risk with your own craziness. It either flies or it doesn't, and you can lose years of your life if it doesn't; but if you are a genuine writer you have to take that chance. It's the only game in town. The alternative is sharecropping other people's ideas, movie novelizations, and becoming the next Lin Carter. Thank you, no. I'd rather become a used-book dealer or peddle T-shirts with rotting bodies on them and the legend TIBETAN

OLYMPIC CORPSE-WRESTLING TEAM. ($16.00 postpaid...from yours truly at 113 Deepdale Rd., Strafford, PA 19087)

"Hey *wait a minute*," said the author of the Epic Buggery Story. "How can you *say* that after what you told me at that awful workshop?"

The author did not quite use the other famous line from westerns, *Him speak with forked tongue*, but the implication was clear. I was on another spot.

"Sometimes you have to learn when to tell an editor to go to Hell," someone else chimed in.

"No," I said sternly. "Never. Sometimes you have to learn when to politely disregard what you've been told and find yourself another editor. If you sell the story, then you're vindicated. But unprofessional behavior never helps."

Which still ducks the issue.

My criticism in that workshop was in a marketing, not moral sense. I didn't say, "You are an awful person for writing this and therefore shouldn't." I said that as I understood the contemporary science-fiction market, I did not think this story was publishable, because of its content. I did not think any editorial reader would get much further than that particular scene. In this second encounter, I repeated that assertion. I did not think the market would bear this. My immediate, practical advice to this writer was to take up horror, where you can get away with a lot more. A genre that celebrates Rex Miller's *Slob* and the exploits of Hannibal Lector isn't going to mind a bit of buggery here and there.

But what about the particular novel which opened with the protracted rape of a young boy? *Should* the author continue to write it? *That* is the key question.

Yes. If the author must, the author should.

Now hypothesize that the end result, in which that opening scene is typical, and not a lurid lapse, has some artistic validity. Is it going to get published? Probably not. As I read the market, the novel would have to be published, not in the usual science fiction category, but as pornography, and a very specialized, artistically-ambitious science-fictional pornography at that. The book needs the SF equivalent of Grove Press.

Such a market existed once: Essex House, which published Philip José Farmer's *Image of the Beast* and sequels, and Hank Stine's legendary *Season of the Witch*. Were Essex House still in existence, I would have told the author at that Philcon workshop not that the book was unpublishable, but that it should have been submitted to Essex House, and Essex House was its only shot. Alas, Essex House folded around 1972. There has been nothing like it since. So, if our author bravely persists, it is against the slim hope that sometime in the future such a market will emerge again.

Good God. Next to that, I'm as commercial as Piers Anthony. But a writer's gotta do what a writer's gotta do.

1997 Update

Believe it or not, I have maintained friendly relations, both in person and through correspondence, with the author of the Epic Buggery Story ever since, who continues to wrestle with the muse, aspire to write vital and challenging fiction, but has not, to my knowledge ever sold anything. "How about short stories?" I ask. "Short stories are a way to test the market—and your own ability to write at a professional level—at without wasting huge amounts of effort. A novel can take years. A short story can take a few hours to write. How about writing short stories until you start selling, then come back to novels?"

Alas, our author seems to be a born novelist, who doesn't even like to read short stories. I continue to utter words of encouragement, but otherwise the problem is beyond my ability to advise.

My recommendation of the horror market may not be a good one anymore. While Poppy Z. Brite can get away with *Exquisite Corpse* (in which two gay serial killers fall in love, with much explicit detail), most horror novelists can't get away with *anything* these days, since the market has all but collapsed.

I still do not think the writer should give up, but I'm glad that *my* career path is a (relatively) easier one to follow. The novel I described as "the *Huckleberry Finn* of the soul" became *The Mask of the Sorcerer*. It was published in England by New English Library to some acclaim, although as yet it has failed to find an American publisher. I have imported and sold a few hundred copies. At least a dozen readers are deeply fond of it.

XI.

H. P. LOVECRAFT

STILL ELDRITCH AFTER ALL THESE YEARS

(1987)

i.

Precisely fifty years ago, the intellectual and artistic adventure that was Howard Phillips Lovecraft's life came to an abrupt halt. Lovecraft, born in 1890, died on March 15, 1937 from a "grippe," which, undiagnosed almost to the very end, turned out to be intestinal cancer. He would have been forty-seven that August.

Lovecraft had a bad start in the world, his father permanently hospitalized when he was three, his childhood and adolescence smothered by a neurotically overprotective mother who once told him he was so ugly he shouldn't go out much, lest he scare the neighbors. Declining family fortunes and illnesses, both real and imaginary, precluded college, and the first years of his manhood were spent as a virtual recluse, without any sort of job or much contact with any but a very narrow circle of acquaintances. He spent a great deal of his time writing pompously dreadful imitations of eighteenth-century verse. (The age of Johnson and Swift remained a lifelong fascination; Lovecraft always felt that he would have been happier as a landed English gentleman, circa 1740.) His mother encouraged what she thought was his poetic genius. Genius he was, albeit not a poetic one. He had been an amazing child prodigy, reading and giving poetry recitals at three, writing at four, composing passable Latin by seven or so; but it wasn't until he was in his later twenties that he began to develop, either as a writer or as a human being. That was when his mother was finally put away, leaving a bewildered Howard Lovecraft to discover the universe on his own.

And discover he did, becoming vastly self-educated; developing a wide circle of friends, nearly all of whom remembered him as the most remarkable person they had ever known; travelling as far from his native Rhode Island as Québec and New Orleans; surviving a failed marriage in his thirties; and, quite unlike most people, becoming progressively *more* flexible and open-minded as he got older. As his biographer, L. Sprague de Camp, put it, Lovecraft managed to stay out of the madhouse, jail, and bread lines during the worst of the Great Depression. This has to be counted as something of an accomplishment.

But the reason that Lovecraft was anything more than an interesting psychological case-study is that, around 1917, he began to write stories of the weird and terrible. There had been juvenile attempts, but serious efforts began with "The Tomb," a turgid but effective tale of a maladjusted young man who is more at home with, and eventually possessed by, the spirits of his eighteenth-century ancestors. Much better fiction soon followed. "The Rats in the Walls" (1923) was immediately heralded by the editor and the readers of *Weird Tales* magazine as one of the strongest American horror stories since the days of Edgar Allan Poe. Most of Lovecraft's now classic horror fiction, "The Dunwich Horror," "Pickman's Model," "Dreams in the Witch House," "The Shadow Over Innsmouth," and many others, were written within the next ten years. Late in life, he began to produce work which was incontestably science fiction, and startlingly innovative science fiction at that.

Lovecraft eventually wrote enough fiction to fill three thick hardcover volumes. This represents only a small portion of his output, which also includes essays of all sorts, a huge amount of poetry (perhaps five percent of it tolerably good), and more letters than any other literary person in the twentieth century, if not in all of history, has ever composed. Some Lovecraftian epistles run to fifty pages of small print and amount to short books. Merely the *surviving* ones, if printed in their entirety, would fill about fifty standard-sized volumes.

His reputation continues to rest on his fiction. In his lifetime, Lovecraft saw print in amateur journals, and in pulp magazines, especially *Weird Tales*, where he was a valued contributor. One of his very best stories, "The Colour Out of Space," appeared in *Amazing* in 1927. But, aside from one badly-printed, amateur volume and a few anthology appearances, he had no book publication during his lifetime. It was only later that his friends collected his work into book form, August Derleth and Donald Wandrei founding the still-extant firm of Arkham House for this express purpose. Since then, first at Derleth's urging, and then out of sheer inertia as Lovecraft found an audience, numerous paperbacks and hardcovers and translations followed.

This is nothing out of the ordinary. Many venerable pulp writers, nostalgically remembered by their first generation of readers, have made it into book form later. E. E. "Doc" Smith, Seabury Quinn, and Robert E. Howard spring immediately to mind.

But with Lovecraft, something extraordinary has happened. A vast body of critical literature has grown up. There is more secondary material on Lovecraft than any such writer since Poe. S. T. Joshi's monumental *H. P. Lovecraft and Lovecraft Criticism: An Annotated Bibliography*, published by Kent State University Press in 1981, lists six hundred and ninety-two such items, not counting unpublished papers and academic theses. A recent supplement lists many more. Books about Lovecraft seem to appear at the rate of about one a year. A scholarly journal, *Lovecraft Studies*, flourishes. Lately, the leading Lovecraft scholar, Joshi, has subjected Lovecraft to the same sort of rigorous textual scholarship normally applied to Shakespeare, James Joyce, or William Faulkner, and produced definitive versions of the three standard Lovecraft story collections, *The Dunwich Horror and Others*, *At the Mountains of Madness*, and *Dagon and Other Macabre Tales*, weeding out literally thousands of errors, producing versions which, for the first time, give us what the author intended, and prove Lovecraft to be a better stylist than previously suspected.

Critical recognition abroad has been much greater than in the United States. It's a familiar story. Poe, too, was largely ignored at home until the French began to champion him as one of the very greatest American authors. Now Lovecraft is published in Germany in the equivalent of Modern Library or Penguin Classics, alongside major figures of literature and philosophy. A German publisher once announced a plan to publish twelve volumes of Lovecraft's letters, not for some amateur fan audience, but for the general public. (None have yet appeared. However, the first of the French three-volume set of the *Letters* has.) In Japan, Lovecraft is produced in lavish, boxed editions by the chief publisher of Zen texts. A few years ago the city of Trieste sponsored an international Lovecraft conference, flying in experts from around the globe. This was regarded as an important cultural event. The French, as they did with Poe, have heralded Lovecraft as one of the American masters. Foreign critics, French, Spanish, and Italian, have been quoted as saying the most remarkable things (some verified, some not): that Lovecraft may be counted among the four greatest American writers *ever* (the other three being Poe, Ambrose Bierce, and Walt Whitman), or even that he ranks among the ten greatest ever produced by the human race, right up there with Homer and Shakespeare. The perennial Nobel-prize candidate Jorge Luis Borges, when surveying American literaure, mentioned three "science fiction" writers he thought noteworthy: Ray Bradbury, Robert A. Heinlein, and H. P. Lovecraft. When Borges wrote a story in homage to Lovecraft ("There Are More Things," in *The Book of Sand*), this may have puzzled American mainstream critics, but to the original Spanish audience, Borges felt no need to explain. Lovecraft is widely known in Spanish-speaking countries as a standard, classic American author.

All of this is a long way from the pages of *Weird Tales*. After fifty years it is clear that Lovecraft has become major figure on a world-wide scale. No other contributor to the science fiction and fantasy magazines, in Lovecraft's generation or later, has ever achieved such recognition. Certainly people still enjoy some of his contemporaries. Robert E. Howard and Edgar Rice Burroughs may be more widely read. But no one has ever accused either of producing Serious Literature.

What makes Lovecraft so special? This bears serious examination.

ii.

Lovecraft was not fully appreciated in his lifetime, even by his admirers. His champion, August Derleth, was a woefully incompetent textual editor (Joshi reports finding between fifteen and forty-three errors *per page* in *At the Mountains of Madness*, ranging from word substitutions to whole paragraphs missing), but also clearly did not understand the works of his idol. His "posthumous collaborations" (stories written by Derleth from fragments or notes by Lovecraft) read more like painful parodies of Lovecraft, and the subsequent development of the "Cthulhu Mythos" has led to a banal trivialization of Lovecraftian concepts by generations of later writers, under the auspices of August Derleth.

The first major critic to notice Lovecraft was hardly an admirer. Edmund Wilson produced a withering blast in the pages of *The New Yorker*, declaring that the only horror in Lovecraft was "the horror of bad taste and bad art." But Wilson was hostile to virtually all imaginative or popular fiction. He made a complete fool of himself over Tolkien's *The Lord of the Rings*. He tried to murder the entire mystery genre with an essay entitled, "Who Cares Who Killed Roger Ackroyd?" Today his piece on Lovecraft may be found, reprinted for historical interest only, heavily annotated, in *H. P. Lovecraft: Four Decades of Criticism*, edited by the indefatigable Joshi (Ohio University Press, 1980).

More disappointingly, the first generation of science-fiction critics could not see beyond the superficial trappings of Lovecraft's fiction, and regarded him as a gothic anachronism, an embarrassing enthusiasm of a few older, uncritical readers. To prove their maturity, the first science fiction critics bore down hard on the old pulp favorites, Burroughs, Merritt, and Lovecraft. In his classic *In Search of Wonder* (1956, revised 1967), Damon Knight is strikingly and uncharacteristically imperceptive, making no distinction between real Lovecraft fiction and the bogus Derlethian collaborations (the passage he quotes as a horrid example is by Derleth), and showing no awareness at all that Lovecraft was trying to do anything but say "Boo!" to his readers. Intelligent criticism of Lovecraft in the United States is mostly a recent phenomenon. Aside from a few scattered articles, the bulk of it has appeared since the death of August Derleth in 1971, and most of the best books have come in the past decade. Layer after layer of misapprehension has been stripped away, and now it becomes clear *why* Lovecraft, and none of his contemporaries, has had such an extraordinary posthumous career.

Lovecraft was a thinker of uncommon depth. It is possible to call him a philosopher without flinching. He certainly was as much a philosopher as H. G. Wells or Olaf Stapledon, who have always been respected, not merely as fiction writers, but as thinkers. Like them, he infused all his work with a coherent system of belief. His fiction, essays, those mountains of letters, and even much of his poetry form a vast whole. He was, as de Camp has put it, a formidable exponent of his own brand of mechanistic materialism.

Despite his reputation as a supernaturalist, Lovecraft never had the slightest faith in the supernatural, either of the conventionally religious or occult varieties. His outlook, almost from childhood, was that of a scientist. He wrote that life is merely an electro-chemical process, which ceases utterly at death. Man is a random occurrence in a random and chaotic universe, and as modern science—especially Einstein's theories of Relativity—reveals ever vaster mysteries, we cannot escape the conclusion of mankind's utter insignificance.

His fiction is uniformly an expression of this view. He wrote to the editor of *Weird Tales*:

> All my stories are based on the fundamental premise that common human laws and interests and emotions have no validity or significance in the vast cosmos at large. To me there is nothing but puerility in a tale in which the human form—and the local human passions and conditions and standards—are depicted as native to other worlds or other universes. To achieve the essence of real externality, whether or time or space or dimension, one must forget that such things as organic life, good or evil, love and hate, and all such local attributes of a negligible and temporary race called mankind, have any existence at all.

Like Poe, Lovecraft expounded his literary/aesthetic theories at length, then practised what he preached. His famous "The Colour Out of Space" is about an intrusion from the vast Outside (as Lovecraft was fond of calling it) in the form of a meteorite which displays no known spectrum or chemical properties, and emits a force (which may or may not be considered alive, but is certainly not organic in any earthly sense) that proceeds to absorb and destroy pigs, cows, trees, humans, grass, and insects with complete indifference before renewing itself and taking off for the stars again.

Lovecraft's supernaturalism is mechanistic. Since he did not believe in ghosts or demons, he could not write about them convincingly, and was forced to develop a whole new kind of horror story, which, more often than not, bordered on science fiction. The most exquisite horror for a thinking person, according to Lovecraft, is the intrusion of some representative of the vast and uncaring universe into the placid little world of human existence. The frightening abnormality is not that of shambling zombies or chain-clanking ghosts as much as a suspension of natural law. Fear comes not so much from the immediate danger of being chased by spooks, as from what it would have to *imply* if such spooks existed. Lovecraft's characters go to great lengths to deny what they see, to cling to some shred of rationality, only to be overwhelmed. His vastly original monsters (nothing so *trite* as a zombie or a vampire in evening dress) are utterly inhuman beings which symbolize the forces of the uncaring cosmos. The irony of our existence, says Lovecraft, is that we are precisely clever enough to discover how helpless and unimportant we are. The belief in any sort of deity who will look after us is therefore sheerest wish-fulfillment.

Fritz Leiber has called Lovecraft "a literary Copernicus," because he turned the horror story away from the mankind-centered world, toward the whole universe. Some wit has suggested that Lovecraft was the first person to experience Future Shock. Some of his more philosophically-inclined admirers try to make him out as a pre-Existentialism Existentialist.

Lovecraft himself might have called himself an Epicurian. (He was a classicist, and knew precisely what that meant.) He held that the sole purpose in life is *aesthetic* pleasure. In daily living, this meant clinging to tradition and traditional ideas of decorum. In literature, this meant writing which appeals to a sense of beauty, or adventurous expectancy, or other basic, deeply-felt emotions. He did not write fiction to preach, or even to expound his philosophy. He believed in Art for Art's sake, as did Poe and Oscar Wilde, and quoted Wilde to this effect. ("All art is basically useless.")

Lovecraft took his writing seriously. It was, after all, the focus of his life. There is a playful element in Lovecraft, even a wry sense of humor (tipping the hat to his friend and fellow *Weird Tales* author Clark Ashton Smith by referring to him in "The Whisperer in Darkness" as "the Atlantean priest, Klarkash Ton"), but, in an environment of hack formula-writers and lowest-common-denominator publishing (pulp magazines, as a class, had a terrible reputation, much of it deserved), he wrote carefully, measuring every word. He had stylistic faults, certainly. Too often he would synopsize, rather than develop a dramatic scene; and he was addicted to rare adjectives: squammous, rugose, and most especially *eldritch*, which he loved dearly. At his worst he wrote some of the most florid prose *to survive* from the pulp magazines, but he was vastly more sophisticated than his contemporaries. He believed that atmosphere, rather than jaunty action, was the key element of a fantastic tale, and strove for subtle aesthetic effects when most of his fellow writers, not to mention the readers, scarcely understood such concepts, much less cared about them.

For example, Jack Williamson, writing in *Amazing* in 1930, opened his serial "The Green Girl" in the approved pulp manner:

> At high noon on May 4, 1999 the sun went out!

Lovecraft begins "The Colour Out of Space" with a rolling, cadenced description:

> West of Arkham the hills rise wild, and there are valleys with deep woods that no axe has ever cut. There are dark narrow glens where the trees slope fantastically, and where thin brooklets trickle without ever having caught the glint of sunlight. On the gentler slopes there are farms, ancient and rocky, with squat, moss-coated cottages brooding eternally over old New England secrets in the lee of great ledges; but these are vacant now, the wide chimneys crumbling and the shingled sides bulging perilously beneath low gambrel roofs.

Lovecraft's is not a modern style. Reading him, it is hard to remember that he is a contemporary of Ernest Hemingway. His prose was modelled on the writers of his beloved eighteenth century, Samuel Johnson, Addison and Steele, and Edward Gibbon; and also on Poe and two contemporary fantasists he admired tremendously, Arthur Machen (1863-1947) and Lord Dunsany (1878-1957). But he wrote that way deliberately, composing his tales as carefully as sonnets. He wrote what he had to say as well as he could, and refused to make any concessions to popular taste or commercial formulas. He tried to convince himself that he didn't care if anyone but a few friends ever read his efforts, but never managed to do so. (He took rejections badly, and went into fits of depression which he wouldn't have suffered if he truly didn't care.) Rather than "sell out," he did overt hack-work, revising for pay the mostly hopeless efforts of amateur writers. He certainly made career blunders—failing to submit most of his stories, even when rejected, to magazines other than *Weird Tales*, and, incredibly, failing even to type up his superb novel, *The Case of Charles Dexter Ward*, when a major hardcover publisher asked to see a novel from him—but he managed to keep his art pure and undiluted. By a happy coincidence, he happened to be a better and more substantial writer than he ever knew he was. The integrity of his work was important to *him*.

The work itself, it turns out, is important to a wide readership all around the world.

So Lovecraft's reputation seems secure. He was certainly not as great as Homer or Shakespeare. Such statements are absurd, if the foreign critics who are alleged to have made them actually did. He is not one of the top four American writers either, but he might fit well in a list of the top hundred. He is, so far, the leading American supernatural horror writer for the twentieth century. He has already overtaken all the writers he once regarded as his ineffably superior masters—Dunsany, Machen, Algernon Blackwood, M. R. James—and is well on his way to at least matching Poe. He is certainly the most important writer ever to contribute to the science fiction and fantasy genre magazines.

In a broader sense, he is on a level with Borges or Franz Kafka. If Borges's endless Library of Babel and Kafka's character transformed into a giant vermin are essential touchstones of twentieth-century experience, then so, too, is Lovecraft's vast cosmic alienation myth. In Lovecraft we see the mankind, isolated on the tiny speck of the Earth, amid incomprehensible, limitless darkness. Even the galactic empires of science fiction, on Lovecraft's scale of things, are local, trifling affairs.

iii.

The most important Lovecraftian publications in recent years have been, without a doubt, the Joshi-edited revised texts. Arkham House has issued handsome new hardcover editions of *The Dunwich Horror* and *At the Mountains of Madness* (1984 and 1985, respectively), with *Dagon and Other Macabre Tales* to follow shortly. These three comprise the entire body of Lovecraft's fiction, outside of some revisions of other people's work (which amount to collaborations) and assorted fragments, prose poems, parodies, etc. A forthcoming *Miscellaneous Writings*, edited by Joshi, will contain his major essays. Five volumes of *Selected Letters* (representing about five percent of the extant letters) were published between 1965 and 1976. All but Volume III are currently in print. A supplemental booklet, *Uncollected Letters*, also appeared from Necronomicon Press (1986).

The most interesting critical study in the past few years has been the Starmont Reader's Guide #13, *H. P. Lovecraft*, by the ever-industrious Joshi, which might be called *Lovecraft the Philosopher*. It does an admirable job of demonstrating the overall coherence of Lovecraft's thought and work. Donald Burleson's *H. P. Lovecraft: A Critical Study* (Greenwood Press, 1983) is more a matter of *This Is What Lovecraft Wrote, and This Is What Donald Burleson Thinks of It*, a mass of story synopses and short comments, without any overall plan;

far less useful, but factually accurate, and with occasional insights and rare nuggets of information.

One of the stranger developments is that Lovecraft is the protagonist in two new novels. He has appeared in fiction before. Since Lovecraft playfully wrote his friends into his stories sometimes, it isn't surprising that they returned the compliment. Robert Bloch killed him hideously in an early story, "The Shambler from the Stars" (*Weird Tales*, 1935), provoking the similarly ghastly demise of *Robert Blake* in Lovecraft's "The Haunter of the Dark" shortly thereafter. Clark Ashton Smith used Lovecraft as a character once.

But these were essentially in-jokes, not for the general readership. In two recent books, the figure of Lovecraft is very deliberately evoked, the interest deriving from a continuing fascination with his personality, quite aside from what he wrote. This is facilitated by the awesome, almost stupefying detail in which his life has been documented. (So much so that a joke title in a Tim Kirk cartoon, *H. P. Lovecraft, His Choice in Socks*, is not as ridiculous as it sounds; they were probably black or a plain, conservative grey. In any case, we know how Lovecraft managed to survive on $1.80 worth of groceries a week, where he stayed, what his opinions were on every conceivable subject, when was the last time he rode a bicycle, what books were in his library, what movies he saw and with whom, etc., etc., etc.) He exists on paper in far more detail than most fictional characters, and as novels with famous people in them are always popular, the result is inevitable.

Peter Cannon's *Pulptime* (Weirdbook Press, 1984) has proven so successful it's in its second printing. In this one, H. P. Lovecraft meets Sherlock Holmes, as the Great Detective, now in his seventies, comes to New York circa 1925 and enlists the help of Lovecraft and his circle in a particularly difficult case. Cannon, a Lovecraft scholar of note, has gone to great lengths, incorporating *real* Lovecraftian conversations and excerpts from Lovecraft's letters into the dialogue, using as many authentic incidents, characters, and settings as possible. It's all in good fun, and thoroughly convincing, highlighted by an outrageous scene in which Lovecraft and the fantasy writer Frank Belknap Long nearly have their covers blown in a speakeasy by the tipsy poet Hart Crane. The plot, however, leaves a lot to be desired. It lacks complication. The villain gives up much too easily.

By contrast, *Lovecraft's Book* by Richard A. Lupoff (Arkham House, 1985) has opposite flaws and virtues. Lupoff is a professional fiction writer and knows how to plot. His story moves, and is a pretty good mystery/intrigue effort in its own right. But the Lovecraft character is no more convincing than the H. G. Wells of the movie *Time After Time*, a famous name and little more. There is even a scene in which Lovecraft gets drunk (during Prohibition, no less!), when the real H. P. Lovecraft, like Dracula, never drank...wine. (Actually, he was more fond of a cup of coffee with five lumps of sugar.) The plot, involving the early Nazis and the Ku Klux Klan, makes entirely too much of Lovecraft's alleged racism. Lovecraft's attitudes toward foreigners and minorities were like Shakespeare's toward Jews in *The Merchant of Venice*. They passed without comment at the time, but have since become unacceptable. And as he got older, and met more people of different backgrounds, he began to shed his prejudices one by one. At one point he even naively wrote of blacks, "certainly no one could wish them *any harm*." The Lupoff novel, while adequate as fiction, only distorts the memory of Lovecraft the man, but at the same time underlines his importance, trading as it does on instant recognition of the name.

1997 Update

Since this essay appeared in *Amazing* (hence the several references to Lovecraftian connections to *Amazing*, that venerable publication (the first all-science fiction magazine in the world, founded in 1926), has been allowed to perish by a neglectful publisher. Lovecraftian studies, needless to say, have continued.

Joshi supplemented his corrected editions of the standard Lovecraftian canon with a new edition of *The Horror in the Museum*, Lovecraft's collected "revisions" (frequently stories wholly ghosted for amateur writers, or written from the barest notes or outlines) in 1989. This is actually the most drastically changed of the Arkham House standard set. It drops one story and adds several more on the basis of recent discoveries of who wrote precisely what.

Miscellaneous Writings appeared from Arkham House in 1995.

Donald Burleson's Lovecraftian criticism has, to my mind, ceased to be of any use at all after he converted to "Deconstructionism" and began writing amazingly nit-picking essays which can take a trivial, ten-line poem by Lovecraft, go on about it for five thousand words, and leave the reader seemingly *less* enlightened than before. He is, however, a far more lucid proponent of this sort of criticism than, say, Samuel R. Delany (science fiction's most prominent Deconstructionist casualty). Indeed, Burleson's deconstruction cannot be dismissed as incomprehensible gibberish at all. It is *comprehensible* gibberish. But for those who take such things seriously, one can recommend Burleson's *Lovecraft: Disturbing the Universe* (University of Kentucky Press, 1990).

The chief Lovecraftian journals, *Lovecraft Studies* and *Crypt of Cthulhu*, continue to flourish. Both are published by Necronomicon Press, P.O. 1304, West Warwick, RI 02893.

Necronomicon Press has also brought out what must surely be *the* Lovecraftian tome for the '90s, S. T. Joshi's massively monumental biography, *H. P. Lovecraft: A Life* (1996), which, in 704 pages of tiny print, begins with the comment that Lovecraft is one of the best-documented human beings of all time and proceeds to prove it. This is probably not a book for the beginner, but for the *aficionado*. It is virtually a rediscovery of Lovecraft, shedding more light on HPL's writing, philosophy, and life than virtually all that has gone before, *in toto*. Published almost simultaneously was Joshi's vast expansion and revision of his Starmont House book, *H. P. Lovecraft*, now called *A Subtler Magick: The Writings and Philosophy of H. P. Lovecraft* (Borgo, 1996). Both would make ideal textbooks for a graduate course on Lovecraft. One of Joshi's conclusions is that Lovecraft's racism was more than alleged (something I took Richard A. Lupoff to task for), and that it *did* evoke a certain amount of challenge from Lovecraft's contemporaries, but it must be seen in the much larger context of the author's life and times.

XII.

ABOUT "THE WHISPERER IN DARKNESS"

i.

It is well that H. P. Lovecraft's "Vermont hell-beater," as he jokingly called it, "The Whisperer in Darkness," was published in one piece in the August 1931 *Weird Tales*. The story had originally scheduled for serialization in the July and August issues, but, in the depths of the Great Depression the magazine started skipping issues. Henceforth, it would be a bi-monthly, and there would be no more serials, presumably after editor Farnsworth Wright was done with Otis Adelbert Kline's Tarzan imitation, *Tam, Son of the Tiger*, which began in June/July 1931 issue, part one of six.

Actually, *Weird Tales* resumed monthly publication with the August issue, but meanwhile the scheduling shift had given the readers an unexpectedly massive treat.

It is hard to imagine a Lovecraft story less suitable to serialization than "The Whisperer in Darkness." A masterful example of his later, restrainedly-realistic mode, the story is almost a tone-poem contemplating the mysteries of the unknown cosmos, building gradually from hints of strange, alien bodies seen floating in flood-swollen rivers in southern Vermont, to the final horror, of which, despite his testimony in the first few lines, the protagonist saw quite enough in the end—the abduction of Henry Wentworth Akeley by fungoid beings from Beyond, his still-conscious brain carried into the Void in a silver canister, his body either safely stored under a neighboring hill, or, quite probably, carved up for props when an alien impersonates him.

(The ending of the story, which the *Weird Tales* illustrator brainlessly gave away, the discovery that "the things in the chair, perfect to the last, subtle detail of microscopic resemblance—or identity—were the face and hands of Henry Wentworth Akeley" represent an image Lovecraft returned to again and again, the seemingly human mask behind which *otherness* lurked. But it has always puzzled me. Were the fungoid Yuggothians so skilled in surgery that they physically removed Akeley's face from his skull, eyes and all, then managed to so preserve it that one of their number could wear it as a mask, or did they merely make some sort of artificial likeness? A clever and devious bunch, those Yuggothian Outer Ones. We will never be sure.)

The effect of the story is cumulative. Any attempt to break it in the middle would have surely been disastrous.

ii.

The technique of "The Whisperer in Darkness" is familiar, yet at the same time interesting and unusual. It is quasi-journalistic, less a matter of dramatic scenes and characters *doing things* than a summary of slowly accumulating facts. The imagery comes in glimpses, a single phrase from a report of newspaper clipping (or the narrator's summary of one) tantalizing the imagination with the merest hints: the bloated, pinkish corpses in the floodwaters, a squadron of the winged crab-things wading in a stream, a single specimen seen leaping into the air from a lonely hilltop.

This is one of the most difficult ways there is to write a story. From an unskilled hand, the result would be dull synopsis. Writing instructors always pound the rule of *show, don't tell* into their students. A conventional story, ideally, contains *no* exposition, and is entirely made up of scenes, action, and dialogue. The purpose of such narration is to take the reader into the story, to make him vicariously experience the events therein. But in "The Whisperer in Darkness" we experience the story only at a distant remove, sharing not Akeley's nightmarish siege in the remote farmhouse as the forces from Outside descend upon him, but the narrator Wilmarth's suspense and uncertainty as, indeed, the facts come together and letters from Akeley arrive by post—or fail to. It is as if we, like Wilmarth, "did not see any actual visual horror," but only *heard about it* and were left to imagine more than any author could actually describe. Certainly "Whisperer" is one of the most *suggestive* of all Lovecraft's stories.

Lovecraft had learned this method from Arthur Machen, whose most elaborate pseudo-journalistic story, "The Great Return," served as the structural model for "The Call of Cthulhu." "The Whisperer in Darkness" recalls "The Novel of the Black Seal" from *The Three Impostors*. But in Lovecraft's hands, the technique served a specific purpose, *to make the unreal real*. "I am convinced," he wrote to Clark Ashton Smith, "that a solidly realistic framework is needed in order to build up a preparation for the unreal element," in such a story. "My own rule is that no weird story can truly produce terror unless it is devised with all the care & verisimilitude of an actual *hoax*. The author must forget all about 'short story technique,' & build up a stark, simple account, full of homely corroborative details, just as if he were actually trying to 'put across' a deception in real life."[2]

The thematic content is all Lovecraft's own. The restrained, relatively un-adjectival prose is characteristic of his mature period, when he strove to write coolly and objectively about the *phenomena* which were central to his interest. The humans in such a story are always spear-carriers, or observers, as if *Moby Dick* contained only Ishmael and the whale, with the doings of the other *Pequod* crew members only glimpsed in passing. It is far removed from the florid gibbering of such early stories as "The Hound," which he described to Clark Ashton Smith as, "one of the poorest jumbles I have ever produced...written in 1922, before I had begun to prune down the verbal extravagances of my earlier prose."[3] And prune them he did, with the grim determination of a 500-pound man on a life-or-death diet, and the result was a lean, clear language suitable for the expression of quasi-science-fictional themes. The Gothic mode was far behind him.

Only once or twice does his old manner betray its presence, especially when Wilmarth is being driven deep into the Vermont woods on the way to Akeley's farmhouse by Noyes, an agent of the Yuggothians. Something seems wrong, notably that Akeley himself did not meet Wilmarth at the train station, and his letters made no mention of Noyes. The very landscape seems haunted, as it does so often in Lovecraft, who found his imagination stimulated by the adventurous expectancy of the outdoors. One thinks of the descriptions of the strange, desolate country in "The Dunwich Horror," seen if one takes "the wrong fork" in the junction of a highway, or of the sinister backwoods of "The Picture in the House," where all manner of evil may breed. But in this sort of passage in "Whisperer," Lovecraft sometimes overplays his hand. The reader is left wondering how the sound of a brook can seem "insidious," except perhaps to a psychologically devastated survivor of the Chinese water torture, or how an ancient covered bridge can "linger fearsomely."

The slip is only momentary. The story itself was inspired in part by Lovecraft's visit to the very countryside he describes, which, indeed, to this day remains the sort of wild country of "dense, unvisited woods on those inaccessible slopes" which might conceivably hide "alien and incredible things." Especially in the dusk, it is easy to understand how Lovecraft could have described the hills around Brattleboro, Vermont as if they "held some strange and aeon-forgotten meaning, as if they were vast hieroglyphs left by a rumored titan race whose glories live only in rare, deep dreams."

He wrote to Alvin Perry that the story's genesis came from "two initial compelling concepts: the idea of a man in a lonely farmhouse besieged by 'outside' horrors, & the general impression of weirdness in the Vermont landscape, gained during a fortnight's visit near Brattleboro in 1928."[4]

iii.

"The Whisperer in Darkness" is not so much a story of New England as of outer space. It is one of the most purely cosmic of all Lovecraft's tales, further inspired by the then brand-new discovery of the planet Pluto in 1930. He wrote to a correspondent that April that the discovery excited him "more than any other happening in recent times." And as he wrote that letter, he was in the midst of composing "The Whisperer in Darkness."

"The first real planet to be discovered since 1846, & only the *third* in the history of the human race!" he rhapsodized. "One wonders what it is like, and what dim-litten fungi may sprout coldly on its frozen surface! I think I shall suggest its being named *Yuggoth!*"[5]

Certainly outer space held both fascination and horror for Lovecraft. Astronomy was a lifelong interest, but throughout his fiction the vastness of the interstellar void remains a symbol for the chaos surrounding the insignificant world of mankind. A pure materialist, without any trace of religious feeling, Lovecraft could only regard Terrestrial life as a random accident of nature, and our Earth as a speck floating for just an instant on the black sea of infinity. Beyond the atmosphere, he seemed certain, man could barely venture at all. The universe was just too vast, too uncaring, mankind too irrelevant. He once described a plan for an interplanetary tale, most of which built up to the protagonist's crushingly awful realization that he is *actually on another planet*. Surely a sensitive man would go mad...

Yet we are drawn to such mysteries as is a moth to a flame. This is the liberating purpose of fantasy, as Lovecraft explained it in the same letter to Smith, to "give the imagination a ground for limitless expansion, & to satisfy aesthetically the sincere & burning curiosity & sense of awe which a sensitive minority of mankind feel toward the alluring & provocative abysses of unplumbed space and unguessed entity which press upon the known world."

Lovecraft was one of that sensitive minority. So, probably, was Henry Wentworth Akeley, as is, certainly, Wilmarth, through whose viewpoint we appreciate the awesome temptation of the offer the Yuggothians eventually make: a virtually endless voyage through the universe, congress with beings on otherwise unknowable worlds, near immortality as one's disembodied brain is borne through the interstellar darkness.

The genius of the story is how deftly this temptation is balanced against the horror. Part of us knows perfectly well that the Outer Ones mean Akeley—and possibly all of mankind—no good, but we desperately want to believe the claims in the "final" Akeley letter that they are godlike and wise, and offer infinite knowledge to those humans who will only trust them. That final letter subtly wrenches our emotions. The story is only half done, and it would seem the climax has been reached—the siege of the farmhouse is coming to an end. The aliens must surely win. Then comes the letter, assuring us it was all a misunderstanding. There are more than a few hints that it is a forgery, or at least written under mind-control, but, in one of the most delicate maneuvers in all Lovecraft's fiction, he plays hope and wonder off against logic and horror.

It is interesting to compare "Whisperer" to the Professor Jameson series of Neil R. Jones, the first installment of which, "The Jameson Satellite," appeared almost simultaneously in the July 1931 *Amazing Stories*. That Jones was a much inferior writer to Lovecraft goes without saying. He is barely remembered today, and certainly has no critical reputation at all. But the adventures of Professor Jameson and the alien Zoromes were popular in *Amazing* in the 1930s, and even enjoyed a brief revival in paperback in the 1960s. As late as the mid-1980s, Jones was still trying to peddle them to subsequent editors of *Amazing*, having, pathetically, made no artistic progress at all since 1931.

In "The Jameson Satellite," the late professor's corpse is put in orbit, presumably freeze-dried forever. But the metal-bodied Zoromes, creatures which discover him aeons hence, place his brain in a body like their own, and the lot of them blithely soar off to explore the universe, story after story. The Professor's attitude toward being carried off into realms beyond utterly human imagination and experience might be summed up as a shrug of, "Well, gee, that's interesting..." He seems to have so little emotion that at times it is hard to tell him from the indistinguishable, numbered Zoromes.

But Lovecraft approached the same material with a deep sense of awe, and was able to make such a bargain as alluring and terrifying as Faustus's deal with the Devil. "I *know*," he wrote, "that my most poignant emotional experiences are those which concern the lure of unplumbed space, the terror of the encroaching outer void, & the struggle of the ego to transcend the known & established order of time...space, matter..."[6]

For Lovecraft the materialist, for whom there was no hope of rebirth or the hereafter, the physical immortality of those brains-in-canisters and the chance to explore the "outer void" and know its unknowable secrets, coupled with the brains' utter helplessness and dependency on the dubiously-motivated Outer Ones, plus their total loss of Earthly culture, familiar settings, and associations, and everything that made them human, must have been as close as he could come to imagining heaven—and hell.

Thus "The Whisperer in Darkness" is the quintessential Lovecraft story, the one cosmic vision which sums up the entirety of his aesthetic agenda and philosophical thought. If he had written no other fiction, he would be remembered, I think, and rated highly, for this one.

XIII.

H. P. LOVECRAFT'S FAVORITE MOVIE

H. P. Lovecraft's letters show him to be a frequent, albeit seldom enthusiastic movie-goer. There are occasional references to this or that film, often forgotten comedies, seen in the company of Frank Belknap Long and or other friends. One further recalls the two poems "To Mistress Sophia Simple, Queen of Cinema" and "To Charlie of the Comics." There are also a couple of stronger references in a letter to Farnsworth Wright dated Feb. 16, 1933—to a disgusted HPL walking out of the Lugosi *Dracula*, "seeing red" out of "posthumous sympathy" for Mary Shelley upon viewing the Karloff *Frankenstein*.

In general, HPL had a low opinion of weird films and radio plays, particular ones based on published stories (the actual subject of the letter to Wright is a polite refusal to have "Dreams in the Witch House" adapted for radio), and recommends "as a thorough soporific... the average popularly 'horrible' play or cinema or radio dialogue." At the same time he concedes that weird drama can be written, "when the author starts out *from the first* to utilize the dramatic form."

Not surprisingly, Lovecraft's favorite film—certainly his favorite *fantasy* film—is an adaptation of a stage play, which would thus lose somewhat less in translation to the screen.

The 1933 time-travel film *Berkeley Square* (Twentieth Century Fox, directed by Frank Lloyd, starring Leslie Howard, Heather Angel, Alan Mowbray, and Irene Browne) gave the Old Gent "an uncanny wallop," as he describes in a letter to J. Vernon Shea dated February 4, 1934. It is an adaptation of John Balderston's stage-play of the same title, and concerns a reclusive, world-weary twentieth-century man who slips back into what he imagines to be the age of elegance and paradisiacal simplicity, Britain in the late eighteenth century.

The story managed to—in the modern parlance—push every one of Lovecraft's buttons. "It is the most weirdly perfect embodiment of my own moods and pseudo-memories that I have ever seen—for all my life I have felt as if I might wake up out of this dream of an idiotic Victorian & an insane Jazz age into the sane reality of 1760 or 1770 or 1780...the age of white steeples & fanlighted doorways of the ancient hill, & of the long-s'd books of the old dark attic trunk-room at 454 Angell St. God Save the King!"

Berkeley Square was very nearly lost. I managed to see a rare showing at a Philadelphia film society, the print having been made in a laboratory by the man who showed it, a copy of a copy of what was probably the last, crumbling original in the world. It came out quite well, considering, restored to what was described as "eighty-percent" quality, with one or two jerky splices and occasional graininess.

Since then, *Berkeley Square* has edged back from the brink of oblivion. In the originally published version of this article, I pronounced gloomily that the film was not commercially available in any form, did not seem to have been shown on TV in the VCR era, and therefore seemed likely to perish. I am grateful to T. E. D. Klein for pointing out that it is available from Foothill Video (P.O. Box 547, Tujunga, CA 91043). The Foothill copy is not as good as the one I saw in Philadelphia, at perhaps "seventy-percent" quality, with a couple of frames clearly missing and the visuals about the level of a silent movie of ten years earlier. The sound is pretty good.

The play of the same title is occasionally revived. I saw an Off-Off Broadway production about fifteen years ago, starring no less than Christopher (Superman) Reeve in the leading role as Peter Standish. The text was published as a book by Macmillan in 1929 and went through several printings.

It is clear from Lovecraft's letter to Shea that he had *not* seen or read the play, although Wilfred Blanch Talman and Frank Long had told him that the movie version was "slightly inferior." The play is still useful to Lovecraftians because of the rarity of the film, in order to get an idea of what the story is like. The adaptation, by John Balderston and Sonya Levien, is fairly faithful. The actual writing differences primarily consist of scenes shortened or lines of dialogue left out. I have now seen a performance of the play (albeit twenty years ago), read the printed text of the play, and seen the film, and can with some authority compare all three.

Berkeley Square is the story of Peter Standish, a scholarly young man who, were he not romantically involved with a lady, might be described as a typical Lovecraftian protagonist, socially withdrawn, bookish, and more alive in the past than in the present. He has inherited from a remote relative a fine Queen Anne-era house in Berkeley Square, London, which an ancestor of his built. Virtually nothing has changed inside the house between 1784 and 1928 save for a few minor rearrangements of furniture and the addition of electric lights. It is the world outside which has changed so much. The one other significant detail is a portrait of the ancestor (also named Peter Standish) by Joshua Reynolds, hanging in the twentieth-century "morning" room, which, in the play, serves as the scene of all the action. (The film, of course, moves around.) Surely many of us have had the feeling that in such a place the past is still alive, that at any moment people in eighteenth-century garb might come in through the doors, or that a toga-wearing figure might casually appear in some exceptionally well-preserved Roman building, or that perhaps one might slip out of the present, into some past era.

Sure enough, twentieth-century Peter *does* go back, switching places with his eighteenth-century ancestor. The method is never completely explained, but apparently his researches have led him to this possibility. It is not even clear whether he switches minds, occupying the *body* of his ancestor, or whether he goes back physically, and somehow arriving in eighteenth-century garb, with his hair grown long in eighteenth-century fashion. Before leaving, he warns his associates in the twentieth century not to be too alarmed if he seems a bit odd for a few days (*i.e*, his twentieth-century self is being impersonated badly by eighteenth-century Peter).

He apparently materializes inside the house, back in 1784. The people there have seen eighteenth-century Peter (a rich American relative who is to marry one of the daughters of the house) alight from his carriage in the pouring rain. Someone goes to the door, but he is not there. Then twentieth-century Peter comes into the room, *in dry clothes* (eighteenth-century Peter presumably arrived in the twentieth century wet, in twentieth-century clothes, his hair short). In the film this transition is finely handled, with what must have been for the time a quite sophisticated interplay of light, shadow, and background sound. Gradually twentieth-century traffic noises give way to hoofbeats on cobbles.

The dry clothes constitute the first of several "slips" Peter has to explain away as, guided by letters and a diary he found in the twentieth century, he attempts to impersonate his eighteenth-century forebear. Things do not go well, as he often refers to things which haven't happened yet (a painting Reynolds has only begun, a gift shawl one of the daughters hasn't unwrapped yet), and seems decidedly uncanny to the eighteenth-century characters. Worse yet, he follows his own emotions rather than following the "script" of his ancestor's diary and falls in love with the wrong daughter. It is an impossible, heart-wrenching situation, particularly after he takes the maiden into his confidence and gives her a vision of the terrifying twentieth century. (This may be the weakest point in both the film and play, but I confess I can think of no more satisfactory way to do it: the girl looks into his eyes and sees twentieth-century skyscrapers, an auto race, a collage of World War I scenes—and all along everyone else has been distinctly *afraid* to look Peter straight in the eye.) Eventually he returns to 1928, only to learn from a tombstone that his beloved died three years after he knew her, in 1787, possibly pining for him. To both the eighteenth- and twentieth-century supporting cast, "their" Peter Standish has recovered from some sort of delusion or mania once the reverse-transition has taken place.

Berkeley Square is a fine film in its own right, certainly one of the best time-travel films ever. The performances by Leslie Howard in the lead, and by all the supporting cast, are far beyond the awkwardness of the cast of *Dracula* or the scenery-chewing melodramatics of Colin Clive and Dwight Frye in *Frankenstein*. Lovecraft saw *Berkeley Square* three times, twice on his second visit, though one suspects that he was drawn more to the supernatural/slip-into-the-past aspect than the romantic plot. (Though, uncharacteristically, he didn't *object* to the romantic elements.) He also would have enjoyed the depiction of eighteenth-century life in the film, which constitutes one of the most convincing portrayals of a past era in any film up to that time.

Berkeley Square is rich in period details, which, naturally, no one other than twentieth-century Peter finds at all odd: for instance, each gentleman arriving at a party first places a paper cone over his face, then submits to having his wig powdered.

The movie adds a prologue-scene not in the play. Eighteenth-century Peter stops at a tavern on his way to London, where he hears news that a Frenchman has just flown across the Channel in a balloon. "It's starting," he says, "this age of speed which we will never live to see." This neatly underscores the theme of the whole film.

Some of the nastier details are left out. Twentieth-century Peter becomes disillusioned by the filth, squalor, and cruelty of the eighteenth century, finding himself "buried alive," as he puts it, in an alien era. But we encounter very little of that filth, other than an exchange with an obnoxious character over Peter's "eccentricity" of bathing, and a reference to Peter's turning his back "rudely" when a prince blows his nose with his fingers. One detail I vividly remembered from the performance of fifteen years ago, which isn't in the film, was Peter's outrage when he learned that a gentleman had paid three guineas for a window seat to see a woman burned at the stake (for counterfeiting). Everyone regards him as laughably squeamish (p. 66-67 of the published play).

There is also an amusing bit in which Peter, ever the antiquarian, is admiring the lovely Queen Anne furniture, and the lady of the house says, "the wars have impoverished so many of us here, dear cousin, alas, we cannot afford to rid ourselves of our old rubbish."

Lovecraft makes several interesting points in his letter to Shea, the most significant that when eighteenth-century Peter returned to the eighteenth century, he should have been changed by his experience. Yet he wrote his diary (which twentieth-century Peter uses as a guide) making no mention of his adventure, even though that diary clearly goes on for years beyond the period of the trans-temporal exchange. He seems to have just gone on as an ordinary eighteenth-century man.

Lovecraft wants to know what the eighteenth-century Peter was doing in the twentieth century, while our attention was elsewhere. We get something of an explanation, as the housekeeper tells of drunken fits, gambling, bawdy old songs, and even an episode in which her master tried to force his way into a club claiming to be a member, only to be thrown out. Lovecraft tries to explain this as the behavior of twentieth-century Peter in a deranged state *after his return*, but I don't see anything in either the film or the play to support such a view. Eighteenth-century Peter was a bit of a rake, and *he* was the one who belonged to that club. As he is thrown out, he proclaims that the people around him won't be born for a hundred years. No, the person who so upset the housekeeper is eighteenth-century Peter. Lovecraft specifically disagrees. The reader may find the printed play (which is not at all scarce) and see for himself.

The significance of *Berkeley Square*, and particularly of Lovecraft's having seen it when he did, is that it must have been on his mind when he was writing "The Shadow Out of Time," which, according to the now widely-accepted Joshi chronology found in the new edition of *Dagon and Other Macabre Tales*, was begun in November 1934. Many of the film's elements Lovecraft discusses in his letter are present: a modern man changing places with a counterpart in the past, some mystery about what the person from the past has been doing in the twentieth century in the meantime, and even a specimen of writing discovered by the twentieth-century man which provides a crucial key. Of course, the logic-lapse of the diary is precisely the point which bothered HPL. He much improved on the motif, when *his* time-traveller finds writing from the remote past *in his own handwriting*. Balderston didn't think of that. Twentieth-century Peter never does find anything which he himself wrote back in the eighteenth century.

The major difference, of course, is that the protagonist of "The Shadow Out of Time" changes places with a non-human creature whose body might best be described as an animate salt-shaker with tentacles. So, where Balderston is vague about whether or not Peter Standish has switched minds with his eighteenth-century counterpart, or just walked through a door into the past, Lovecraft must be explicit. And of course, too, Lovecraft's version is vastly more cosmic, complete with lost races and cities, weird alien beings and menaces, and lacking pretty girls.

Berkeley Square also contains uncanny parallels to *The Case of Charles Dexter Ward*. Twentieth-century Peter is very much like Charles. He, like Charles, discovers a portrait of an eighteenth-century ancestor which bears a striking resemblance to himself. He, like Charles, seems to have dabbled in the paranormal, leading him to an attempted recovery of the past. And, once his eighteenth-century ancestor is impersonating him in the twentieth century, everyone notices how changed he seems.

Unfortunately there is no way *Berkeley Square* could have influenced *The Case of Charles Dexter Ward*. According to the chronology, *Ward* was written between January and March 1927. (Even without the chronology, this is easy to established from published Lovecraftian letters. See *Selected Letters II*, p. 106.) The Balderston play bears a *1929* copyright, and in any case it is clear from HPL's letter to Shea that he had *not* seen the stage version. Therefore he could not have been familiar with *Berkeley Square* prior to 1933. It is an amazing coincidence, but no more than that.

And it is, too, one more reason why Lovecraft found the film to be "the most weirdly perfect embodiment" of his own moods and feelings he had ever encountered. Independently, he had already written his own version.

XIV.

M. R. JAMES AND H. P. LOVECRAFT

THE GHOSTLY AND THE COSMIC

i.

For all that the writing of ghost stories played only a small role in the life and career of medievalist, scholar, and educator Montague Rhodes James (1862-1936), he had distinct views on how such stories should be written and what they should contain. Four key documents articulate virtually everything James had to say on the subject: the preface to *More Ghost Stories of an Antiquary* (1911), the introduction to *Ghosts and Marvels*, edited by Vere Henry Collins (1924), the introduction to James's own *The Collected Ghost Stories* (1931) (called *The Ghost Stories* in later editions), and an essay, "Some Remarks on Ghost Stories" (1929).

James wrote his stories almost as parlor tricks. For many years he produced one each Christmas, to be read aloud to a circle of friends. Later, when Provost of Eton, his Christmas readings entertained students. He only sought publication when his friends urged him to. He was never, in any sense, a professional writer. That he was extraordinarily talented is undeniable. His best stories are masterful tone-poems of dread which resonate as effectively on the tenth reading as on the first. There is something almost outrageously enviable about a man who can, on an agreed-upon schedule, casually put aside his weightier concerns and toddle off to produce one more undying classic, however minor that classic may be in the overall literary scheme of things.

"The sole object" of ghostly fiction, he wrote, is that of "inspiring a pleasing terror in the reader."[7] In the introduction to *The Collected Ghost Stories* he further suggests (echoing Dr. Johnson) that the public is the only judge of fiction's merit: "if they are pleased, it is well; if not, it is no use to tell them why they ought to have been pleased."

As for what constituted a "pleasing terror," James had what would seem to a modern reader somewhat prudish standards. He did *not* approve of physical gore, his "Some Remarks" essay dismissing the pulp writing of "some Americans" (including, quite possibly, H. P.

Lovecraft) found in such anthologies as *Not at Night* as "merely nauseating," and even Ambrose Bierce as "unpardonable."[8] A discussion follows, delineating which writers remain on the right side of "the line" and which do not. "I should remove one or two that leave a nasty taste," he says of the contents of H. R. Wakefield's *They Return at Evening*. A. M. Burrage gets James's approval, as does F. Marion Crawford. R. H. Benson he finds "too ecclesiastical." (Curiously, E. F. Benson is not mentioned.) Erckmann-Chatrian and J. Sheridan Le Fanu are particularly championed. At the very end, James admits having read Henry James's *The Turn of the Screw*, but then refuses to comment on it.

The introduction to *Ghosts and Marvels* sets down the "rules" of the ghost story, although James is astute enough to realize that no writer follows "rules." These are, rather, "qualities which have been observed to accompany success." The key ingredients, then, according to James, are "the atmosphere and a nicely managed crescendo." The characters should be introduced in a realistic setting, going about their ordinary business. Gradually, the supernatural begins to intrude. By the climax of the story, the supernatural manifestation is quite unambiguous. The "loophole for a rationalistic explanation" is ultimately "not quite practicable. You are sure that the ghost did intervene, but sometimes you will find it quite difficult to put your finger on the moment when it did so."[9] (If he ever read it, James must have particularly admired Edith Wharton's "Afterward," in which the ghost is only recognizable in retrospect, after it has gone.)

James had slightly peculiar ideas on *when* the ghost story should be set. The detective story, he explains, thrives on the modern, on the latest techno-gimmickry, but for the ghost story, "a slight haze of distance is desirable." Nevertheless, that distance is to be slight. In "Some Remarks on Ghost Stories" he explicitly rejects the use of costume settings:

> ...the belted knight who meets the spectre in the vaulted chamber and has to say, 'By my halidom," or words to that effect, has little actuality about him. Anything, we feel, might have happened in the fifteenth century. No, the seer of ghosts must talk something like me, and be dressed, if not in my fashion, yet not too much like a man in a pageant, if he is to enlist my sympathy.[10]

Although one of his slighter tales ("There Was a Man Dwelt by a Churchyard") is set in Elizabethan times, otherwise James seems to define a sufficiently "modern" setting as any period after the Age of Reason, when the manifestation of the ghostly will seem a violation of the order of things, rather than a natural part of it. He doesn't hesitate to go back into the middle of the eighteenth century (the main action of "The Ash Tree" is set about 1755), but even at such a relatively slight temporal distance, James recommends finding some way to "bring the reader in contact" with the past era, such as the finding of old documents, a device he employs effectively in "Count Magnus" (which takes place in Sweden, about 1840).

The idea, ultimately, is to "put the reader into the position of saying to himself, 'If I'm not very careful, something of this kind may happen to me!'"[11]

Further, James felt that the ghost itself should remain distinctly *supernatural*. Several times he warned against the use of pseudo-scientific occultism, which "call into play faculties quite other than the imaginative."[12] He had some reservations about Algernon Blackwood's *John Silence, Physician Extraordinary* on this point. He didn't want elaborate explanations of *how* the ghost performs its hauntings:

> ...the greatest successes have been scored by authors who can make us envisage a definite time and place, and give us plenty of clear-cut and matter-of-fact detail, but who, when the climax is reached, allow us to be just a little in the dark as to the working of their machinery. We do not want to see the bones of their theory about the supernatural.[13]

The "bones" of such a theory, of course, is exactly what "occultism" would provide. It would dissipate the wonder by making the supernatural something which can be routinely accepted and understood.

To sum up the Jamesean ghost story quickly then: a familiar, realistically presented setting, into which a malevolent "ghost" intrudes subtly but definitely, until a horrific climax is reached. It's useful to mention that James was at his most imaginative when producing his specters, which are often quite other than returning revenants of the dead. Many Jamesean spooks might be loosely described as demons, squat, hairy, and, as H. P. Lovecraft noted, frequently *felt* before they are seen. James was capable of far more than a fleeting figure in a winding sheet.

ii.

H. P. Lovecraft, of course, was well familiar with James's work and addressed him as one of the "Modern Masters" in *Supernatural Horror in Literature*, for all he sometimes found him lacking in atmosphere:

> Dr. James has, it is clear, an intelligent and scientific knowledge of human nerves and feelings; and knows how to apportion statement, imagery, and subtle suggestions in order to secure the best results with his readers. He is an artist in incident and arrangement rather than in atmosphere, and reaches the emotions more often through the intellect than directly. This method, of course, with its occasional absences of sharp climax, has its drawbacks as well as its advantages; and many will miss the thorough atmospheric tension which writers like Machen are careful to build up with words and scenes.[14]

This passage tells us as much about Lovecraft as it does about James. While no opinion of Lovecraft by James has been recorded (and if James only read Lovecraft in the *Not at Night Series*, he was at the time of his "Some Remarks" essay, only familiar with "The Horror at Red Hook"[15]), he would probably have found Lovecraft's work labored, unsubtle, and definitely "over the line" of nastiness. Lovecraft seems a little dissatisfied with James's economy of style; yet there is no denying that James could often draw a more powerful effect in a single paragraph (or even a sentence) than most other writers, including Lovecraft, could in a full page. Lovecraft, for all his many merits, was not succinct.

The irony is that, so many years later, Lovecraft's reputation and popularity have so vastly outstripped James (letting the public decide, to cite James's own criterion of success), that very possibly a large percentage of James's present-day readership discovered him through the description in Lovecraft's essay. Critics, in the years since James's death, haven't had much to say. To the mainstream establishment, he is an undisputed master of a specific type of story, safely acknowledged, put on a shelf, and allowed to gather dust, a footnote in the history of literature. To the specialist critic of the weird, James is likewise little explored; yet the amount written on Lovecraft now dwarfs his own work. New books on Lovecraft appear at least yearly, and there seems no end in sight.

So, what are the differences between James and Lovecraft? Why is Lovecraft the more (posthumously) successful, both critically and popularly, by several orders of magnitude? While it is easy to argue that James is, technically, the superior writer, it doesn't seem particularly illuminating to do so.

First, the most interesting area of inquiry is what the two writers have *in common*.

Lovecraft's views on the aesthetics and technique of the weird tale are too well known to reiterate in any great detail here. Certainly it is unnecessary to produce a long array of quoted passages, even to the extent done above for James. The reader is merely referred to such essays as "Notes on Writing Weird Fiction" and *Supernatural Horror in Literature*, and also to Lovecraft's letters, which expound his aesthetics again and again. He is often at his best when tutoring some promising young weird-fiction writer, as in his recently published *Letters to Robert Bloch*.

Atmosphere, rather than action or character, was for Lovecraft the focus of the weird tale, the whole point being "a vivid picture of a certain type of human mood."[16] The setting should be realistically depicted, the details as cleverly and convincingly compiled as if the author were constructing a hoax—one reason Lovecraft's stories frequently contain vast amounts of genuine historical and geographical data. The purpose of this realism, is of course, to make the fantastic intrusion plausible, the marvel itself being "treated very impressively and deliberately." The horror comes from "a convincing picture of shattered natural law," the impossible becoming possible so that "its mere existence should overshadow the characters and events."[17]

This is *not at all incompatible* with M. R. James's "qualities which have been observed to accompany success." Both writers prefer stories set in the modern-day, or at least close enough to the modern-day that the habits and customs of the characters should not be much different from those of the reader. Both opt for the use of prosaic detail, realistically presented, to create a convincing milieu into which an unnatural abnormality will then, subtly, intrude.

Both prefer a plain style. James achieved this at once, although it is ironic to note that James's stories, because they were meant to be read aloud, are more obviously told in the author's voice. They contain numerous vocalisms, even to the point of intrusion. The effect is that, for all James's prose is by far leaner, he seems a more old-fashioned writer than Lovecraft, hearkening back to the early Victorians with their "Dear Reader" devices.

Lovecraft began very floridly, his whole career being an uphill struggle toward a simpler, less pulp-influenced style. He began to approach his own ideal standards in such later tales as *At the Mountains of Madness* and "The Haunter of the Dark." Lovecraft did prefer more fulsome descriptions than James, and devoted more wordage to the deliberate building-up of atmosphere, but note that James, too, cited atmosphere, along with a well-managed climax, as the key to the ghostly tale.

Both Lovecraft and James liked an explicit, but not *too* explicit climax. Lovecraft was a bit more given to physical gore, as in "The Rats in the Walls" and "The Thing on the Doorstep," but he, like James admired the sort of "pleasing shudder" which lingers, by the story's implications, well after the reader has ceased reading. Both writers recognized, and stated explicitly, that (contrary to Lovecraft's comment about James's appealing directly to the intellect) the desired effect is an emotional one, James's "pleasing shudder," Lovecraft's "picture of a certain type of human mood."

In short, Lovecraft and James would, if they'd ever had the chance to discuss the matter, have found that they had a great deal in common and very little disagreement over the method of the weird tale. Aesthetically, they are not far apart.

Philosophically, however, they are very far apart indeed. The difference between the two is to what *use* they put their spectral fictions. S. T. Joshi, in *The Weird Tale*, makes impatiently short work of James, because, as most other critics have found, there really isn't a lot to be *said* about James. His stories were composed to make himself the life of the party at Christmas. They proved popular and became an annual tradition. Otherwise, James was seldom moved to write ghost stories. Some of his tales ("There Was a Man Dwelt by a Churchyard" most explicitly of all) are merely elaborate methods of saying "Boo!"—of making the reader or hearer jump. James's stories carry virtually no philosophical or thematic freight. They aren't, on a deeper level, *about* anything.

This very lack of substance may in part account for his limited acceptance by the mainstream establishment. Fantastic fiction as unambitious as that of M. R. James is hardly going to threaten the prevailing view that realism constitutes the only valid, "serious" literature. James knows his "place" as practitioner of an avowedly minor, generic form.

Lovecraft's work, of course, is far more challenging. He is as rich and complex a writer as Wells or Stapledon. Most obviously, his stories express a distinct view of the cosmos and mankind's place in it which is *very* threatening to complacent humanism: that all is the indifferent, random result of natural forces, galaxies forming out of dust, planets forming, then being destroyed as stars explode; the feelings, aspirations, and moral standards of such organic life as may have evolved on those planets in the meantime being of no lasting or more than local importance.

The ramifications of this go on and on. The more Lovecraft's thought is studied, the more facets of it appear. His is a complete world-outlook, which he thought through and expressed in great detail. Lovecraft's fiction is a natural and integral part of the rest of his writing and thought. James's fiction is the seasonal hobby of a man whose main interests lay elsewhere.

But we have to admit that the horror-reading public, the very public which has chosen Lovecraft so overwhelmingly over James, didn't necessarily do so out of admiration for the intricate points of Lovecraft's mechanistic materialism. It may well be that Lovecraft's *popular* success is for the very reasons James wouldn't have approved of him. Lovecraft is a more *extreme* writer than James, although this is a divergence of degree rather than kind. Lovecraft goes into vast detail describing Joseph Curwen's sorcerous doings in *The Case of Charles*

Dexter Ward, where James merely hints, at some distance, what Count Magnus may have been up to. And nowhere in James is there any imaginative feat as vast as Lovecraft's sweeping vistas of ancient civilizations and past epochs in "The Shadow Out of Time" or *At the Mountains of Madness*.

One way to put it is to say that where James presents the tip of the iceberg, Lovecraft produces the whole iceberg. Where James leaves most of the details out, Lovecraft puts them in. Lovecraft is, to use Clive Barker's term, an inclusionist.[18] While including everything imaginable in vast detail may sometimes overwhelm the story (as it does in Barker's novels, and, candidly, in some of Lovecraft, particularly the last half of *At the Mountains of Madness*), it has the effect of satisfying the jaded reader. James's subtle glimpses whet the appetite for increasing frightfulness, more than James is willing to produce. Lovecraft delivers.

But there is more to Lovecraft, even to Lovecraft's popular success, than sensationalism. Undeniably, Lovecraft produces a stronger "thrill" in more people than does James. *Why?* Their stated aims are so similar, as are their taste and aesthetics.

We come back to the thematic content. Lovecraft is more convincing because he is more *relevant*. That is, few modern (American, at least) readers have ever *seen* a medieval cathedral, much less entertained much belief in shuffling Things summoned from the vaults by the decipherment of a moldering Latin manuscript. But thoughtful modern readers *do* believe in the universe at large. Lovecraft is facing, without flinching, the chief philosophical problem—and fear—of the twentieth century: the revelation, through science, of a godless, meaningless cosmos, in which mankind exists by chance, in which there are no absolute moral standards and no external source of justice or comfort.

James, by contrast, with his antiquarian spooks, is merely quaint.

XV.

RICHARD MIDDLETON

Beauty, Sadness, and Terror

i.

"...he was the Bohemian personified," editor John Gawsworth wrote. "One of the 'rare' spirits in the Elizabethan, jovial sense of that antique adjective. Simplicity—the keynote of his art—was also the keynote of his Alsatian mode of living; for all his learning, for all his passion, he could not 'grow up.'"

Arthur Machen praised his genius and wrote of the title story in his principal collection, "I would exchange this short, crazy, enchanting fantasy for a whole wilderness of seemly novels."

Lord Alfred Douglas found him "a witty and whimsical talker."

But in 1911, Richard Barnham Middleton, the author of "The Ghost Ship," one of the most cheerful pieces of supernatural *fun* in English literature, killed himself in his sordid lodgings in Brussels by drinking chloroform. He had been ill for some time, had suffered the pangs of unrequited love, and was apparently in despair over the future of his literary career. He was twenty-nine. Machen was writing the introduction to a memorial volume.

Middleton's friends at the time doubtless asked "Why?" Today the same question gives his work an added, if morbid fascination, quite apart from its very real merit. We search it for suicide notes, as surely as we do Robert E. Howard's poetry. We find a great deal about death, unhappiness, and despair; the answer is as simple as that and also more complex. That one famous story, "The Ghost Ship," wonderful as it is, is quickly seen as amazingly atypical.

ii.

Richard Middleton was born at Staines, England on October 28, 1882. His father, an engineer, provided a stable home environment. Schooling seems to have been ordinary enough for a middle-class boy of that period, save that Middleton, brighter and more sensitive than his fellows, became that archetypical, suffering object of cruel fun found among every group of schoolboys. These agonies are chronicles in his story, "A Drama of Youth," which is, indeed, about a superior boy put through hell by his peers, who finds it better to stay home sick. So chicken pox becomes a cause for celebration.

In real life, when the pressures on him became too great, Middleton's father removed him to another school, from which, in 1899, he passed his matriculation examination for the University of London. There he studied Elementary and Additional Mathematics, English, and what was still called "Natural Philosophy." He did well, but for some reason his college career was cut short, and he became a clerk. Office work was a painful drudgery, endured for six years while he read the classics and dreamed of freedom. He began to write, and joined an informal society of literary men, The New Bohemians, of which Machen was a member.

This was his chance. He made a break for freedom, resigned his job, and became a full-time literary man, without ever having, apparently, made a shilling from writing. It was the classic mistake of the would-be writer, but one which many writers have managed to survive.

Middleton's social connections did him good service. Lord Alfred Douglas (the same who, years before, had been Oscar Wilde's unindicted partner in iniquity) made him a book reviewer for *The Academy*, which he edited. Edgar Jepson made him sub-editor of *Vanity Fair*. By 1908 he was being published fairly widely in British periodicals, although book publication eluded him. He developed a following as a poet. Austin Harrison of *The English Review* called him "the carol-boy of English poetry...our Verlaine."

This was at least a modest level of success. However discontented Middleton may have been, there were doubtless thousands of struggling hopefuls who never got as far as the pages of *Century* or *Vanity Fair*. He did not make much money, but then, as now, serious money was in novels and book-length nonfiction. Middleton's work consisted of short stories, prose sketches, essays, and poems, and, while he had little difficulty placing them, it was only natural that it would take time for his reputation to grow. Book publication would have come eventually, if he had only been patient.

Of course he was not patient, and it is very easy to lecture a man long dead about how he should have run his career. Logically, Middleton should have held whatever jobs he could which would still enable him to write, then gone on that way until he was earning enough from writing that he could afford to go full-time. Perhaps he would never have made a living from writing. Many writers, even great ones, don't. All Middleton needed was a job, and his poverty and subsequent sufferings could have been avoided.

But he was no more logical than most of us. His passions and ambitions drove him, and perhaps too some deep-seated urge he did not understand. He was the living stereotype of the Romantic poet, a wildly impractical seeker-after-beauty who never manages to adjust to the prosaic world and hurts when the world fails to adjust to him. Gawsworth tells us he even looked the part, "...a sturdy, broad-shouldered man with the darkest and shaggiest of black beards, his thick lower lip gleaming like a wet cherry from out its opulence...his pockets bulged with drafts of poems scrawled upon old envelopes, the stories illegibly recorded on the backs of bills." Middleton did not plan his life. He lived it, and things, in time, did not work out happily.

It is not entirely clear with whom he was in love, but there were bad love affairs which depressed him, and he was already that sort of person whose emotions ran in a roller-coaster ride from wild elation to deep melancholy and back again. He wrote love poems to a prostitute, which only fits the Romantic image. Gawsworth says, "he could find in the eyes of the most degraded wanton...the picture of 'the best sort of fairy' and, further, celebrate this finding of purity amid defilement in flowing music." One wonders if the prostitute ever knew she was the object of such affections. The image of the Romantic poet and the living man become difficult to separate. Perhaps Middleton couldn't do it either.

He moved to Brussels in 1911 and continued to write, mostly prose by this time, as the failed love affairs seem to have silenced his muse. His work continued to appear in various magazines, but the real world began to close in on his dream of freedom from everyday cares. He was desperately short of money. His health worsened, and he had increasing attacks of neuralgia. (That is, a sharp pain from a variety of causes; neuralgia being one of those ailments, like dropsy, which turns out to be a miscellany of symptoms rather than a specific disease. It is even possible in Middleton's case that the pains were psychosomatic.) He had been prescribed chloroform, and, on December 1, 1911, when there seemed no other way out, he drank some. To the end he maintained a cheerful façade, but it was indeed only a façade. His last message to his friend Henry Savage was, "Goodbye, Harry, I'm going adventuring again."

It was a cruel irony, which he no doubt would have expected, that as soon as he was dead, Middleton was proclaimed a lost, neglected genius. Five memorial volumes appeared within two years: *The Ghost Ship and Other Stories* (his best fiction), *Monologues* (essays), *The Day Before Yesterday* (reminiscences of childhood in the manner of James Barrie's *The Golden Age*, and two volumes of poetry. More followed: a play, a collection of letters to Henry Savage, and finally, in 1933, *The Pantomime Man*, a gathering of uncollected stories, essays, and sketches edited by Gawsworth, who had become his champion. There are further uncollected stories in Gawsworth's anthologies, no less than six in *New Tales of Horror by Eminent Authors* (1934). Vincent Starrett's *Buried Caesars* (1923) contains an essay about Middleton which examines, then dismisses, the idea that genius is somehow inherently self-destructive. Middleton's death, Starrett muses, "must have been, partially, in the nature of a protest...[his] beautiful writings were placed in covers *after* his death.... Suppose someone had whispered a few words of sympathy and appreciation, and it had been a bit less difficult for him to live and write and sell his tales!"

If only. Richard Middleton's life and death were a long series of if-onlys. There is a great deal about death in his work, but, as Starrett points out, there usually is in the writings of youth. Quite unlike fantasy fiction's other famous suicide, Robert E. Howard, Middleton seems to have been a basically healthy personality. There was no horrible fixation driving him inexorably to his doom. Middleton's suicide probably came as a surprise, even to Middleton. He merely failed to get past one particularly difficult stretch of living.

If only—

Middleton was still young when he died, and his talent was perhaps not fully developed, but it was already abundantly clear that the loss to literature was very great. His enormous promise had already yielded enormous accomplishments in many areas, not the least of which were his tales of the fantastic and grotesque. Starrett said that Middleton "looked out of a window and dreamed fantastic dreams."

Indeed he did, and some of those dreams were nightmares.

iii.

"The Ghost Ship" is a jolly tale about a phantom galleon blown into a turnip patch in a respectable English village. In time the rowdy specters have so upset the villagers' sense of propriety that the specters must leave, taking all the local ghosts with them. The once richly-haunted place is left without the barest wisp of ectoplasm. Without a doubt, this is one of the most successful humorous ghost stories of all time. It used to be a standard item in anthologies, and it deserved its fame. More remarkably, it hasn't aged at all. Humor often fails to hold up over even a few decades.

Most of Middleton's fiction, however, is beautiful and sad. There is a pervading sense of helpless melancholy, as if he were aware that life would never conform to his beautiful notions. "The Soul of a Policeman" is about precisely this conflict. The policeman is so ready to see the good and the beautiful that he forgives criminals and can't meet his arrest quota. "The Poet's Allegory" is more of a direct polemic, about a poet who sings of beautiful things and is ignored, then turns scurrilous and develops a huge following.

About a quarter of Middleton's stories have clearly fantastic elements. Many more have the "feel" of fantasy, and are right on the edge of non-reality. "Children of the Moon," for example, is about two children in search of "magic" (in the broadest sense) by moonlight.

Anything they see, presumably, is entirely in their minds, but the point is a sad irony: only an escaped lunatic can understand their quest.

In "The Bird in the Garden," a child dwells in a fabulous garden and waits with almost messianic expectation for "a bird of all colors, ugly and beautiful, with a harsh sweet voice." But one day the child disastrously "awakens" into the mundane world: a sordid basement tenement with a few flowerpots hanging from a grating.

This child, like many of Middleton's characters, is trapped by life. It is no one's fault. Things merely are. The boy-tramp in "On the Brighton Road" coughs out an account of his wanderings. He seems very ill, perhaps dying. It turns out that he has already died many times along the road, and is condemned to repeat his death over and over. (The story makes an interesting contrast with the realistic "The Boy Errant," in which a fourteen-year-old vagabond seems happy with his lot, until his fears are briefly and poignantly revealed.) The inept magician in "The Conjurer" tempts fate in his one last, desperate attempt to save his career. He succeeds in making his wife disappear, but can't get her back. There is no moral reason for this. It is a fluke of cruel, existential weirdness. Similarly, there is no explanation for the sinister activities of "The Coffin Merchant," who only gives his handbills to people who will be needing his services soon. Middleton's world never offers an easy answer. "Shepherd's Boy" was neglected by his drunkard father and killed in a stupid accident, but his ghost still tends the sheep. Why? There is no reason.

Middleton was capable of straight-out grue. The title object of "The Hand" is found severed on a tabletop by a character groping around in the dark. "Wet Eyes and Sad Mouth" is a chilling study of the mind of a murderer as he contemplates the woman he has just strangled. In "The Luck of Keith-Martin," a traveller comes to the darkened residence of an old friend. A woman's voice bids him leave. He persists and turns on the lights, only to discover that the woman has murdered his friend and is drenched in his blood. Even more bizarre is "The Making of a Man," in which an immature wimp of a clerk comes upon a woman in need of help—she has just murdered a man and needs help chopping up the body. So the clerk pitches in and finally "caught her in his arms and kissed his boyhood away on her hot face." More pathetic is "Who Shall Say—?," about two small children who must decide what to do, now that their father has announced that he has murdered their mother. Grue and helplessness come together to an absurd degree in "The Murderer," in which the suicidal protagonist casts himself before an oncoming train. But inexplicably, after he feels himself run over, he finds himself alive and under arrest for murder, having pushed a duplicate of himself in front of the train. His last recorded words are, "Can a man die twice?"

The boy on the Brighton road knew the answer.

iv.

All this comes into focus when we remember that the author was a suicide, as if Middleton's death formed an artistically correct conclusion to his career. But his work can be appreciated without any knowledge of who the author was or how he died. At his best, Middleton was a master of form. He wrote beautiful prose, and, as in "Shepherd's Boy," he could create a vivid, dark miniature in only a few hundred words. He had an exquisite aesthetic sense, a little commoner in his generation, perhaps, but rare in any. Oscar Wilde, Lord Dunsany, Walter de la Mare, and a few others shared it. More than that, Middleton wrote with passionate conviction. The unrealty shimmering at the edge of the ostensibly realistic stories is genuine, not an affectation. Middleton saw life as an uncertain thing. Like the boy on the Brighton road, we go on and on, past all miseries, but, like the child in "The Bird in the Garden," our circumstances might become much worse if we suddenly "awaken."

Arthur Machen considered Middleton to be a great artist because he understood that the universe is a "mystery." But Middleton, unlike Machen, never learned to live with the mystery.

XVI.

HOW MUCH OF DUNSANY IS WORTH READING?

I don't make a practice of responding to reviews—as de Camp has always pointed out, there is little to be gained that way—but let me make a case for an exception:

The critical response to my *Pathways to Elfland: The Writings of Lord Dunsany* has been gratifying for the most part. The book was even nominated for an award. But there have been a few reviewers who have completely missed the point, notably a dimwitted academic who seemed utterly befuddled by the absence of effusive praise on every single page. Schweitzer, he concluded, must not like Dunsany at all, and have scribbled this treatise grudgingly, and in a hurry to get it over with. (Actually it took fifteen years. But never mind.)

More worthy of respect, but just as misleading, is a recent comment by Richard E. Geis, "...apparently most of his fiction and plays were flawed in one way or another...Lord Dunsany was a kind of 'Johnny one note' writer, a man with one thin vein of excellence which quickly played out."

Wrong on all counts. What people think of *Pathways to Elfland* hardly matters, but this sort of misconception about Lord Dunsany, who in his way was one of the very greatest fantasy writers, needs to be cleared up. Readers expecting a panegyric in place of criticism will have to continue to be disappointed, though. I recall how the late Lin Carter once commented that he could never write a book about Dunsany, "because it would be nothing but a long love letter."

A serious examination of *any* writer's work and career has to be more than that. No writer is uniformly great. Even Shakespeare wrote *Titus Andronicus*. Even God...if the Bible is the inspired Word, merely taken down by human hands but the product of the divine Will and more correctly entitled *The Collected Works of God*, then we must conclude that not all The Almighty's chapters are up to snuff.

How much of Dunsany is worth reading? The answer is, most of it, but at varying degrees of interest. Geis is completely wrong that Dunsany was a "one-note" writer who exhausted himself early. The whole source of Dunsany's strength, and the reason why he was able to publish in each of the first six decades of the twentieth century—and do meritorious work in every one—was that every time he exhausted one "note," he swiftly found another. It is true that he tended to do his best work in any given vein early, but the pattern of his career is one of successive exhaustions and renewals. As late as 1955 he was doing superb work. The still uncollected Jorkens story, "Near the Back of Beyond" (*Ellery Queen's Mystery Magazine*, November, 1955) is a masterpiece of grue, about a wrongfully condemned man who escapes Death Row by killing two guards, switching clothes with one of them, and mutilating the faces of all three, *including himself*. The idea is that a recovering prison guard with his face in bandages will be much less hotly pursued if he vanishes from a hospital than an escaped murderer. This is clearly the Dunsany of "Two Bottles of Relish" with undiminished powers.

He is best known, of course, for what are usefully called the "wonder books," beginning with *The Gods of Pegana* in 1905. This particular vein can be described as pure gold, almost perfect tales of wonders and terrors in imaginary-world settings, told in language of extreme and exquisite beauty. The "wonder" stories are the ones we evoke when we call something "Dunsanian"—for all Joshi, in *The Weird Tale* points out this is a misnomer, and a late Jorkens story is just as Dunsanian as *The Gods of Pegana*—and they are the ones which have had the widest influence, on Lovecraft and subsequent writers down to the present day.

In among the stories of gods, heroes, and ironic cosmic dooms are other gems: "The Highwayman," a beautiful and charming story of superstition, about criminals who bury a hanged comrade in the tomb of a bishop so the dead rogue can make it to Heaven; "Where the Tides Ebb and Flow," a remarkable nightmare of a man who cannot be buried, and several tall tales which prefigure the later Dunsany, such as "The Three Sailors' Gambit" (the Devil and chess), "The Exiles' Club" (the waiters are deposed kings; the members, upstairs and never seen, are former gods), and "A Story of Land and Sea" (how Shard the Pirate put his ship on wheels and sailed across Africa).

Suffice it to say that *The Gods of Pegana*, *Time and the Gods* (1906), *The Sword of Welleran* (1908), *A Dreamer's Tales* (1910), *The Book of Wonder* (1912), *Tales of Wonder* (1916; American title, *The Last Book of Wonder*), and *Tales of Three Hemispheres* (1919) are all musts for any *aficionado* of fantastic literature. They contain much of the very finest short fantasy fiction ever written. It is hard to say which is best. All have their partisans. Lovecraft preferred *A Dreamer's Tales* because it was more unadulterated in its sense of cosmic awe, as opposed to *The Book of Wonder*, which is more sophisticated and ironic, often veering close to self-parody. *Tales of Three Hemispheres* is definitely the weakest of the lot, but it too contains worthwhile material, especially the two novelette-length sequels to "Idle Days on the Yann" (from *A Dreamer's Tales*).

This early vein of Dunsany's did not so much run out as become a casualty of World War I. After years of horror and the loss of many friends, Dunsany was a changed man, and could not quite write from the same point of view. He only returned to it fitfully thereafter. "The Opal Arrow-Head" (1920, collected in *The Man Who Ate the Phoenix*) is definitely in the old manner, but inferior.

Had Dunsany been unable to write any other sort of story, his career would have stopped there. His achievement would have been great, but he would have been Geis's "one-note" writer who burned out after no more than fourteen years at most.

But Dunsany was more versatile. At the same time as he wrote the "wonder" material, he experimented with short fables, prose poems, and ironic allegories, such as those collected in *Fifty-One Tales* (1915). These are best read a few at a time, because they tend to blend together, but many are very fine. "The True History of the Hare and the Tortoise" is something of a classic and often reprinted.

His first, and best, plays belong to this period. The essential collections are *Five Plays* (1914) and *Plays of Gods and Men* (1917). Most are in the manner of the short stories, filled with exotic situations, poetic language, and irony. *The Gods of the Mountain* contains notable strains of horror, but has a weak ending. *A Night at the Inn* is also a horror play with a touch of parody, about a Hindu idol which comes crawling vengefully after its stolen eye, and was for decades Dunsany's best-known and most often performed theatrical piece. But perhaps the most satisfactory is *The Laughter of the Gods*, about a prophet who foretells doom frivolously, only to have his prophecy fulfilled.

Two books from the early period you can skip are *Tales of War* (1918) and *Unhappy Far-Off Things* (1919). Both contain good writing, but they are World War I propaganda, and of associational interest only.

The First World War marks a major watershed in Dunsany's life, much more so than the Second, because he was too old to see active service by 1939. In the changed world of the '20s, he was not quite the same writer.

He turned to novels, a major departure for a writer who had never previously written anything as long as 10,000 words. *The Chronicles of Rodriguez* (1922; American title, *Don Rodriguez: The Chronicles of Shadow Valley*) is a rambling, romantic adventure set in an idealized Renaissance Spain, rather like *Don Quixote* with the satire removed. It is not a wholly satisfactory performance, beautifully written, of course, with several impressively imaginative sequences and some grue. (Who can forget the sinister inn where the "doorbell" consists of a rope attached to a hook lodged in the guts of some unfortunate, whose shrieks summon Mine Host?) But ultimately the story fails to come together, and concludes with an absurd intrusion of Robin Hood and his Merry Men, who have somehow wandered into the wrong book. This is one for the Dunsany "B-list."

The King of Elfland's Daughter (1924), on the other hand, is a masterpiece, one of the great fantastic romances, on a par with E. R. Eddison's *The Worm Ouroboros* or even Tolkien's *The Lord of the Rings*. It is flawed only by excessive unicorn-hunting scenes, though this seemed natural enough to Dunsany's generation, which thought there to be no finer activity for a gentleman than ranging across a beautiful countryside, admiring the wonders of nature, and blowing the heads off God's creatures. But, hunting scenes or not, *The King of Elfland's Daughter* is strikingly original in its conception of Elfland as a mystical realm which can "flow, as the tide over flat sand," overwhelming the world of men or else withdrawing to such distances "as would weary the comet." It is Dunsany's one completely successful revival of his pre-war "wonder," and an evolution of that mode into something else.

The next novel, *The Charwoman's Shadow* (1926) returns to Spain and is an ostensible sequel to *Don Rodriguez*, but superior to that work in every way. The story is coherent—about a young man who sells his shadow to a magician—and contains many excellent touches. It shows some advance over *The King of Elfland's Daughter* in its tighter structure, without unicorn-hunting or any other sort of padding.

The Blessing of Pan (1928) is more sharply realistic, with better characterization and more elaborate dialogue. It is the first Dunsany novel to be set in the "real" world (Kent), and deals with a clergyman who first resists, then surrenders to the lure of pagan music from the hills. By the end, he's sacrificing to the old gods. Some people like this one more than I do, but I find it too long and too simple, and regard it as being of secondary importance, though definitely worth reading.

The Curse of the Wise Woman (1933) is another masterpiece, Dunsany's first (and finest) Irish novel, about witchcraft, political terrorism, and commercial exploitation. The characterizations are the best Dunsany ever did, the writing itself is spare and far removed from the Biblicism of *The Gods of Pegana*, but still impressively beautiful, particularly when dealing with nature, and the climax builds up considerable suspense. There is, incidentally, no explicit fantasy element in the story, though the characters clearly *believe* that supernatural things are happening. *The Curse of the Wise Woman* is pivotal in a development which I discuss in *Pathways* and Joshi explores in *The Weird Tale*: the rejection of Elfland, that is, a growing tendency to dismiss the fantastic as the quaint delusions of simple-minded people. In the first three novels, the supernatural element is unquestioned, though at the end of *The Charwoman's Shadow* the assorted wizards and magicians withdraw from the world forever. In *The Blessing of Pan* the fantastic is present, but never seen, and by *The Curse of the Wise Woman* it is clear that witchcraft and the Celtic paradise of Tir-nan-Og exist only in the minds of the believers.

Later Irish novels continue this progression, through *Up in the Hills* (1936), and *Rory and Bran* (1936), down to *The Story of Mona Sheehy* (1939), in which a child is suspected of being a changeling, but this is explicitly denied on the first page. These later novels all have their moments—the opening chapter of *Up in the Hills* is very good satire—but are of secondary interest.

One other novel of the '30s is *My Talks with Dean Spanley*, a well-imagined and well-written joke about a clergyman who, when drunk on a rare brandy, can remember his previous incarnation as a dog. Dunsany wrote superbly about nature and about animals, and there are many fine passages, but the whole is perhaps not as great as the sum of the parts. Another one for the B-list, worth reading, but not of primary importance.

As detailed in my book, Dunsany's career as a playwright simply ran down during the 1920s and '30s. Fashions changed. Literary politics (and real-life politics) went against him, and he was soon alienated from the Irish Renaissance. Perhaps he was merely losing interest. *If* (1921) was a great success in its time and still would probably perform well today; it's a comedy about magically-induced time-travel and what might happen if we could go back and change our own past. All the later play collections, *Plays of Near and Far* (1922), *Alexander and Three Small Plays* (1925), *Seven Modern Comedies* (1928), and *Plays for Earth and Air* (1937), and the three-act children's play *The Old Folk of the Centuries* (written 1918, published 1930), are of varying degrees of interest, though it must be admitted that if Dunsany had written only these plays, he would not be remembered.

Two full-length plays published in the 1930s but written in the early '20s are a bit stronger: *Mr Faithful* (1935) is about a young man who cannot marry his true love unless he can prove to the girl's father he can hold a job. So he finds an ad in the *Times* offering fifty pounds for a watchdog and *applies for the job*, sleeping in a barrel, barking at the mailman, and so on. The results are quite amusing.

Lord Adrian (1933) begins very well as an elderly nobleman rejuvenates himself with ape glands, then sires an unnatural son (the title character) who has more affinity for animals than for humans. The dialogue is witty and things move briskly—think of it as *Man and Superman* meets Tarzan—but the ending is weak, leaving *Lord Adrian* an interesting but seriously flawed work.

But while Dunsany's theatrical career was winding down, he was mastering a new type of short story which was to serve him for the rest of his life. In *The Gods of Pegana* and the other early collections, the viewpoint is remote and cosmic, the language poetic and Biblical; but as early as "Poor Old Bill" (a curse, pirates, and cannibalism) in *A Dreamer's Tales*, Dunsany was experimenting with something much more intimate: the story told in dialogue, usually in a bar as the narrator gets more and more tipsy.

The adventures of Mr. Joseph Jorkens, the world's greatest liar, began in 1925 and fill five volumes, all of which contain many fine stories of fantasy, humor, and credulity-stretching. The joke is that Jorkens, who seems an endless source of amazing reminiscences about his widely-travelled youth, can never be proven wrong, as in "The Black Mamba," which involves seemingly impossible survival after a snakebite. The members of the Billiards Club (the setting for the entire series) demand to see the scar. Jorkens removes his shoe and sock. There is no scar. "You're looking at the wrong foot!" he exclaims, and everyone is too embarrassed to demand to see the other.

Some Jorkens stories are slight, but there is very little decline in quality from the first to the last. The later ones tend to be more concise, the earlier occasionally a bit long-winded.

So, on the A-list: *The Travel Tales of Mr. Joseph Jorkens* (1931), *Jorkens Remembers Africa* (1934), *Jorkens Has a Large Whiskey* (1940), *The Fourth Book of Jorkens* (1948), and *Jorkens Borrows Another Whiskey* (1954).

The 1940s saw no more plays at all, but a lot of Jorkens and more novels. *Guerrilla* (1944) marks the end of the rejection of the fantastic that had begun in the earlier novels. Alas, Dunsany had little talent for plain realism. This superficial, implausible World War II melodrama, written in a month for a contest, is one of the least rewarding of all his books.

Jorkens aside, the best book of the decade was *The Man Who Ate the Phoenix*, a collection of stories dating (as far as bibliographers Joshi and Schweitzer are able to tell) as far back as 1920, but with most of the material from the mid-'30s. The title novella is in the manner of the middle novels, a gentle rejection of the fantastic, concerning a rustic who ate a common pheasant but is convinced he has devoured the very Phoenix itself, and has numerous (rationally explained) encounters with ghosts, banshees, and so on. "The Widow Flynn's Apple Tree," about a boy transformed into a goose, contains some of Dunsany's best nature descriptions. "The Return" is a classic ghost story in which the narrator discovers that *he* is the ghost.

Actually one of the best shorts of this decade was only recently discovered and remains uncollected: "The Story of Tse Gah" (*Tomorrow*, December 1947, and since reprinted in *Worlds of Fantasy & Horror* #2), in which a small boy in an obviously Himalayan country is carried off by priests who designate him a god incarnate. He lives a wretched life, cut off from all normal human activity. Then there is a revolution; the priests are killed, and the boy-god pathetically attempts to call down lightning on the revolutionaries. Nothing happens.

The 1950s brought three more novels: *The Strange Journeys of Colonel Polders* (1950) mixes Jorkens with Dean Spanley. The snobbish colonel opposes the entry of an Indian magician into his club, so the Indian transforms him into various animals to prove the point. The bulk of the book consists of the animal episodes. While many of the episodes are quite good, the book goes on long enough to become repetitious and a little dull. Another one of secondary interest.

The Last Revolution (1951) is an inept science-fiction novel, of interest in the context of Dunsany's other work and for what it shows of his thought, but very weak on plausibility and internal logic.

His Fellow Men (1952) is no more plausible, but very interesting for its thematic content. It is a true oddity in the Dunsany canon, the story of a "modern saint" who tries to be tolerant to every political, religious, and ethnic faction, and ends up offending everybody, because, of course, no one can stand to be that tolerant. In the end he adopts the Ba'hai faith because of its universal tolerance.

But Dunsany's best work in the 1950s was in the short story, in the later Jorkens stories, and in some of the miscellany I collected in *The Ghosts of the Heaviside Layer and Other Fantasms* (1980). The title story is about an ill-advised attempt to clean out a haunted house with a psychic vacuum-cleaner. "Autumn Cricket" is a fine sentimental ghost story with a sporting motif. "Told Under Oath" rivals the best of the Jorkens stories for its exploration of the "liar paradox." "The Ghost of the Valley" presents the novel concept of a ghost destroyed by air pollution.

The other great curiosity of the decade was *Little Tales of Smethers* (1952), which collects Dunsany's mystery fiction, some of it written much earlier, some of it virtually new, and including the most widely-reprinted of all his tales, "Two Bottles of Relish" (1934). The other stories are clever parodies of conventional crime fiction, and are highly regarded by mystery critics. Ellery Queen listed *Little Tales of Smethers* among the top hundred mystery books of all time, and "Two Bottles of Relish" among the top twenty crime stories.

A variety of miscellaneous items deserve mention. Dunsany wrote three autobiographical reminiscences, of which *Patches of Sunlight* (1938) is the best, filled with charming anecdotes and observations. As autobiography, it is evasive, since Dunsany never gets very personal or introspective, but this volume in particular yields a vast amount of information about his work and career. Later autobiographical volumes, *While the Sirens Slept* (1944) and *The Sirens Wake* (1945), are more of the same, though somewhat padded with accounts of how many small birds Dunsany shot each day as he wrote. *The Sirens Wake* does contain an account of an epic journey out of Greece, across Africa, and back to England, this roundabout route being necessary to escape invading Germans during World War II. (A typical detail: Dunsany fled Athens wearing two hats because he didn't see any point in leaving one behind for the Nazis.)

My Ireland (1937) reads like a series of stray chapters from the autobiographies, again evasive (particularly about the Irish political situation) and charming without achieving much substance. *If I Were Dictator* (1934) is mildly satirical, and of interest for displaying some of Dunsany's pet hates and crotchets, but, again, hardly a major work; it was written as part of a series of books by different hands, all with the same title. *The Donnellan Lectures* (1945) is an important source for Dunsany's aesthetics. The book contains three lectures, on prose, poetry, and drama.

His *poetry* as a whole is wretched, unfortunately, such book-length effusions as *A Journey* and *The Year* being so intensely and unremittingly bad that they inspire an undeniable, if stupified sense of awe. There are a few good lyrics in *Fifty Poems* (1929) and *Wandering Songs*, (1943), and *To Awaken Pegasus* (1949) is an acceptable offering from a minor poet, but on the whole Dunsany's verse is scarcely better than the bulk of Lovecraft's. It often reads like the sort of filler magazine and newspaper publishers used to use before advances in printing made the reproduction of cartoons easier—and that's exactly what it is.

To sum up, in the 1900s and 'teens, Dunsany wrote brilliant fantasy, from *The Gods of Pegana* on through *Tales of Three Hemispheres*. He also wrote his best plays then.

In the 1920s, he began the Jorkens series, and wrote two superb novels, *The King of Elfland's Daughter* and *The Charwoman's Shadow*.

In the 1930s, more Jorkens, other very fine short fiction ("The Return," etc.) and several good-to-fine novels, highlighted by the superb *The Curse of the Wise Woman*, which is arguably his best.

In the 1940s, even more Jorkens. Other worthy short fiction. "The Story of Tse Gah." *The Man Who Ate the Phoenix*. In *To Awaken Pegasus* (1949), incredibly, some quite presentable verse, notably the title poem.

The 1950's: *Little Tales of Smethers*, *His Fellow Men* (a startling departure for a writer then seventy-four years old); yet more Jorkens; "Told Under Oath," "The Ghosts of the Heaviside Layer," and other excellent short fiction.

This is only a brief survey. It does not show a "one-note" writer, or someone whose "one vein of excellence was quickly played out." No, not at all.

XVII.

COUNT DRACULA AND HIS ADAPTERS

Would Bram Stoker recognize his most famous creation these days?

I reread the original novel *Dracula* recently, amid all the discussions of the alleged authenticity of Francis Ford Coppola's curiously mistitled film, *Bram Stoker's Dracula*. That it was found necessary to hire Fred Saberhagen to novelize the script, rather than just reissue the Stoker novel as a tie-in book, is but the first of many danger signs. Needless to say, *Bram Stoker's Dracula* is more the equivalent of the Christopher Isherwood-scripted telemovie, *Frankenstein: The True Story*. While it borrows many *incidents* from the novel, it is the *most variant* adaptation yet to appear. In spirit, and particularly in its presentation of the characters, *Bram Stoker's Dracula* is a wholly original creation.

The 1897 novel is still a grand read after all this time. If perhaps some of the impact of certain key scenes has faded with over-familiarity, the text's continuing power is undeniable. The book is admirably structured: vast and atmospheric, yet unified and fast-paced, like the very best Victorian adventure novels. While no one would claim it is High Literature, it is certainly high pop-literature at its grandest, something of a late nineteenth-century specialty. This is a yarn worthy of sitting on the same shelf with Rider Haggard's *She*, Doyle's Sherlock Holmes stories, and *Treasure Island*. It will still be read with enjoyment for centuries to come.

It's also, from a writer's point of view, a perfect specimen of the horror *novel* as opposed to the book-length, padded short story. The first four chapters introduce Count Dracula, establish his character, and, most importantly, firmly and unambiguously establish that he is, indeed, a vampire, a supernatural creature of evil. Stoker then gets on with business, spinning out his plot without his characters spending half the book trying to discover or deny the reality of vampirism, while the Count remains at the periphery of our vision, glimpsed at a distance or in a seeming dream, the almost invisible driving force against which all the other characters react.

Of course there are other strategies for writing horror novels, but this is the classical one. Were all the secrets revealed in the first ten percent, or even the first half of a shorter work, we'd say that the author had shot his bolt prematurely. Arthur Machen observed that *The Strange Case of Dr. Jekyll and Mr. Hyde* goes flat as soon as we know what is going on. The supernatural short story may indeed dely its revelation to the very end, and resonate on a final, shocking discovery. But the longer horror tale, particularly a *novel*, can only delay so long. Then it must *continue*, well after the spectral cat is out of the bag. What Stoker wisely chose to do was to establish the menace of the Count early, then use it as a foil for the rest of the book, before reader impatience could diminish interest.

There are minor, but definite problems for the late twentieth-century reader: some of the speeches, particularly those of Dr. Van Helsing and the crusty old fisherman at Whitby, are too long and too tortured in their syntax for easy reading. More seriously, the heroes are entirely too one-dimensionally noble. Next to them, the Fellowship of the Ring begins to resemble the Dirty Dozen. *Not one* of the all-purpose good guys, the young men who assist Van Helsing in his quest (Jonathan Harker, Quincey Morris, Arthur Holmwood, and Dr. Seward), has the slightest doubt, or failing, or moment of weakness, save for Jonathan's understandable stress-related problems after his ghastly experience. (By no coincidence, Jonathan is the only one to develop much personality.) That there are four such heroes hardly matters. There could have been two, or ten, and it wouldn't have made much difference, a fact which stage and film adapters used to their advantage.

And one has the sinking feeling that Quincey Morris, the American cowboy, contains more than a trace of one of the more offensive Victorian stereotypes, the lower-class or racially-inferior sidekick (Morris is less educated than the rest, perhaps near-illiterate, the only one of the major characters who does not further the plot with diaries, notes, memoranda, etc.) whose main function is to be stalwart and true until the end, then die a noble and moving death. (Sure enough, Quincey is the only one killed in the fight with the Count's attendants at the end.) A clear example of this is the character of Job in *She*, a comic yeoman (rather like Tolkien's Samwise) whose heart gives out at the climax of the novel, leaving only the stouter, aristocratic Leo Vincey and his grizzled mentor Holly to see it through to the end. As one critic observed, the sidekick could readily be replaced by a reasonably intelligent dog.

The contemporary reader may also balk at some of the medical impossibilities in *Dracula*, particularly the all-purpose blood transfused into Lucy from anyone who happens to be available, and the way, after the shock of seeing the Count force-feeding Mina his own poisonous blood, Jonathan's hair *turns white overnight*. The former is just unfortunate dating. Blood-typing was not well understood when Stoker wrote. (And transfusions were a lot riskier.) Instantly white hair is a superstition, impossible because, once the hair has grown out of the follicle, it remains inert. Even the hair of a corpse won't change color. White hair must grow out from the root, replacing the older, darker hairs. Even if Jonathan's hair *did* turn white from the shock, it would take several weeks for this to be apparent.

Then there are seeming lapses of internal consistency. Possible explanations for everything are present in Stoker's text, but the reader may still wonder why, if Count Dracula *can* move about in the daytime, albeit without his powers, he must lie helplessly in his box in the last few pages, waiting for the sun to go down, even though the gypsies have delivered him to the courtyard of his own castle and his existence is in gravest peril. The whole climax of the novel turns on this. Stoker's editor needed to say, "Make it clear the Count is *exhausted.* He hasn't had any blood lately. He's lost his power from being carried over running water from the sea and river journeys. Van Helsing likes to lecture. Let him say that." Indeed, Dracula by daylight does seem at a disadvantage. In Chapter XXIV, having been rooted out of his last London refuge, the Count shows up at a shipping office to arrange passage back to Transylvania wearing a *straw hat*. Now, audiences would laugh at the sight of Bela Lugosi or Christopher Lee in a straw hat, but it makes perfect sense. One can well imagine the Count, almost blinded by this forced exposure to the afternoon sun, making do with whatever is at hand, grabbing a straw hat from a street vendor.

Here's another one: the Russian ship comes ashore at Whitby, filled with corpses and Dracula's boxes of earth. Dracula must rest in those boxes by day. But, instead, he leaps on shore in the form of a huge wolf and lurks about the neighborhood for several days before the boxes are secured. Van Helsing does explain the vampire's limitations regarding water. He must attain the land as quickly as possible. Had the ship not run aground, the Count would have been trapped. But where is he hiding before he can get back to his boxes? Look very closely in Stoker's text. Later on, Van Helsing must sanctify Lucy's tomb, lest the Count find refuge there. The vampire can hide in any unhallowed grave. At Whitby, he takes shelter in the grave of a suicide, which, by some coincidence, happened to be Lucy's favorite perch on the cliffs above the harbor.

David Skal's admirable *Hollywood Gothic: The Tangled Web of* Dracula *from Novel to Stage to Screen* explains how most adaptations of *Dracula* derive from the 1924 play by Hamilton Deane. It was a bad play, filled with ludicrous dialogue, sacrificing both the powerful opening and the climax of the novel to both the limitations of the stage and the conventions of the time.

Theater-goers in those days expected elaborate, massive sets, which took a long time to build and couldn't be switched around easily. No one would tolerate abstract or minimalist sets, theater-in-the-round, or other modern methods of rapidly shifting scene and setting. It's no coincidence that one of the standard genres of the time was the "drawing room" play, the entire action of which took place in one room.

Dracula became a drawing-room mystery. It was trashed by the critics but enormously popular nevertheless, enlivened by magic-show effects, even a trick corpse that crumbled into dust at the end. One gimmick provided an essential element of the subsequent Dracula iconography: the Count wore a black cape with a rigid, upturned collar. The collar served to hide the actor's head when, in darkness, he turned his back to the audience and dropped down a trapdoor, seeming to vanish into thin air. Most Draculas have sported that cape and collar ever since.

It is with the Deane play that the most important change begins to occur, in the character of the Count himself. Someone who has only seen the movies and goes to the novel for the first time is in for a shock: Stoker's Dracula is not a doomed, romantic lover. He is *vile*, a creature evoking disgust. He tries to be polite to Jonathan Harker at first, but the patina of his humanity proves very thin indeed. He is first seen as a very old man, dressed all in black, with a shock of white hair and a beard. (Reduced to a drooping moustache when he reaches London.) His lips are unusually red, and his teeth—all of them—are noticeably sharp. (Though he does most of his work with the canines, and leaves the characteristic twin bite of the movie vampire.) Indeed, Felix Hoffman, the illustrator of the Heritage/Limited Editions Club edition (1965) depicts him as buck-toothed.

Dracula's breath is foul. His eyes seem to glow at a distance, as when he is spied at sunset atop the cliffs at Whitby in Chapter VIII. As he drinks blood, he grows younger. Toward the end of the book, much harassed by his pursuers, he begins to age again.

In Chapter II, he actually does speak the line, "Listen to them—the children of the night!" which Bela Lugosi made so famous, then quickly, as Lugosi did not, reassuring the disconcerted Harker by adding, "Ah, sir, you dwellers in the city cannot enter into the feelings of the hunter."

When driving the three vampire women away from Jonathan, he also has this exchange, from which later script-writers have derived possibly too much:

> "You yourself never loved; you never love!" On this the other women joined, and such a mirthless, hard, soulless laughter rang through the room as almost made me faint to hear; it seemed like the pleasure of fiends. Then the Count turned, after looking at my face attentively and said in a soft whisper:—
>
> "Yes, I too can love; you yourselves can tell it from the past. Is it not so? Well, now I promise you

> that when I am done with him you shall kiss him at your will. Now go! go! I must awaken him, for there is work to be done." (Chapter III)

To appease his female vampire slaves, the Count gives them an infant to devour (a detail too shocking to be filmed until the 1977 BBC version). His potential as a lover is never alluded to again. For the women he attacks later on in the book, Lucy and Mina, he is something out of a nightmare worse than anything they have previously been able to imagine. He gets no sympathy from anyone, save when, under his power, Mina suggests that perhaps the Count, hunted by all, is to be pitied. But the other characters are outraged and she rapidly retracts, acknowledging the vampire's totally monstrous nature, which must be expunged. Toward the end, she, like everyone else, seems intent on revenge for the Count's atrocities, not his redemption.

But a wholly diabolic, physically repulsive Dracula would not work on stage, at least not in the imagination of Hamilton Deane, within the conventions of a drawing-room mystery. The Count had to be made presentable, so that the title character could be on stage more of the time. Otherwise the role becomes minor, Dracula almost a prop, for all his unseen presence must dominate the whole story.

So the first step had been taken from Stoker's hideous monstrosity to the matinee-idol characterizations of Frank Langella or Gary Oldman (of *Bram Stoker's Dracula*). Ironically, the unauthorized 1922 German version, Murnau's *Nosferatu: eine Symphonie des Grauens* (which Stoker's widow tried to suppress) features a "Dracula" even *more* ghastly than the original. Max Schreck, as "Count Orlock," resembles nothing so much as an enormous, half-human rat. (Indeed, he is associated with rats, bringing plague wherever he goes.) While Stoker's Dracula gives people the creeps, and is anything but pleasant company, he can at least pass for human long enough to walk into a shipping office and conduct business, something the rat-like "Count Orlock" could not—and probably wouldn't feel inclined to do anyway. The nosferatu Orlock is also totally allergic to sunlight, and is the first of many cinematic vampires to be destroyed by staying up past his bedtime.

Judging the Deane version to be too crude for American audiences, Horace Liveright, who acquired the American stage rights, called in John L. Balderston, the author of the fantasy play *Berkeley Square*, one of the most prominent stage and film writers of the time. (Balderston also scripted or co-scripted many of the Universal horror classics of the '30s, including *Mad Love* and *The Mummy*.) The Balderston/Deane "collaboration" proved the basis for the 1931 film with Bela Lugosi, who had also played the role many times on stage.

While the opening fifteen minutes or so of the film are a very faithful, very capably-mounted adaptation of the Stoker material, the rest of it is very far removed from the original. Again, it is the character of the Count that changes the most. He is suave, sophisticated enough that he can be invited to high society parties, even if he has to hypnotize the occasional flunky to gain admittance. Dr. Van Helsing must solve the "mystery" of who, among the company present, is the vampire preying on Miss Lucy. Only a mirror determines that the charming, exotic Count is the culprit. Otherwise, Lugosi's Dracula seems entirely human, as Stoker's character never did for more than a few minutes.

The logic of the story begins to change. Ask yourself: if Renfield is the deranged, grovelling servant of the vampire, the object of (apparently) a considerable amount of Count Dracula's attention, what actual service does he perform?

The answer is that *Stoker's* Dracula is so hideous that only a lunatic would invite him inside, and, according to the lore, the vampire must be *invited* in before he may enter any inhabited place. So he must use Renfield to gain access to Mina, who is staying in Dr. Seward's rooms at the sanitarium. He is not somebody you rub elbows with at a cocktail party! (And, once Dracula has been invited in through the window of Renfield's cell, the treacherous vampire has no further use for his "servant," and soon kills him.)

In the 1931 film the characters of Jonathan Harker and Renfield have become fused. It is *Renfield* who travels to Transylvania to help the Count with his real-estate dealings. He goes mad as a result of his experiences, and is discovered on the derelict Russian ship at Whitby, hopelessly insane.

That's not Stoker, but it's an understandable change. As we examine all the stage and film adaptations of *Dracula*, we find changes in two areas: the Count's character, as noted, and in the scope and cast of the rest of the book. Certainly *Dracula*, with its four heroic stalwarts, its vast geographic scale and rapid changes of scene, not to mention the train, boat, and horseback chase back to Transylvania, wasn't going to work as a drawing-room mystery, or in an hour and a half running time. There is an inevitable need to condense and contract. Characters become fused or eliminated altogether. As for the setting, the 1931 film follows one strategy: *keep it all in London*. The 1958 Hammer film, *Horror of Dracula* (the first Christopher Lee Dracula) kept it all in eastern Europe, often at the expense of geography and logic.

But there was no actual need to have the whole thing take place in London. The 1931 film was *needlessly* dependent on the stage-play. Then, as now, a trip across Europe might be cheaply depicted with a rapid succession of stock shots of ships and trains, and a line moving across a map. Indeed, the opening *does* take us to Translyvania, to the very elaborate Castle Dracula set, and the Count's journey to England is shown in the expected manner, with a stormy sea and a (not very convincing, admittedly) model ship. The ending could have just as readily taken place in Castle Dracula as in Carfax Abbey.

The 1931 film also had censorship problems. No disintegrating corpses this time. Bela Lugosi is staked entirely off-stage, and all we hear is a grunt. Nothing more than that was allowed. And we never actually see him bite anybody. There is not a drop of blood in the whole film, save when Renfield/Harker cuts himself shaving during his initial visit to the Castle. (A scene out of the novel, reproduced faithfully in virtually all later adaptations, a very good way of showing, *early*, that the Count is not what he seems.)

After the 1931 *Dracula*, the changes came thick and fast. Lugosi, never quite got to play the role again, though he reprised it in all but name in *The Mark of the Vampire* (1935) and once more in *The Return of the Vampire* (1943). *The Mark of the Vampire* was a adaptation of the 1927 silent, *London After Midnight*, the producers of which, afraid of legal trouble with the litigious Mrs. Stoker, changed the ending so that the "vampires" all prove to be impostors involved in a contrived plot. By 1935, no one had bothered to fix the ending, and it's a tremendous come-down. *The Return of the Vampire* made interesting use of the London Blitz as a background, but is otherwise inconsequential and seldom shown today.

Nevertheless, it was Lugosi's Dracula, not Stoker's, which was imprinted on the public consciousness. Dracula in his cape, with his charming manners, had become as instantly recognizable as Tarzan in his loincloth (particularly Johnny Weissmuller's characterization, which is quite different from Edgar Rice Burroughs's) or Robin Hood in his Lincoln green. After that, any film or novel had to react against the public expectation of what Dracula "should" be like.

The adaptations of the 1940s continued negligibly, though it must be admitted that John Carradine at least *looked* the part in two of the later Universal "monster rally" mish-mashes, *House of Frankenstein* (1944) and *House of Dracula* (1945) (both of which strove to feature as many of the stock Universal-trademarked monsters as possible). But these films, along with the 1943 Lon Chaney Jr. opus, *Son of Dracula*, made no attempt to utilize Stoker's material.

We can draw a discreet shroud over Bela Lugosi's humiliation in *Abbott and Costello Meet Frankenstein* (1948) and merely shudder at the thought of *Old Mother Riley Meets the Vampire* (1952), even as the Turkish *Drakula Istanbulda* (1953) remains a mystery. John Carradine played the Count one more time on television in 1956. The renown of this performance has not travelled down the years, nor did Francis Lederer's performance in *The Return of Dracula* (United Artists, 1957) have much impact.

The next meaningful adaptation occurred in the 1958 Hammer film, *Horror of Dracula* (British title, *Dracula*). This is the film that made international stars out of Christopher Lee and Peter Cushing. It is a classic in its own right, and manages, largely, to break free of the encumbrances of the Hamilton Deane play. In many ways, it remains the best Dracula to date.

A close rewatching, now possible in the VCR era, reveals strengths and flaws. The script is often weak. The production values are cheesy. Editing is poor, to the point that the staked corpses sometimes can be seen to breathe. For all the Count doesn't have a staff of servants and even must carry Jonathan Harker's luggage himself, the Castle Dracula, with its curiously Italian architecture, is always spotless and well-lit. (Stoker, more plausibly, describes the castle as a ruin. So it is presented in that superbly atmospheric, cobwebby introductory scene in the Lugosi version.) But Terence Fisher's direction is wonderfully fluid and the performances of Lee as Dracula and Cushing as Van Helsing are superb. They carry all before them. They do Bram Stoker proud.

Once more, the plot, cast, and geographic scale have been condensed. It is indeed Jonathan Harker who first visits the Castle, but this time he is sent *by Van Helsing* (whom he did not originally know in the book; Van Helsing was Dr. Seward's old mentor) as an assassin, to kill Dracula. His "cover" is that he is the new librarian. Why Dracula should suddenly require a librarian or fall for this ruse is never clear. (In the novel, he *does* need a real estate agent, and someone to help him with his English.) The three vampire women have been reduced to one, a lady who runs around in her slip with much cleavage visible. She begs for Jonathan's help, but also tries to bite him.

The Count promptly puts a stop to the lady's attempts, and to the lady. He is seen frothing blood, carrying her off through a secret door in the library. All this within the first ten minutes of running time. This film is, if nothing else, fast-paced. Of course, *audiences*, being familiar with Dracula on the screen for decades, could not possibly be teased with any mystery of the Count's nature. So screenwriter Jimmy Sangster took a nod from Stoker, established the basics fast, and got on with the plot.

That's about the last we see of Jonathan. He proves a most incompetent vampire-hunter in an admittedly chilling scene wherein he descends into the crypt, drives a stake through the vampire-lady (she of the scanty slip and heaving cleavage), then turns to the Count's coffin only to find him gone. It's sundown. Harker, having been bitten by Dracula (or someone) the previous night, slept through the day. He is sure he can't survive another night, and so does what must be done, regardless of the risk. Alas that he, a trained vampire hunter, didn't bring a crucifix or garlic, or anything else along to protect himself.

Later, Van Helsing visits the castle by daylight and is nearly run over by a hearse galloping out the front gate. The hearse carries one coffin, which contains, of course, Dracula. Who is driving, we can only guess. Van Helsing finds Jonathan, now a vampire, in the crypt, and stakes him.

Dracula then attacks Lucy, who dies, rises again, and is destroyed; and then he sets in on Mina. But none of this happens in England. For some reason all these English people are living in eastern Europe. The geography of the film is extremely fuzzy. Much of the action takes place in Klausenberg, which is the German name for the Romanian town of Cluj, which *is* in Translyvania and not completely inappropriate. But all the "natives" seem Bavarian rather than Slavic or Latin. They speak pidgin-German, often with Cockney accents. Dracula's coffin is stored at an undertaking establishment in Friedrichstrasse.

The German elements come from a superficial reading of the novel. Transylvania in the late nineteenth century was part of the Austro-Hungarian Empire, the main language of which was, indeed, German. Jonathan Harker, knowing none of the local languages of Romania, makes do with German as best he can. Innkeepers and the like call him "Herr." But of course they are not speaking their native tongue. Used to dealing with tourists, or at least officials, they speak German as a *second language*. Harker hears peasants muttering about the Count in their own languages. He jots down a few words and looks them up in a dictionary, to disconcerting results. ("Ordog." Satan. "Stregoica." Witch. etc.) Nevertheless, this German element dominates all the later Hammer films, often to ludicrous results. (Then again, this is the English film company, which, in their version of *The Mummy* couldn't even make *England* convincing.)

The thrilling climax of *Horror of Dracula* updates, not Stoker's novel, but *Nosferatu*. After a carriage chase and a wrestling match with Van Helsing, the Count is destroyed by sunlight, crumbling away into dust.

All-in-all, this isn't great art, but it is grand entertainment, even if it doesn't bear close critical examination.

That fuzzy geography again: all these English people (Mina, Arthur Holmwood, Lucy) are living *within a few miles* of Castle Dracula. The Count, interrupted in his attack on Mina in the middle of the night, kidnaps her, steals a coach, and drives back to his refuge *before dawn*. He crashes through a border-post (where?) upsetting the comic porter who seems to have stumbled right out of *Macbeth*.

We cannot help but remark on the curious burial customs in Transylvania, or wherever this is supposed to be. Corpses are laid out in concrete troughs, without coffins, or even lids. And, of course, when the sun comes up and Van Helsing tears away the curtains to destroy the count, it seems remarkably bright, and the angle of the light suggests it must be about 11 AM on a clear day.

What this film does so splendidly is restore the *evil* of Count Dracula and convey his uncanny power, even despite a near-crippling lack of a special effects budget. This Dracula cannot turn into a wolf or a bat or fog—a "common misconception," Van Helsing assures Holmwood. When Dracula goes forth in search of victims, he strides purposefully down the road from the castle. But Lee (who said in an interview that he had never seen the Lugosi film before acting the role) does not play Dracula as a suave party-goer. He is Stoker's monster, clean-shaven admittedly, without any trace of Lugosi's accent (then again, after his first scene, he has no dialogue), yet purely predatory, never treated sympathetically, and often very physically violent, capable an almost animalistic frenzy. He hurls Jonathan Harker across a room. He hauls Mina off as if she were a child. And he has a menacing glare Stoker would have appreciated.

This film also makes use of a handy plot-device Stoker didn't think of, but which tends to show up in later versions, particularly the romantic ones. Dracula, while still playing the polite host, admires a picture of Harker's *fiancée*. (Lucy, this time. Mina is here the wife of Arthur Holmwood and Lucy's sister-in-law.) He becomes fixated and deliberately seeks her out. In Coppola's *Bram Stoker's Dracula* it's Mina's picture (she being, as in Stoker, Harker's intended) and he seeks *her* out. (Lucy is just the pause that refreshes.)

There's no such picture in the novel. Therefore, the plot depends on the rather large coincidence that the Count, out of the hundreds of women available at Whitby or the millions in all of England, *just happens* to attack someone Jonathan Harker knows, Lucy, the best friend of Harker's *fiancée*. She *just happens* to be staying at this seaside resort town, and just happens to sit on the suicide's grave which provides the Count his first refuge in England.

For all the deviations in geography, incident, and the secondary characters (there's also no Renfield, nothing to do with a lunatic asylum), *Horror of Dracula* does follow the outline of the book. Stoker's novel can be broken down into three key sequences: the revelation of Dracula's evil, the vampirization of Lucy and her destruction, and the pursuit and destruction of the Count. All the rest is apparatus and filler.

Sloppy as he was in many respects, scriptwriter Sangster got right to the essentials of the story. *Horror of Dracula* delivers three knockout punches—Dracula's first entrance as a vampire; Lucy as vampire, shrieking as Van Helsing's crucifix burns her forehead; and the Count's amazing dissolution. These scenes work so well that little else matters. Lee is a great Count Dracula.

Cushing is a wonderful Van Helsing. The two of them are perfect adversaries. The script may not make much sense at times, but this *plays*.

Christopher Lee, fearing for his career, refused to don the cape for several years afterward. Ultimately numerous Hammer sequels followed, each one resurrecting and destroying the Count in a more ridiculous manner than the last. But these are not based on Stoker. Toward the end, the vampire is little more than a prop, although whenever he can, Lee does give us something of the Count's character. In the last couple of installments, though, the sympathetic viewer is hard-pressed to find even five minutes' worth of the old magic.

Lee also starred in the multi-national 1970 rendition, *Count Dracula*, directed by Jesus Franco. This film is noteworthy for an attempt to present the Count as close to the Stoker original as possible (bearded, youthening), but as drama, it is a flat failure, often incoherent. Klaus Kinski made a fine Renfield, but had too many scenes to no particular purpose.

The next genuine Dracula was Jack Palance, in the 1973 telemovie called, simply, *Dracula*, scripted by Richard Matheson. Here, for the first time, an attempt is made to link Count Dracula with Vlad Tepes, the Impaler of fifteenth-century Wallachia. Stoker's text supports this, but makes little of it. (Dracula tells Harker vivid stories of battles long ago, allegedly the deeds of his ancestors.) But the characterization is not particularly memorable, and that the Count dies impaled to a table with a spear only hints at the other liberties taken with the material.

In 1977 the BBC did a far better job with a miniseries, *Count Dracula*, which tried very hard to be faithful to the text and went out of its way to film scenes no one ever had before.

For the first time on the screen we see Lucy and Mina vacationing at Whitby, sitting in the graveyard, conversing with the Old Salt who tells them some of the sinister legends of the place (*e.g.*, about the suicide). The chase back to Castle Dracula is faithfully recounted. Van Helsing and Mina ward off the three vampire women in the forest where they've camped, and Van Helsing has created a protective circle of crumbs of the Host. For the first time we see the vampire, as Stoker described him, clambering down the wall of the castle *head downward*. (The effect looks silly on camera. His cloak must have been pinned to his ankles, lest it fall down over his head.)

Yet Louis Jourdan's Count is far from Stoker, effective in its own right, and very popular with female viewers—not a repulsive rapist/monster, but a seducer, a decayed, romantic beauty. As in virtually all previous versions, he has more on-stage time in the film than he does in the novel, which only makes commercial sense. As the Hammer Dracula films proved, people go to Dracula films to *see Dracula*.

The stage was (in more ways than one) then set for the 1979 Frank Langella version, *Dracula*, based on a Broadway revival of the *Script That Wouldn't Die*, the Deane/Balderston play. (The Broadway version was campy, with sets by Edward Gorey.) Here we are almost as far from Stoker's original creation as it is possible to get, as if Rudolph Valentino has somehow usurped Bela Lugosi's role. Langella is *so* romantic that the ladies (on screen, and even some in the audience) virtually swoon when he makes an appearance. He is a tragic figure, or tries to be, but the film slides into soap-operatic absurdity so often that one is almost ready (and cringing) for him to break out into crooning song. (Be thankful for small favors. He doesn't.)

This film even managed to waste an actor as great as Sir Laurence Olivier (as Van Helsing). As *horror*, it must be considered a total failure, since it fails to frighten. But as *romance*, more akin to *Dark Shadows* than anything by Bram Stoker, it had considerable impact. The Langella image and the romantic vampire novels of Anne Rice surely played far more of a role in the genesis of *Bram Stoker's Dracula* than did Bram Stoker.

Despite all the hype, the Coppola film is not Stoker at all and it is barely Dracula. Certainly it intersects Stoker's storyline at many points—the scenes with Renfield, the chase back to Transylvania, etc.—but the whole spirit of the original is gone. Coppola, in tossing out the accumulated baggage of a full *seventy years* of Dracula films (ever since *Nosferatu*, 1922), also threw out Bram Stoker's character.

When Jonathan Harker (Keanu Reeves) first encounters the old Count in Castle Dracula at the beginning, he meets a shrivelled, almost androgynous figure dressed in bright, fantastic clothing, sporting a hairdo of elaborate coiffure and an ankle-length braid. Dracula (Gary Oldman) looks like a demented version of some Renaissance portrait of a Venetian doge. Admittedly, the crawling-down-the-wall scene is done very well, with the Count scrambling like a large, bright red rat.

But once Dracula is in London, he's established as the last word in tragic, romantic vampires, in appearance what we might call a Byronic hippie, twenty-ish, fashionably dressed, with shoulder-length curls and smoked granny-glasses. He weeps for his lost love, killed in fifteenth-century Romania, now reincarnated in Mina. Shades of Rider Haggard. This is Ayesha, She-Who-Must-Be-Obeyed, with a gender-change.

Not knowing the strange Count is a vampire, Mina falls genuinely and passionately in love with him, then nobly breaks off the affair because she has promised to marry Jonathan. After she *does* know he is a vampire, she *still* loves him and *forces herself* upon him in a total perversion of that scene in Stoker's novel which turned Jonathan's hair white in sheer horror.

Mina begs to be made immortal, so she can be with Dracula forever. He tries to avoid her, warning her of the terrible fate of the vampire. She *willingly* drinks his blood, whereas the Dracula of the novel had to hold her, helpless, to the wound on his chest. (Stoker: "The attitude of the two had a terrible resemblance to a child forcing a kitten's nose down into a saucer to compel it to drink.")

Stoker's Mina reacts to this with utter, despairing horror ("...my God, pity me! He placed his reeking lips on my throat!"). Coppola's Mina (played ably enough by Winona Ryder) weeps for

Dracula because of his terrible loneliness. The whole meaning of the scene changes. In Stoker, this is the final abomination which drives the heroes beyond a selfless crusade to rid the world of evil, into a personal quest for revenge. In Coppola, it means that Mina and Dracula's love transcends all else. At the end, not so much under the Count's hypnotic influence but acting of her own accord, Mina holds off the other pursuers at gunpoint and helps the wounded Count back into his castle, where he can expire with dignity in the chapel where he last saw his beloved.

Gary Oldman gives an interesting, eccentric performance as the Count, but this tale of the Great Love That Never Died is not Stoker's *Dracula* at all. Bram Stoker, were he undead, would be spinning in his grave at this point, or, after sundown, rising up to wreak horrific vengeance. The film has its merits, but they are those of an original creation. It should be entitled *Francis Ford Coppola's Dracula.* In imagery, character, and tone it is entirely new.

So, what have Dracula's adapters done to him? What else? The same thing that the adapters of Frankenstein's monster have done. They've changed him beyond all recognition, so that the popular, public image of the character bears virtually no resemblance to the original. Bela Lugosi, in his opening scene only, on the steps in the great hall of the castle (when he walks *through* the cobwebs without disturbing them), and Christopher Lee, in perhaps twenty minutes of on-screen time in *Horror of Dracula*, have captured some of the character's essence. But none of the other impersonators have came remotely close. Nor are any likely to in the future, with the continual burden of the Jourdan, Langella, and now Oldman portrayals to be contended with.

The "real" Dracula, written by Stoker, is one of the most unmitigated fiends in all of literature. He is *not* the romantic figure the films have made him. The whole subtext of the novel is one of disease and contagion. Stoker's vampire evokes, not merely horror, but disgust. Like his charnel breath, he is *unclean*.

As for what that strange statement to the vampire women ("I too can love!") really means, my own guess is that the Count, wholly a monster, intends to show those ladies, and the reader, just what he means by love: the brutal destruction and degradation of the innocent Lucy.

The modern movie-goer would never recognize Bram Stoker's original Dracula. He is *not* someone you'd want invite into your parlor.

Note: The author would like to thank Eva Schegulla for providing data on two relatively recent stage versions of *Dracula* performed in New York. These are:

1. *Count Dracula*, by Ted Tiller. Equity Theater. Lucy is already dead at the beginning of the play. She was a *patient* of Dr. Seward. Dracula lives in a nearby castle (no explanation). Dracula gains entrance to the sanitarium by befriending Seward's sister, Sibyl, who invites him home for dinner, possibly unaware of his specialized dietary requirements. Dracula manipulates Sibyl through hyponosis, kills Renfield, and preys on Mina. The heroes (mostly Seward and Harker; Van Helsing's role is much reduced) chase Dracula back to his castle, then follow Mina's footprints to Dracula's coffin. The vampire is staked. When Mina comes under the Count's influence, she is sexually liberated. When she is "cured" by his death, she is repressed once again. William Shust played Dracula.

2. *The Passion of Dracula*, by Bob Hall and David Richmond. Cherry Lane Theater. Opened September 27, 1977. No synopsis available. The credits note, "A Gothic Entertainment" in three acts. The action takes place in England during the autumn of 1911 in the study of Dr. Seward's home. Dracula played by Christopher Bernau.

Both of these ran opposite the Frank Langella revival of the Balderston-Deane play, and were apparently buried by it.

XVIII.

PHILIP K. DICK

ABSURDIST VISIONARY

In the first months of 1974, Philip K. Dick, already established as one of the leading science fiction writers on the planet, singled out by Ursula K. Le Guin in *New Republic* as "our own homegrown Borges," began to have visions. He had had visions of quite another sort during the Sixties, when he had experimented with psychedelic drugs and consumed an awesome amount of amphetamines, but it would be grossly unfair to this brilliant, imaginative, and intellectually adventurous man to just say, "Fried his brain. Saw God. Big deal."

By 1974, Dick was off drugs. He had already written the first draft of a harrowing anti-drug novel, *A Scanner Darkly* (1977), and his personal life, chaotic from divorces and failed relationships and the deaths of friends, was beginning to come together. Suddenly, he was blinded by a flash of pink light, and he felt his mind invaded by what he later described as *transcendent rationality*. It was the opposite of most mystical experiences: something supremely comprehensible, bursting into a life and a universe which, for Dick, had never previously made sense. All his earlier work, including such now classic novels as *The Man in the High Castle* and *The Three Stigmata of Palmer Eldritch*, grappled with the eternal question of what is real.

(Moviegoers can get a hint of this in *Total Recall*. The first twenty minutes bear slight resemblance to a Dick short story, but a genuinely Dickian moment occurs later, when, after much carnage, Arnold Schwarzenegger's character is approached by the company psychiatrist, who informs him that it's all been a psychotic fantasy, and his only hope of returning to reality is to cooperate and take these two pills. How can Arnie be *sure?*)

Dick spent the remaining eight years of his life trying to correlate the data received in that one flash of light. He wrote an enormous and still largely unpublished *Exegesis*, a kind of diary, notebook, and inchoate theological masterwork in which he explored every conceivable explanation of what had happened to him, except, curiously, the most obvious one that, since he had been hospitalized for high blood-pressure around this time, he had actually experienced a series of small strokes.

Dick's life improved thereafter. He repeatedly claimed he had been healed by conversion, just as St. Paul had been on the road to Damascus. This, as Lawrence Sutin points out in *Divine Invasions: A Life of Philip K. Dick* (Harmony Books, 1989), is virtually unique in the annals of American literature. American writers aren't supposed to have visions from the Beyond. In another age, one might add, Philip K. Dick might have been a saint, or, considering the eclecticism of his theology, which veered from various forms of Christianity to Zoroastrianism and Gnosticism to everything in between—including, but not limited, to three-eyed aliens, an artificial intelligence disguised as a discarded beer, possession by extraterrestrial spores, time-reversals, and a "Fifth Savior" who is already alive in our time, hideously mutilated and scarred by our degradation of the environment—he would have more likely been burned at the stake as a heretic. He was a spiritual disciple and close friend of the maverick Episcopal bishop James Pike, who died in the Judean desert seeking the true nature of Christianity, and had even participated in Pike's séances in which he tried to contact his dead son.

All this was intensely important, intensely serious, but the element of the trickster always remained. Phil Dick could embrace, then discard mutually contradictory theories at an enormous pace. He delighted in rendering people unsure whether he was revealing vast truths or having them on. So we shall never know, shall we?

What is now loosely known as "the *VALIS* trilogy," has been reissued by Vintage Books as a matching set of trade paperbacks. These three novels are the product of the last period of Dick's life, in which he began to shape what he called his "2-3-74" (February-March 1974) experience into literary art. They are best read in conjunction with the Lawrence Sutin biography, because by this point Dick was living a P. K. Dick novel, and his novels were woven out of the raw stuff of his own experience.

What really happened? In *VALIS* (the title means Vast Active Living Intelligence System) there is a writer character "Philip K. Dick," and another, "Horselover Fat." (Philip is Greek for "Horselover"; Dick is German for "Fat".) "Philip Dick" tells us unequivocally, "I am Horselover Fat, and am writing this in the third person to gain much-needed objectivity" (p. 11). But Fat co-exists with Dick. They talk, go driving together, meet with their friends Kevin and David (based on writers K. W. Jeter and Timothy Powers). The four of them debate why God allowed Kevin's cat to be run over by a truck. It is Fat who has the "pink light" experience. Arcane theological speculations right out of (real life) Philip K. Dick's *Exegesis* fill page after page as Fat tries to figure out what is going on. As a result of these revelations, Fat's son Christopher is saved from a hitherto unsuspected brain tumor, even as (in real life) Philip K. Dick's son Christopher was saved from a previously undiagnosed and potentially fatal inguinal hernia. But later, the characters see a movie (condensing into a few pages the first draft of *VALIS*, later published as an entirely different novel, *Radio Free Albemuth*) which seems to confirm their experiences. In the presence, of a girl who seems to be the Messiah, "Philip K. Dick" is cured of incipient madness and "Horselover Fat" ceases to exist. But when the child is killed in an experiment with a laser beam, Fat comes back to life and is last heard from travelling in remote lands, seeking the Savior's return.

Dick's editors and readers were nearly as amazed by this as his characters, and may have found at least the first few chapters of the sequel, *The Divine Invasion*, a reassuring return to form. It begins in a typical Dickian cartoon future, in which insignificant people struggle to survive in a world both like and unlike our own—1960s America, but with flying cars, robot cabbies, interplanetary travel, and the world ruled jointly by the Christian-Islamic Church and the Communist Party. As strict, scientific speculation in the Arthur C. Clarke manner, none of this is even slightly convincing. But Dick's agenda is elsewhere. Our hero finds Yahweh alive and well on a desolate planet (God having been driven from our world after the fall of Masada in AD 72), and plots to smuggle the Messiah back to Earth. The forces of Belial plot back. Is our hero dreaming all this while in cryogenic sleep and being bombarded with endless replays of *Fiddler on the Roof*? We are never certain. Possibly Emmanuel is born on Earth, amnesiac, and recovers his memory with the aid of a miraculous girl who may embody the female half of the Godhead and (in a Kabbalistic sense) personify the Torah. Mankind is redeemed in the end. The dual Godhead is reunited. Our hero's dreams of becoming the lover of his favorite female pop singer (based on Linda Ronstadt) are fulfilled. Maybe. It might all be a dream of Belial.

The Transmigration of Timothy Archer was Dick's last novel, written with "a powerful sense of having endured temptation" after he had turned down a huge amount of money for the degrading job of novelizing the film *Blade Runner*, which was already based (loosely) on his novel, *Do Androids Dream of Electric Sheep?* Sutin suggests that Dick suspected he didn't have much time left. It was more important to set into artistic form his relationship with Bishop Pike and his final theological speculations. Again, the results were surprising. *Timothy Archer* was Dick's only realistic novel to find a major publisher in his lifetime. (Several others, too unconventional for mainstream publishing in the '50s and '60s, were issued posthumously.) It is Dick's version of Pike, his failed life and searches for the ultimate truth, told from the somewhat caustic point of view of the widow of "Bishop Archer's" son. Dick writes himself into the novel (sort of) as the schizophrenic son of Archer's mistress, who believes himself possessed by the spirit of the dead bishop. The narrator finds this foolish. For all his bravery in "trying out every possible idea to see if it would finally fit," Bishop Archer misses out on the basics of happiness—tenderness and caring for others—and is destroyed. The novel is about the human cost of religious obsession. Once more Dick has stepped outside himself and is looking in.

This wasn't supposed to be the end. Dick was planning *The Owl by Daylight*, another novel based on "2-3-74," when he died of a stroke in 1982.

Inadvertently, the *VALIS* trilogy, along with the *Exegesis*, became his last testament.

These books are not, despite Dick's startling black humor and breezy California-speak style, for the uninitiated. They grapple intricately with themes which obsessed the author throughout his entire career and represent the climax of a long progression. Think of them as the graduate course in Dick Studies, to be approached chronologically through his earlier works, the way you start with *Dubliners* to work up to *Finnegans Wake*. The effort will be rewarded. You will have spent quite a while in the presence of one of the most original literary minds of our time.

XIX.

KIPLING'S SCIENCE FICTION[19]

There can be little doubt that the work of Rudyard Kipling, as much as that of H. G. Wells, and probably more so than Jules Verne's, is one of cornerstones of science fiction. The number of writers influenced by him over the course of several generations, openly proclaiming him to be a formative influence on their own careers, is impressive, even though Kipling did not actually write a great deal of SF. Here John Brunner has assembled what may well be the entire Kipling SF canon, and it barely fills a thin book.

It's also clear that he was a genuine world-class writer, a master, with an artist's eye and a linguist's ear. His work is richly textured, with great depth of authentic detail.

Quite possibly, too much so. Time has not been kind to Rudyard Kipling, and he is now the most difficult of all nineteenth- or early twentieth-century British authors. Most of his contemporaries, Wells, Bernard Shaw, Arthur Machen, Conan Doyle, or whoever, can still be read easily. Maybe every few thousand words the modern American reader may encounter a phrase or an allusion that could use a footnote, but in Kipling's case such discontinuities occur on virtually every page. Whole paragraphs go opaque. He needs to be almost as heavily annotated as a translation of Dante, in which you read the introduction to each canto, puzzle out a the text with one finger in the footnotes, and only gradually does the undiminished excellence emerge from obscurity.

Kipling's narrative techniques are archaic, not just the rambling openings characteristic of Victorian fiction, but showing a complete disinterest in staying in viewpoint. Here's something that today would be a textbook example of what *not* to do:

> "And be sure I shall treasure this"—she touched the beads—"as long as I shall live."
>
> "I brought—trusted—it to you for that," he replied and took his leave. When she told the Abbot how she had come by it, he said nothing, but as he and Thomas were storing drugs that John handed over in the cell which backs on to the hospital kitchen-

chimney, he observed, of a cake of dried poppy-juice: "This has the power to cut off all pain from a man's body."

"I have seen it," said John. (p. 145)

At which point the reader does a double-take. It would practically require a Deconstructionist to make sense out of that passage. The lady receives the beads from the aforementioned John (the protagonist), who makes the reply in the third line. John leaves. The viewpoint shifts to the lady, then to the abbot, so that the "he" making the observation about the poppy-juice is not the speaker of the beginning of the paragraph at all, but the abbot. John is then written back into the scene. We've had three point-of-view shifts, two scene shifts, an exit, and an entrance, none of them properly delineated, in three sentences.

But consistent point-of-view was not required in Kipling's day, any more than it was against the rules to break viewpoint altogether and address the reader directly. The above excerpt is from a gem of a story called "The Eye of Allah," about medieval monks who discover, and suppress, the microscope.

Possibly because Kipling was writing about the historical past, an act of deliberate imagination which required planting informational cues for the reader's benefit, this story is more lucid than most, and for once we can see why the author's influence on science fiction has been so strong. "The Eye of Allah" (the title refers to a magnifying lens, gotten from the Arabs) is *knowledge fiction* of a high order, about scientists and artists both chafing against the restrictions of orthodoxy and superstition, and about the excitement of discovery. More surprisingly, it contains an extremely sensitive study of an artist—novel-quality characterization in a short story—and then applies genuinely science-fictional genius as the artist applies knowledge of micro-organisms and a greater understanding of disease to medieval manuscript illustration. Kipling has managed to show how this "anachronistic" discovery would have excited the imagination of a creative mind of the thirteenth century. Here we can see all sorts of beginnings, themes recurring in *Pavane*, *A Canticle for Leibowitz*, and arguably, *The Foundation Trilogy*. There's even a very good description of what a medieval microscope would have been like.

Another highlight of this collection is "A Matter of Fact," with its echoes of William Hope Hodgson and Ray Bradbury, about a sea monster roused from the deep by an undersea earthquake and attracted to a ship's foghorn. Then, deftly, Kipling turns the whole situation on its head as the journalist characters agree that this report can't be printed in England, because the English are too conservative, or in America, because the Americans are so credulous that one more monster story wouldn't matter. So the third man proposes to write it as fiction, which is presumably what we've just read.

John Brunner has done an admirable job as editor. His prefaces to the stories sometimes go on for several pages, attempting to explain all that has become difficult for a modern reader to understand (as, again, it is not necessary to do for *any other* British writer of the same period), but sometimes this just isn't enough. Kipling's two most famous SF stories, "With the Night Mail" and "As Easy as A.B.C.," will probably defeat most readers today. Both of these stories are set in an elaborately-realized future. In any such story, the author works from a set of contemporary perceptions—we all agree what "reality" is—and then distorts those perceptions, inventing slang, allusions to future events and culture, and so forth, giving the illusion of an era other than our own. Kipling probably did this better than anyone prior to the early Heinlein, but the effect is as if Geoffrey Chaucer had written *Beyond This Horizon*. The whole narrative vanishes into alternate-universe technobabble. Even a careful reading has no more than the effect of skimming. We can make out only a broad outline, thirty or forty percent at best. The lack of controlled viewpoint prevents us from getting into any character's head long enough to straighten things out.

Viewpoint shifts prove the undoing of a speculative medical story ("Unprofessional," from a book published as recently as *1932*). We never share anyone's thoughts, and it becomes virtually impossible, for pages at a time, to understand *why* the characters say and do *what* they say and do. A good deal of the conversation seems to consist of non-sequiturs, as it almost certainly did not to Kipling's original readership.

Admittedly, some of the others, notably the famous "Wireless," manage to stay in focus better, almost by accidents of stagecraft. In "Wireless" the entire action consists of a small cast of characters sitting around a chemist's shop listening to someone fiddle with a radio—which picks up voices from the past. So there is little opportunity for meandering viewpoints or murky transitions, the only narrative static being occasional strange referents.

There seems to be something of a Kipling revival going on in science fiction of late. First, Baen Books publishes two volumes of science-fiction writers' tributes to Kipling, now this, not to mention a companion, *Kipling's Fantasy*. But I don't think it can be a truly popular revival. The texts, as an Elizabethan once complained about Chaucer, are just too "dark."

There may be a lesson here for writers overly determined to make their work absolutely up-to-the-minute, dropping brand-names, cultural referents, quoting rock & roll songs—is this what Stephen King is going to read like in seventy-five years?

Kipling's Science Fiction is still an undeniably important piece of literary archaeology, but only about half its contents can actually be read for enjoyment.

XX.

THE BLACK FLAME

Here's a historically significant volume which takes us, in more ways than one, all the way to the beginnings of the genre SF in America. The Tachyon Publications edition of Stanley G. Weinbaum's *The Black Flame* is a crude piece of book-making, a good ten years behind the state of the art in desktop publishing (unjustified right margins, copyright page in the wrong place, and pages sewn from the side rather than in signatures so the book cannot be laid flat) with an amateurishly retro dustjacket which would not have been out of place among the small-press SF of the late '40s. Artist Michael Dashow's clumsy efforts to depict the seductive stance and expression of the title character would never have made *Thrilling Wonder Stories* or *Fantastic Adventures*, but he would have been right at home at the early Fantasy Press or F.P.C.I. In a way, such an inept drawing is absolutely perfect for this volume, the first complete publication of a novel written in 1934, by a writer whose tragically short career (eighteen months) revolutionized the field, but to whom the passage of time has not been entirely kind.

Metaphor time: sure, this is a milestone, but it is a milestone long passed. It is important to remember that early American pulp SF was the creation of Hugo Gernsback, a science-hobbyist of no literary understanding whatsoever. In his day, the walls of the SF ghetto were hermetically sealed against even the influence from other pulps, much less literature and culture at large.

Therefore, it was not particularly hard to revolutionize science fiction in 1934. Imagine the inhabitants of the SF ghetto as crippled dwarves. Weinbaum was a dwarf who could stand on his own two feet and even hobble a bit. But he could not dance, and outside the ghetto walls they were dancing.

Sam Moskowitz's introduction ably captures the perspective of the early genre when he bemoans an early editor sacrilegiously altering the prose of "one of the finest science fiction stylists the field ever produced." Yet this fine stylist is capable of writing: "He rose and followed his escort down the dim corridor, into a dusky chamber at whose far end stood the grim and shadowy throne of death," when he actually means that his hero followed the guard down the hall to the electric chair.

No, Weinbaum was arguably the finest stylist produced in the American SF pulps up till 1934. But he was nowhere near as good as such contemporaries or near-contemporaries as Raymond Chandler, Talbot Mundy, or even Robert E. Howard, not to mention such non-pulp folks as F. Scott Fitzgerald, Ernest Hemingway, or Lord Dunsany. In the SF field, the early work of Sturgeon, Leiber, and Heinlein was only five years away. So, while Weinbaum caused a significant revolution within the field, it was still a teapot tempest.

To be fair, here we have a self-taught writer in a field almost totally devoid of competent narrative technique, where such technique was not appreciated or even understood, where characters were stock, most images and ideas already prefabricated, and most areas of human experience completely taboo. Weinbaum, who made his mark with genuinely imaginative funny-alien stories such as "A Martian Odyssey," had accomplished quite enough already by breaking the stranglehold of Edgar Rice Burroughs on the interplanetary romance. Henceforth, the inhabitants of Mars didn't have to be leftovers from Lost Race novels, beautiful princesses, evil high-priests, mightily-thewed swashbucklers, etc. Now they could be creatures that existed entirely on their own terms, and, incidentally, littered the surface of Mars with pyramids by shitting silicate bricks.

With *The Black Flame*, Weinbaum tried something even more ambitious, and the field wasn't ready for him. What he did was try to propel pulp SF out of its short-pants era, into genuine adolescence. That was when the trouble started.

He could not sell the result in his lifetime. Even after his death, with the pulps so hungry for the Weinbaum name that they'd feature Weinbaum's sister Helen on the covers in huge type (she wrote a few unexceptional stories), various agents had a great deal of trouble selling what was clearly the author's best novel. The great editors of the day, F. Orlin Tremaine, even John W. Campbell, turned it down as "not the right type," though Campbell later regretted doing so. Eventually the work appeared in the launch issue of *Startling Stories*, dated January 1939, and the various editors' hesitation was proven to be folly. The fans loved it.

It takes quite a lot of historical positioning to understand what the problem was. *The Black Flame* should have been a pulp editor's dream. The hero on the way to the electric chair doesn't die. He wakes up in the future. He is one of those tough Irish heros who abounded in pulp fiction and movies of the time, the sort of guy who doesn't express emotions well but for his occasionally explosive temper, who talks with his fists and otherwise doesn't have any threatening depth of character. He is stalwart, true, brilliant, handsome, and straight out of Central Casting. The future he finds himself in features gadgets galore and enormous, towering cities right out of *Metropolis*, a "girl" (not a "woman" for all she's in her twenties) there to play the role of passive love-object, and a gang of immortals who run the world with a system of benevolent Fascism. Oh yes, don't forget the elderly scientist. There's one of those too. Our hero, the scientist, another regular guy from the village, the "girl," and a horde of peasants embark upon a revolution against the immortals. The hero, with more political savvy than is typical for pulp protagonists, has serious doubts that this is a good idea.

And at this point, the formula story is starting to jump the rails. It is not a wish-fulfillment power fantasy in which the good guys triumphantly defeat the thirtieth-century Caligula and set everything right in a trice. No, the social forces are more complex than that. The revolution fails in minutes. Our hero has even more doubts, and by the end of the story he's changed sides, and fallen in love with Princess Margaret of Urbs, the Black Flame of the title.

For all that this sort of romance had been going on in the Burroughs Barsoom series for some time, the fans of *Wonder Stories* and *Astounding* wouldn't have it. Seventeen-year-old editor Charles Hornig of the Gernsback *Wonder Stories* firmly rebuked, "Love, to many of the young minds who read our mag, is a weakness in a man."

Or maybe it was something those "young minds" found too scary to think about. Certainly *The Black Flame* isn't *Madame Bovary*. Quite bluntly, had it been written by John Doe and published ten years later in *Startling Stories*, readers would probably have found it a little clichéd, and nowhere near as good as the best of Henry Kuttner or Murray Leinster. The novel might have had a couple paperback printings, maybe as half of an Ace Double in the '50s, and that would have been the end of it.

It's one of the embarrassments of science fiction (to use Tom Disch's phrase) to recognize how truly revolutionary *The Black Flame* was, even in 1939. Those dwarves were just beginning to hobble. This one could almost walk. Certainly, the romance of Tom Connor and the Flame is not a mature relationship. It is very true to the spirit of late-'40s pulp covers, the ones showing scantily-clad, sometimes whip-wielding ladies, in what seemed to be metal bikinis.

Actually, whips are the operative motif. The pulps wouldn't dare describe a healthy sexual relationship, but a little sado-masochism was often okay. Margaret of Urbs is a fantasy dominatrix who dresses to match. She torments and destroys men, and has more in common with Zsa Zsa Gabor's character in the *Queen of Outer Space* than most Weinbaum advocates would care to admit. Our hero earns her respect by physical abuse. In the end, he marries her and lives happily ever after, but by then she has been tamed, and agrees to become mortal for a few years to bear children. One can easily envision her in her futuristic kitchen, apron around her waist, contentedly puttering away while little flamelets tug at her skirt. We will leave it to Feminist critics to explore the full ramifications, but this is not great characterization, folks. It only seemed to be, for a little while, in our shabby ghetto.

Much more interesting is the character of Evanie, the passive love-object "girl" back at the rebel village. She is fearful of a possible mutant strain and afraid of her body. In the course of the action, she undergoes an awakening, falls out of love with our hero, and marries the regular village chap who has been smitten with her all along.

This is the crux of Weinbaum's marketing problem, and precisely *why* this book was revolutionary. The characters *change*. More than that, the development of the plot turns on character change. The Flame remarks on page 170 that "to be human is to love and suffer," and *that*, to the "young minds" of SF fandom, was terrifying heresy. *The Black Flame* was probably the first pulp SF novel in which the characters are driven, not so much by a need to save the world or perfect the Extra-Cosmic Thingamabob, but by their intimate, personal feelings. It was a genuine achievement that, even posthumously, Weinbaum could get away with such a notion. It is an indication of the rapid growth of the pulp SF field as it moved *into adolescence* in the late '30s that in just a few years, *The Black Flame* wouldn't seem like anything more than a colorful pulp melodrama, and such stories as C. L. Moore's "No Woman Born" (1944) or "Vintage Season" (1946), not to mention the mature work of Ray Bradbury, were possible.

The textual history of *The Black Flame* is complicated. An earlier version, called *Dawn of Flame*, with more "sex" and less gadgetry, also failed to sell in Weinbaum's lifetime, and was sufficiently different that it has been published as a separate story, first in 1936 in the Weinbaum memorial volume, then in *Thrilling Wonder* in 1939, somewhat abridged and combined with the main story in the 1948 Fantasy Press and 1969 Avon editions. *The Black Flame* itself appeared in *Startling Stories*, cut by about 12,000 words and somewhat rewritten by editor Mort Weisinger, who may have been concerned that, for all the story moves along at an already zippy pace, we don't actually meet the title character until more than halfway through. In 1939, Forrest J Ackerman bought the original manuscript at the first Worldcon, and was able to see the extent of the changes at a glance. Incredibly, he did not take any such responsibility as might be expected of the owner of the *only copy* of a significant text, such as making several copies, dispersing them just in case the house burns down, and putting the original in a safe place. Instead, he allowed the original to be stolen. When Avon proposed to bring out the unabridged text at the end of the '60s, the cry went out through fandom. The manuscript did not turn up. A carbon since has, in the possession of a Weinbaum relative, and now, a full fifty-nine years later, the book is in print as Weinbaum wrote it.

That it is brought out by a specialty press again takes us once more back to the very beginnings of the genre.

Tachyon Publications is a private firm devoted to preserving the backlist of science fiction, which has been abandoned by the major publishing houses. In the '40s, fans ploughed their G.I. Bill money into ventures to preserve favorite pulp stories of a decade earlier, which general publishers by and large would not touch. We are back to that situation. The next Tachyon book, already announced, is *The Best of Clifford Simak*. Twenty years ago, it would have been inconceivable that such a volume would not have come out from Putnam or Del Rey or any of Simak's other publishers, even as Avon would have been perfectly willing to publish an unabridged *Black Flame*, had the text not disappeared.

So, whatever its limitations, Tachyon Publications deserves our thanks for doing the job, when nobody else seems willing to.

The original trailer-blurb for this review read:

Darrell Schweitzer originally read The Black Flame *in* Startling Stories *in his youth, although he hastens to point out that the magazine was a collector's item even then.*

XXI.

ON BRIAN ALDISS'S *BAREFOOT IN THE HEAD*

Innovations are the common property of all writers. Whenever anybody comes up with a new technique, be it the realistic narratives of Defoe and Richardson, controlled point-of-view as pioneered by Poe and Maupassant, Joyce's stream-of-consciousness, or even something as elementary as the flashback, this becomes a standard tool which any subsequent writer may take down off the shelf and use, for whatever purpose, to the best of his or her ability.

But there's more than one shelf. Prior to the New Wave, most science-fiction writers had found themselves confined to the lower, pulp-magazine shelf. Only once in a great while did some prankster like Alfred Bester snatch something off the mainstream, Real Literature shelf up top.

What the New Wave did was spill the upper shelf, deliberately, as an act of rebellion. As the contents scattered over the floor and everybody scrambled for them, the result was a flurry of "experimental" work, particularly in *New Worlds*. These experiments were nothing new to general literature, but they were *new to science fiction*. Think of the New Wave as remedial catch-up on the culture of the twentieth century.

Some of these effusions were downright embarrassing, the sort of thing you'd expect in undergraduate literary magazines, but there were solid successes: John Brunner's pastiche of Dos Passos in *Stand on Zanzibar*, Disch's deliberately allegorical *Camp Concentration*, Ballard's surrealism (which had been present even before Michael Moorcock became editor and the Wave officially started), and, most impressively, I think, Brian Aldiss's *Barefoot in the Head*.

I read this book in high school, and was intrigued, for all I didn't understand very much of it. Returning to it more than twenty years later, I am still intrigued, but it seems an entirely different work from what I remember. Easier to understand too, perhaps because this time I've got the complete text (the 1969 Faber edition) rather than the episodes as published in *New Worlds*, not necessarily in the right order.

Barefoot in the Head takes place in what must have been intended to be the near-future. Europe has been bombed into the Stoned

Age by, of all possible aggressors, Kuwait, the atmosphere saturated with psychedelic chemicals, so that everybody, even in neutral countries, is on an increasingly intense, unending LSD trip. Our hero, Colin Charteris, a rather obnoxious young Serb with an obsession with all things English, deserts his United Nations relief duties in Italy and motors to England. He has a vision that everyone is part of an uncertain perceptual "web," and that external reality is a figment of the imagination. This is an incredibly appropriate message for the time, and soon Charteris has taken over someone else's budding cult and become a messiah, he and his followers caroming along the highways of Europe, many perishing in multiple-car pileups which evoke an erotic, death-wish fixation prefiguring Ballard's *Crash*. "Miracles" begin to happen, and Charteris, the "self-imagined man," passes into legend.

One of the many puzzles of this book is whether or not everything after the second episode is the hallucination of a perhaps dying Charteris. He's been having visions of other selves peeling off and crumpling by the roadside. On page 50 the viewpoint Charteris rushes out of a cottage and sees a duplicate of himself driving off in his car. *He* has become a discarded image. But Charteris-the-messiah would doubtless explain that it hardly matters.

Certainly the first thing the *New Worlds* reader would have noticed is that science fiction had never seen prose like this before:

> Knee-deep in his groins, thin in his increasing thicket, cult-figure Colin Charteris the Simon Temple of himself makes his own mark in the greylight, emerging like a lion from his lair, his mange of hair all about him. Some of his larger jackals call a greeting, the Burtons, Featherstone-Haugh, little Gloria, think dark Cass, Rubinstein with an early reefer glowing. The hero half-coughs in answer, cans craftily the stoned reigns of the beach, checks to see no great sweet jail trees sprang up there in the constabulary of the night, impoisoning them among writhing branches and the rough unshaven cyanightmarine light in the cell-out. (p. 135-136)

What Aldiss has done here is take the techniques of *Finnegans Wake* and adapt them to his purpose. He lacks Joyce's music, but is a lot easier to read; the exercise being no mere stunt, but an ideal matching of style and content, the book opening up with very restrained, conventional (though richly textured) prose, then getting crazier and crazier as the characters get crazier and crazier. Puns abound, multiple meanings pile up like crashed cars, as the characters' thoughts (and the narrative) are no longer able to stick to one linear path, but wander all over the "landskip." At the end of the episode called "Still Trajectories," there is a breathtakingly deft sequence from the viewpoint of a psychotic woman who is "cured" and carried away by Charteris, told in quietly restrained verse. And, since Charteris is a youth-cultured, sex-drugs-and-rock-&-roll sort of messiah, we also get a lot of song lyrics, some quite good, but all properly regarded, like the verse in *The Lord of the Rings*, not as poetry by the author but the effusions of his characters. They add to the overall creation, as products of the Acid Head War era.

One of them sums up the messiah's message and impact in the aftermath of his passing:

> An ambiguity
> Haunted him haunts
> All men clarity
> Has animal traits
>
> The bombs were only
> In his head
> On his memorial tree
> A joker wrote
> KEEP VIOLENCE IN THE MIND
> WHERE IT BELONGS

But of course we can't keep it there, which is why messiahs usually come to bad ends. Sometimes, at least, their story is as vividly recorded as in *Barefoot in the Head*, the Gospel of Colin Charteris according to Brian Aldiss, a unique and specialized pinnacle to which no one else in science fiction has ever ascended.

XXII.

A FISHERMAN OF THE INLAND SEA

This latest collection, boldly subtitled "Science Fiction Stories," should reassure those who still believe the silly canard that Ursula K. Le Guin has somehow hung out with mainstream-literary types for too long, turned in her science-fictionist's badge, and gone native. She has explained away such nonsense before with good humor, in interviews and essays, while producing children's books, poetry, a Nebula-winning fantasy, *Tehanu*, and, yes, one collection of realistic stories from *The New Yorker*, *Searoad*. That her career has always been that varied, is, one suspects, a good thing; most writers go stale if they churn out the same kind of material over and over again.

And now, for those who require it, a book with the words "science fiction" very large in the subtitle. What more could anyone want? Neon lights?

But seriously, the genuinely remarkable thing about Le Guin's "comeback" is that here is a writer in the maturity of her career, someone who began publishing novels almost from the start, (first story, "April in Paris," 1962; first novel, *Rocannon's World*, 1966), with classic novels behind her, entering what will probably be seen as a major phase of her development *as a short-fiction writer*. This is not the normal evolution. SF writers tend to move from shorter to longer forms and stay there. But, suddenly, there have been a lot of Le Guin stories out in just a couple years, in everything from *Asimov's* and *F&SF* to *Playboy*, *Crank!*, *Amazing*, and *Tomorrow*. The present volume collects only a few of them. There is enough out there to fill another book already.

The best news is that these stories show Le Guin at the top of her form, exploring new territories and returning to old. We are back in the Hainish universe. There are passages which might seem mildly incomprehensible to the newcomer:

> Oreth, who had just come out of female kemmer, having thus triggered Karth's male kemmer, all of which, by coming on unexpectedly early, had delayed the test flight for these past five days, enjoyable days for all—Oreth watched Rig, whom she had fathered,

> dance with Asten, whom she had borne, and watched Karth watch them, and said in Karhidish, "Tom-or-row..." ("The Shobies Story," p. 87)

Chances are, very few science fiction readers will come to this volume without having read *The Left Hand of Darkness* first. If they do, they'll probably be able to cope. Le Guin retains the science-fictionist's ability to define in context, to make the strange comprehensible by having her characters take it for granted. (A tradition that goes at least as far back as Heinlein's "the door dilated.")

What is less familiar to SF and, frankly, more refreshing is Le Guin's concept of—to reach for the current cliché—*family values*. She's fully as collectivist as the Heinlein of *Starship Troopers*, or any of countless others in the *Analog*/Baen Books camp, but the difference is that while the individual is subservient to the group, it is within a context of consensus rather than an authority. There is no leader. Everyone has to achieve harmony rather than domination.

In the above-quoted passage we have an extended family of space-travellers resting in the beach before setting out on a dangerous interstellar journey. It is a peaceful moment, the group's last before passing through hyperspace into a chaotic multiple-reality. The harmony of the group proves crucial to survival. The typical SF-militarist character (like Captain Kirk in the *Star Trek* episode "Shore Leave," the one about the alien amusement park where stray thoughts produce material menaces) would stand everybody to attention and *order* them to think only the correct thoughts, maintaining discipline through sheer toughness.

Instead, Le Guin's characters work it out among themselves, like a band of Buddhist monks. This isn't the simple trick of taking something from elsewhere (*i.e.*, outside of the United States), sticking it in the future and calling it alien. These *aren't* Buddhist monks. They think differently than we do. Their norms are different. I am merely grasping for an analogy. What's refreshing is the presentation of a far-future mind-set which is as far removed from our own as ours is from, say, medieval Byzantium. The future will be different. Possibly it will evolve more from the thoughts of Buddhist monks than from those of twentieth-century military officers. In the end, it will resonate to its own harmonies.

This faster-than-light travel is a change for the Hainish universe, a breakthrough based on "churten" technology, which, Le Guin admits in her introduction ("On Not Reading Science Fiction") is scientific nonsense; but it *feels* right, and what one does with gobbledygook in science fiction is exploit it for all its metaphorical worth.

Think of *The Fisherman of the Inland Sea* as a volume of theory-and-practice. In the introduction, Le Guin explains her aesthetic explicitly. The deepest appeal of science fiction, she tells us, to, no doubt, the intentional (but ultimately enlightening) puzzlement of some readers, is its beauty. It is hopelessly primitive to value a story merely for the ideas it contains:

> The beauty of a story may be intellectual, like the beauty of a mathematical proof or a crystalline structure; it may be aesthetic, the beauty of a well-made work; it may be human, emotional, moral; it is likely to be all three. (p. 6)

Certainly this beauty is achieved most clearly in the exquisite title story, which closes the book. Le Guin uses a Japanese fairy tale as her central device, to resonate off the churten technology even as the churten technology resonates off the fairy tale. It's about time-travel, the quest for knowledge, and how a man can live two completely separate lives, like the philosopher and the butterfly, each dreaming of the other and both having an equal handle on the truth.

Think of this book as a spectacular "comeback" from someone who has never been away.

XXIII.

LEXICON URTHUS

Readercon, as most patrons of *The New York Review of Science Fiction* know, is a convention held not quite annually in the Northeast, catering to the needs of a very small, specialized subgroup within the larger context of SF fandom: readers. Not trekkies, whovians, or other assorted media-fen, not costumers or goths or SCA, but people who actually read science fiction and fantasy and like to discuss it. Lots of writers come. It has a certain atmosphere all its own. Its detractors would call it snob-appeal. You might say there is an agreed-upon intellectual decorum at a Readercon.

But at one of the very first Readercons, I was at a room party where the topic of conversation turned inexplicably to *Star Trek.*

"Wait a minute," someone said. "Here we are at this exclusive, oh-so-literary convention, and we're talking about *Star Trek.*"

"We're being iconoclastic," said someone else. (I think it was Gary Farber.)

Sometimes you have to startle people. Hang on, I'm going to approach Gene Wolfe and the subject of Futurity by way of *Star Trek.* There is a method to this madness.

What I've concluded about *Star Trek* (all variants, including, presumably, the animated series, which I have never seen) is that it is a (metaphorical) *cartoon*. It doesn't even attempt to present a realistic, spacefaring future any more than Gary Larson does realistic nature portraits. It provides a crude, almost featureless outline, and tells the audience, "imagine the future here." We *know*, from what we know of biology, cosmology, etc. that if humans ever get to the stars they're not going to find the universe inhabited by "humanoids" who live on planets that look remarkably like California and differ from us only by a facial problem and an attitude. What is a Klingon but a samurai with *really* bad skin?

You may blame some of this on Gene Roddenberry's failure of imagination, or on the limitations of the medium; but if we're fair about it, we have to admit that even Hal Clement's aliens are anthropomorphic constructs. Genuine aliens (as opposed to the sort the popular imagination places aboard UFOs) would be the product of completely different evolution and history. Their appearance and behavior would not consist of re-arranged scraps of things we have already seen before, but things we have *not* seen. They would be, literally, unimaginable, which of course limits the human science-fiction writer's ability to depict them. All any writer can do is fake it, either in a simple-minded, *Star Trek* manner, or something more sophisticated.

Science fiction cannot actually deliver what it promises. This is an inherent limitation of the form. What the writer does is says, "Imagine here, something beyond human experience," and substitutes a cartoon.

Let me suggest that science fiction cannot imagine the remote future either. H. G. Wells projected Marxist class-struggle to the end of time and produced a terrifying, beautiful cartoon. Asimov spread the Roman Empire among the stars. Clark Ashton Smith and Jack Vance, in their stories of the Zothique and the Dying Earth, gave us a mythic, medieval/antique cartoon of an era millennia hence, when the world is haunted by sorcerers and ghouls. We accept, as a kind of literary convention, that this is not what the Year Two Million will actually be like, but that the Year Two Million could not be understood by twentieth-century readers, so this approximation will have to do.

Michael André-Drussi's *Lexicon Urthus* is subtitled "a Dictionary for the Urth Cycle." It is more than that. Yes, you can look up most of the odd words in Gene Wolfe's *The Book of the New Sun* here, and find the derivations of the names. It's a beautifully-produced book, thoroughly researched, often illustrated with useful woodcuts and drawings. I can spot only one factual error, on p. 275, where we are told that Zama is "the traditional site of Scipio's defeat by Hannibal in 202 BC." Surely that is a typo. "By" should read "of." Scipio won the battle.

Otherwise it's a very handy, excellent reference work.

But, paging through it, reading the longer entries, following unfamiliar words from one entry to another, *Lexicon Urthus* becomes a tool for understanding Gene Wolfe's method of creating the most extensive far-future cartoon ever wrought.

The world of the New Sun is a collage of history and myth. The Commonwealth, as Wolfe explained in the interview I did with him for *Weird Tales* (duly cited in André-Drussi's bibliography) is, or approximates, Byzantium, its salient feature being that it is declining, but at such a speed that everybody knows they will live their lives out in the Commonwealth, and their grandchildren will live out their lives in the Commonwealth, and *their* grandchildren will live out their lives. In Byzantium, even after the disastrous defeat at Manzikert in 1071 sent the empire precipitously sliding into oblivion, it still took almost four hundred years. A Byzantine of 1100 might have an outlook similar to that of an inhabitant of Wolfe's Commonwealth, feeling the weight of an enormously ancient heritage, looking forward to the likely destruction of his world, but aware that he is part of a process far greater than a human lifetime.

We discover in *Lexicon Urthus* that most of the characters are named after medieval or late-classical saints:

> MASTER GURLOES. Saint Gurloes (died 1057) was a Benedictine monk, prior of Redon Abbey, who in 1029 became abbot of Sainte-Croix of Quimperle in Brittany.
>
> SEVERIAN. There are five Saint Severians... Outside the Church, "Severian" refers either to a member of an Encratite or Gnostic sect of the 2nd century...or to a follower of Severus, the Monophysite patriarch of Antioch.
>
> THECLA. There are eight Saints Thecla, but the most pertinent is the 1st-century first female Christian martyr...

We also find that many of the political and military terms are Greek, the cosmology derives from the Kaballah, and a lot of the strange animals are extinct, prehistorical mammals, usually very big ones.

Does this suggest, then, that Gene Wolfe is just being sloppy, and giving us a hodge-podge of historical scraps in lieu of actual imagination?

Certainly not. *The Book of the New Sun* is a brilliantly constructed, almost infinitely rich cartoon, which fills in for a remote futurity we cannot truly imagine. And if he *could* imagine it, Wolfe would not be able to describe it from the point of view of a native (Severian) and hope to have twentieth-century readers understand it. History comes in layers. If the contemporary author writes about the twentieth century for the benefit of an ancient Babylonian, he has to leave out, or else completely explain in ancient Babylonian terms, our own past which is still in the Babylonian's future: Greek philosophical ideas, Roman legalities, medieval religious controversies which gave birth to the Reformation and caused social changes through the Industrial Revolution. As *Connections* pointed out, all the early industries in Britain were started by Dissenters, who went into industry because they couldn't become aristocrats or go into politics. Try to explain *that* to the Babylonian, who has never heard of Christ or a steam engine, and then give him a twentieth-century American view on it.... He won't understand it.

And, of course, if the temporal distance is millions of years, rather than just a few thousand, well...forget realism. We're too far back in Severian's remote past for him to (realistically) speak in our terms at all. A cartoon will have to do. A cartoon resonates better anyway. The step beyond cartoon is myth. All the great myths approximate what cannot be described or truly explained. No poet has ever genuinely shared the experience of the dead and come back to tell about it. So we have the story-cartoon of Orpheus instead. Here, imagine it is like this.... After a while it feels right.

Gene Wolfe's ancient and medieval scraps feel right. It's a brilliant stroke to portray this remote Urthian future from the point of view of primitives, who have forgotten most of it. Then Gnosticism, the Kaballah, Greek myth, Catholic martyrologies, and the like resonate, giving Wolfe's Urth a sense of vast antiquity and barely comprehensible detail. One thing you appreciate from *Lexicon Urthus* is precisely how well Gene Wolfe chooses his words. (And no, he didn't make any of them up.)

Okay, you can pretend that Severian's name is really Squggnikk, and that this proper name, common two million years from now, has rich historical and mythic resonances, which, by that point, have been around for fifty thousand years. But it's still in *our* future, so we aren't going to understand it. Therefore the "cartoonist" author has "translated" the name into something from our own past, the Latin name Severian, the name of five saints and a term for assorted heretics. In the same way that all the other notions in *The Book of the New Sun* and its sequels, companion volumes, and satellite stories are similarly "translated." What *Lexicon Urthus* does so ably is provide a key to the "translation."

Admittedly this is more the sort of book that is going to appeal to the typical Readercon attendee than to a *Star Trek* fan. But there is a similarity in the methodology. The trekkies already have a vast library of such reference books. The difference is merely one of texture. Where Gene Roddenberry drew like Charles Schulz, Gene Wolfe draws like Piranesi.

XXIV.

PROSPERO'S DRACULA

Perhaps another viewing will settle the matter. After just one I am unable to make up my mind whether Francis Ford Coppola's sumptuous *Bram Stoker's Dracula* (Columbia Pictures, 1992) is High Art, an intriguing neo-Gothic, neo-Expressionist excursion (the word "masterpiece" comes to mind, but inappropriately), or else an instance of much cinematic expertise wasted on High Kitsch.

It certainly isn't Bram Stoker, Coppola's numerous protestations of authenticity and devotion to the original text to the contrary. His *Dracula* is no more the "true story" than *Frankenstein: The True Story* was authentic Mary Shelley. It is, if anything, despite a dogged determination to reproduce incident after incident straight from the book, the most variant Dracula yet.

Think of it as the vampiric version of *Prospero's Books*, Peter Greenaway's gorgeous, gallumphing, ultimately self-overwhelmed film rendition of *The Tempest*, wherein every shot, every sequence, seemed taken from some surrealistic dream of live-action Renaissance paintings, and—for all it made sense in terms of the whole thing being a, well, tempestuous outpouring from the magic-soaked mind of Prospero—the viewer longed for the occasional realistic scene of shipwrecked seventeenth-century people, in plain, not riotously fanciful costumes, on a real beach. *Bram Stoker's Dracula* has considerably less excuse for failing to touch down in prosaic, Victorian reality, but fail it does: the outdoor sets are so obviously sound-stages, the train steaming through the Carpathians so obviously a miniature, the 1890s' London in its own way as fantastic as Castle Dracula (which itself looks like something out of Tim Burton's *Batman* or *Edward Scissorhands*). Only in movies like this do English ladies of that era wear almost transluscent, almost luminous nightgowns designed by some ancestor of Frederick's of Hollywood or get buried in tombs that ought to be on exhibit in the British Museum, or, worse yet, stroll calmly off the street into a silent movie exhibition of *pornography!* Not that vice didn't prosper, and fester, in the 1890s, but it was discreetly hidden, so that respectable appearances might deceive, which was one of the themes of the Stoker novel missing in this film.

There is nothing of "respectable appearances" here. Coppola has created an entirely new set of Dracula images, owing nothing to Stoker and virtually nothing to prior films. An old man with a drooping moustache, dressed all in black? Hardly. Before a drop of the red revitalizes him, Coppola's Count (Gary Oldman) looks like a demented approximation of a Renaissance Venetian Doge crossed with a large rat (a bow to Nosferatu, perhaps), and very possibly in drag, sporting an incredible coiffure (who or *what* is Dracula's hairdresser?) and a bright red cloak several times as long as his own body. (How does he keep it clean? Doesn't it get stuck in doors?) He transforms several times into impressive monsters, most strikingly, a man-sized, almost hairless, greenish bat. Youthened Dracula, in London, might best be described as a Byronic hippie, right down to the granny glasses, although so immaculately attired that the same team of eldritch hairdressers and laundrymen must spend the rest of their (waking?) hours brushing Native Earth off the old boy.

(And, speaking of servants, have you ever wondered precisely what service the madman Renfield—Tom Waits raving and gibbering in the best tradition of the "*cinéma-lunacé*"—renders the Count in exchange for all those wiggly, scurrying treats? You won't find out here. The dapper Dracula doesn't need some weak-minded soul to invite him into human society.)

What this film needed, what *Prospero's Books* needed, what *Edward Scissorhands* in its own way managed to achieve, was *contrast*. Sure, *Bram Stoker's Dracula* is a technical marvel, something Coppola wastes no opportunity in reminding us, every time we notice that his camera is shooting through a peacock's fan, or that the Count's shadows don't match his motions. There is a *great* shot of Dracula scurrying down the outside of the castle, head downward, in the posture and with the motions of a rat. (Right out of Stoker, yes, but silly when you start wondering why Dracula's cape doesn't fall down over his head in that position. I think it was Louis Jourdan who played the same scene, wheezing along like a flopping, beached fish, with his cape neatly pinned to his ankles.) But Coppola, like so many other film-makers before him, has failed to grasp an underlying principle of fantasy: the unreal must be framed in the real. The supernatural must exist in the context of the grittily convincing, the utterly mundane, so that it seems an *intrusion*. Fine, all well and good, that Castle Dracula should give Jonathan Harker a bloody and erotic experience out of some lunatic's dream, but this will inevitably dissolve into self-conscious camera angles and effects-on-display and thoughts of "I wonder how they did that?" unless we see a *real* railroad train and *real* Transylvanian countryside and a *real* castle, then return again to a *real* London, where Harker may seem safe, awakened from the lunatic dream, until, to his horror, it all starts happening again.

Contrast. Between the real and the unreal. None of that here. Instead, *Bram Stoker's Dracula* opts for a "fairy tale," "once upon a time" look which completely vitiates its power. Nothing horrifies, for all we are treated to a gorgeous parade of Gothic images. The cast (Oldman as Dracula, Anthony Hopkins as a decidedly eccentric Van Helsing, Keanu Reeves as Harker) are so completely overwhelmed by the visual effects, by sets, costumes, everything, that you have to stop and think, yes, these are probably pretty good performances. Worse yet, in a fifteenth-century prologue (again utterly unrealistic, with battle scenes like a series of animated, blood-soaked Kay Nielsen silhouettes) Dracula is established as a Romantic Lover, who renounced God over the loss of his True Love. He is sympathetic. Ladies swoon for him. More like a character out of Haggard than Stoker, he has been searching through the centuries for the reincarnation of his Beloved. (Guess who?) There is no sense of *evil* anywhere in the film, except possibly in the very striking encounter between Reeves and Dracula's three "wives"—and in the end Mina (Winona Ryder) saves the Count's dignity, gives him peace, and weeps for him. Stoker, or his original readers, would be among the last to recognize the final scenes.

It's a visual feast, a fantastic art gallery of a film, but it is not Stoker and it is barely *Dracula*. It is certainly not, hype to the contrary, the definitive anything.

After over a hundred *Dracula* films, we still haven't one fully worthy of, or faithful to, Bram Stoker's novel. What is the best? I still hold out for the 1958 Hammer opus, *Horror of Dracula*, which, despite cheesy production values and occasional plot stupidities (so, Jonathan Harker, you are a professional vampire-killer sent by Van Helsing to bump off the Count, and you went down into the crypts precisely at sundown, *without carrying a crucifix?*) still delivers a horrific jolt the Coppola extravaganza cannot: precisely because the characters are center-stage, and terrific performances by a marvelously menacing Christopher Lee and a heroic but still human Peter Cushing seize our attention and won't let go. If Terence Fisher ever framed a shot through peacock feathers, I didn't notice.

XXV.

CTHULHU 2000

Are the Great Old Ones laughing?

Understand that we have here, in Arkham House's very official compilation, a gathering of the very best modern Cthulhu Mythos material. Editor Jim Turner deftly lifts everything worthwhile from the otherwise unsuccessful Weinberg/Greenberg *Lovecraft's Legacy*, takes a few tales from Arkham House's own 1980 volume, *New Tales of the Cthulhu Mythos*, adds several otherwise uncollected items, wraps it all in a resplendent Bob Eggleton dustjacket, and the result is undoubtedly the State of the Art in matters Cthulhuvian.

I spot only one real stinker (by Basil Copper), and one piece so opaque it's hard to say what it is (by James Blaylock), but otherwise this is a good collection, filled with (perhaps, disconcertingly) smiles, laughter, warm remembrances, and very few authentic shivers.

Are the Old Ones laughing? Lovecraftian humor is *so* easy to do. Right before composing this review, your Humble Reviewer, in semi-delirium from a nasty summer flu, was still able to compose a bit of bucolic verse, "Wilbur Whateley's School Days," about the eight-foot-tall juvenile shambler from "The Dunwich Horror" ("I was the only kid in the first grade class / with tentacles under his arms") and send off same to *Crypt of Cthulhu*, an august journal which has leavened its learned contents with such cosmic cacklings for 93 issues now.

In *Cthulhu 2000* we are treated to Esther Friesner's lovely tale of the Gothic romance publishing industry, "Love's Eldritch Ichor," Lawrence Watt-Evans' somewhat weaker "Pickman's Modem," and Gahan Wilson's "H.P.L.," this last a true fan's touching tribute, in which the Old Gent of Providence (along with his buddy Klarkash-Ton) has survived his reported 1937 death and achieved apotheosis with his beloved monsters. Fred Chappell's "The Adder" is a clever, funny story about the dread *Necronomicon* of the Mad Arab, Abdul Alhazred. It seems that if you place the awful tome next to another book, it will begin to devour the text of that other book, from every copy in the world, and from the memory of everyone who ever read, say, Milton, whose poetical works almost perish in the course of the story's action. Kim Newman's "The Big Fish" is a Sam Spade-type detective story about a Dagon cult in California in the early '40s. It has, in common with all these others cited, an element of knowing satire. The Lovecraftian paraphernalia, like that of the hardboiled mystery, becomes an instantly recognizable billboard on which the author can place something else. Wouldn't it be funny if an lovelorn Innsmouth amphibianess started writing romance novels, or if the detective in the trenchcoat found himself chasing after Spawn of the Minions of the Deep Ones...?

Yes, it might be funny. It might even be good satire. It isn't scary, though.

T. E. D. Klein, not once, but several times, actually managed to raise a few goosebumps out of such knowing, referential fictions. His is a record no one has yet equalled. If there are ten post-Lovecraftian Mythos stories which rival Lovecraft in power and thematic interest, Klein is the author of nearly half of them. Incredibly, he does it by breaking all the rules of horror fiction. His characters know the literature. They're virtually aware they're inside a horror story. They make lots of allusions. In "Black Man with a Horn," the protagonist is loosely based on the late Frank Belknap Long, Lovecraft's best friend, in whose shadow he remained for the rest of a quite extended life. The story reflects on this, the character coming to accept his role as "the hand that shook the hand" of the Great Man. Then, with supreme artistry, Klein manages to make a real story out of such unlikely material, something which rises above the level of adulating pastiche.

Supreme artistry is also present in Gene Wolfe's "Lord of the Land." A fellow writer may examine this tale again and again with envious amazement at how deftly every creak and shadow is in precisely the right place, but, ultimately, when this magnificent mechanism delivers us an Old One who existed as an intestinal parasite in a hyena in ancient Egypt before haunting the American midwest, somehow the cosmic resonance doesn't quite resonate.

With similar skill, Poppy Z. Brite's "His Mouth Will Taste of Wormwood" comments on HPL's "The Hound," resetting HPL's adventure of two jaded necrophiles in the New Orleans punk scene. Where HPL could make noises about decadent aesthetes and their enormities, one was always left with the sense that the Old Gent was making pious noises, and couldn't actually imagine what such "degenerates" actually did or why. Ms. Brite can. It would have given HPL a start: "I had not taken seriously Louis's talk of making love in a charnel house—but neither had I reckoned on the pleasure he could inflict with a femur dipped in rose-scented oil." It's to Brite's credit that this story would actually work for people who have never heard of Lovecraft (or Clark Ashton Smith, whose standard death-by-seduction ending she reverts to, rather than the precise climax of "The Hound"), but the story is still primarily pastiche and commentary. It is art, but built out of recycled parts, like a collage.

Controversial choices, both excellent specimens of writing by any standard, are Harlan Ellison's "On the Slab" and Roger Zelazny's

"Twenty-Four Views of Mt. Fuji, by Hokusai," neither of which, as I read them, have anything to do with Lovecraft. Ellison invokes some old gods, all right, but the myth is that of Prometheus. (Greek myth, as opposed to Lovecraft's Mythos, is human-centered. More on this anon.) The Zelazny tale of death and cyberspace, set in Japan, has one playful Lovecraftian riff about halfway through. It lasts little over a page and ultimately has little to do with the rest of the story. If, as editor Turner chooses to do, we take the two monk-assassins at the end to be emissaries from R'lyeh (are their hands calloused because they are webbed-fingered Deep Ones, or because they practise martial arts; if Dagonites, why the left hands *only*?), the Lovecraftian reading of the story makes no sense. The conflict in the story is human and personal. A dying former secret agent (female) makes a last pilgrimage to Japan to find inner peace, and to thwart her late husband, who has achieved a meddlesome immortality in cyberspace. Why should the Great Old Ones *care?*

The whole essence of Lovecraftian myth, so rarely grasped by post-Lovecraftian writers, is its vision of a vastly impersonal cosmos, in which human values, strivings, and beliefs are of no relevance. The horror in the Lovecraftian tale is frequently evoked as the comfortable façade of human existence is rubbed thin, and someone gets a glimpse beyond, into the unknowable void. It's all summed up neatly in the first lines of "The Call of Cthulhu":

> The most merciful thing in the world, I think, is the inability of the human mind to correlate all its contents. We live on a placid island of ignorance in the midst of black seas of infinity, and it was not meant that we should voyage far. The sciences, each straining in its own direction, have hitherto harmed us little; but some day the piecing together of dissociated knowledge will open up such terrifying vistas...that we shall either go mad from the revelation or flee from the deadly light into the peace and safety of a new dark age.

It is precisely this theme which most post-Lovecraftian Cthulhu Mythos writers, including most of the ones in *Cthulhu 2000*, fail to expand upon.

We now consider those few remaining items in the book which may be reasonably described as horror stories. Ramsey Campbell's "The Faces at Pine Dunes" is not his best. It delivers a few creeps, but ultimately fails to convince as the nice young man who narrates turns out to be One of Them. Michael Shea's "Fat Face" connects with the Poppy Brite tale in its realistic depiction of "decadence," in this case the lives of hookers who get involved with a shoggoth. There's nothing *mythic* here, but one might reasonably wonder what shoggoths (those virtually brainless, amoeboid minions of minions) might do for a living if they survived Lovecraft's aeons-old ruins (as in *At the Mountains of Madness*) and had to make their way in the modern age.

F. Paul Wilson's "The Barrens" delivers workman-like fright, using authentic New Jersey Pine Barrens detail in place of Lovecraft's Dunwich and Innsmouth. There are genuine hints of the Outside pressing in. Wilson, virtually alone of the contributors to *Lovecraft's Legacy*, or even this present book, seems to have actually understood what Lovecraft was about.

But the winner and still champion is Thomas Ligotti's "The Last Feast of Harlequin." While I do not believe that enough thematically serious, non-satirical, non-pastiche, post-Lovecraftian Mythos tales have yet been written to fill a book, this is one of them. If such an anthology ever is compiled, Ligotti may well get the pride of place, as the best of the lot. "Harlequin" may be read as a reflection on (but not a retelling of) Lovecraft's "The Festival." It begins, as do many of Lovecraft's own tales, as a piece of pseudo-scholarship, recounting the researches that went into the correlating of the facts, which led to the searing moment of enlightenment, after which nothing could ever be the same again. It's about strange doings in a small town in the Midwest, which tells us little. There are enormous worms in it, people who aren't quite people, and cosmic forces, barely glimpsed. It's all done without in-jokes, and without, despite an overall similarity of approach, any outright attempt to imitate Lovecraft's style. There are no eldritch, gibbering strings of adjectives. The last line is not in italics. But Ligotti has the real stuff, which makes him virtually unique.

Cthulhu 2000, by its title, implies an attempt to sum up the development of Lovecraftian fiction for the millennium. The results are not entirely impressive. Too many of these stories don't scare us or make us think; they make us smile and remember fondly something we read a long time ago. Lovecraftism has become a familiar trope, something Roger Zelazny can drop into an otherwise serious, unrelated story as a gag. It can become a vehicle for satire (Friesner, Bruce Sterling, Newman, Watt-Evans), for disquieting character study (as Joanna Russ's very human-centered "'I Had Vacantly Crumpled It Into My Pocket...: A Photograph from Life!'"), or even a means for commenting on Lovecraft (Brite, Gahan Wilson), but only very, very rarely has any writer made an attempt to *expand upon Lovecraft's themes*.

Cthulhu 2000 is indeed a very good summation, but what it tells us is that if there is ever going to be a serious literary tradition developing in the wake of Lovecraft, it's barely gotten started.

XXVI.

THE DRAGON PATH

It is the distinguishing feature of fantastic fiction that it can wholly or partially dispense with the "real" world and replace it with a world of the author's imagination, a world whose creation—however much it may draw upon myth, legend, or history—is strictly governed by the author's worldview. Insofar, however, as there is a very obvious if tacit understanding between the writer and the reader that this world *is* purely a product of the imagination, the fantastic universe becomes an aesthetic creation whose entire *raison d'être* resides in its embodiment, almost as a sort of utopia, of what the author wishes the "real" world to be.

—S. T. Joshi,
Lord Dunsany, Master of the Anglo-Irish Imagination, p. 3

Even the Nine Rowers of the boat—those mysterious silent Kings of Faerie he had been with a year and a day since his druids with their magic evoked them from their customary commerce, the portage of the dead, to carry him beyond the limits of the world, even they, he thought, had changed a little in these august surroundings. Though they were silent still, and as ever seemed unaware of him, a light had grown starry and kindly in the inscrutable azure of their eyes; the dark flame that embodied them gloomed more richly; the stars that twinkled and vanished about their heads shone with a larger rhthym. For here was Mountain Tormathrannion within the borders of the World of the Immortals; the light and odor of the Apples of Tormathrannion thrilled all the air of those wonderful regions. One breathed here as the Gods breathe—confident, equal-hearted with the stars.

Then let one's mind be without perturbation; one's hatred.

—Kenneth Morris,
"The Apples of Knowledge,"
in *The Dragon Path*, p. 267

Kenneth Morris is probably the least-known master of fantasy prose in English. There was a time, not too long ago, when he was a truly *legendary* writer, in that one only *heard* of him through word of mouth.

Reference books contain no information about him. Only the most advanced collectors had so much as *seen* a copy of that fabulous rarity, *Book of the Three Dragons*, which, along with William Timlin's *The Ship That Sailed to Mars*, ranked as one of those books which completist collectors gazed upon just once before they died. Well, I exaggerate slightly; in twenty-five years of book-scouting I have turned up two copies, one in a dustjacket, which doubtless makes me an ascended master. I also turned up the only story collection Morris had published in his lifetime, *The Secret Mountain*, and saw another copy ten years later for a mere hundred and twenty-five bucks. Until Newcastle reprinted it in the early 1978, the third Morris book, *The Fates of the Princes of Dyfed*, was even scarcer than the other two. I've seen that too, the only copy even rumored in our field, which its owner generously lent to Newcastle for the reprinting.

No doubt about it, Kenneth Morris's books have been scarce enough that, despite the blurbs that accompany *The Dragon Path*, Kenneth Morris is *not* a writer as important as Tolkien or Dunsany or E. R. Eddison. He could have been. There but for fortune and the vagaries of the market would go one of the grand masters. The problem simply was that Morris's work was too unavailable to have any influence. But for a single mention in Ursula K. Le Guin's "From Elfland to Poughkeepsie," which began the revival of Morris's posthumous reputation, there is no indication that any major figure in fantasy has ever read him.

Morris was a master. Make no mistake about it. He wrote some of the finest fantastic prose we have ever seen, though we (most of us anyway) have only just gotten to see it. If Morris invented Celtic fantasy, as the Tor publicity alleges, alas, the the secret remained well hidden. The current spate of such literature does not stem from Morris, but from Evangeline Walton, Lloyd Alexander, and, quite probably, from people going back to read *The Mabinogion*.

Had Morris's publishing circumstances been otherwise, the whole history of the field might have been different. Call him a lost ancestor. Whether he will *ever* prove to be an important influence is for the future to decide. There will doubtless be some sensitive souls who read *The Dragon Path*, are deeply moved, take Morris as a formative influence, and the results will come into print in about a generation.

That Morris (1879-1937) was a lifelong, devout Theosophist is just the beginning of out difficulties in evaluating him. Most of his stories were published (often under pseudonyms) in Theosophical magazines, and, but for the few included in *The Secret Mountain* (London: Faber & Gwyer, 1926), the rest remained uncollected until Douglas Anderson (after a dozen years of research) gathered them together into the present volume. *The Fates of the Princes of Dyfed* was published by Aryan Theosophical Press in 1914, hardly a path to best-sellerdom. *Book of the Three Dragons* appeared as a children's book from Longmans in 1930, and even had a Junior Literary Guild edition, but, probably because most children's books sell to libraries and are read to destruction, it remained an extreme rarity. Another novel, *The Chalchiuhite Dragon: A Tale of Toltec Times*, remained in manuscript until 1992, when Tor published it.

Morris, when he is written about at all, is most often compared to Lord Dunsany, his "nearest literary relative," as Anderson puts it in the introduction. Both do exactly what Joshi describes in the passage quoted above. They invent allegorical worlds, described in beautiful prose. The difference, other than nationality (for Morris, being Welsh was nearly as important as being a Theosophist; Dunsany, though Anglo-Irish, seldom dealt directly with Celtic materials), was one of *belief.*

Dunsany was a skeptic and a cynic, albeit a romantic one. He wrote of the triumphs of the gods, nature, and time over the trivial workings of mankind. Morris took Theosophy absolutely seriously. He lived in the Theosophical commune at Point Loma, California for many years. Late in life, he founded Theosophical lodges in Britain. He was never troubled by the obvious charlatanries of Madame Blavatsky, her forgeries and plagiarisms, her (repeatedly exposed) fake séances, or the appalling (if sometimes comic) scandals and feuds that shook the Theosophical movement after her death. In his writings, at least, he is a serene and devout believer in the revealed truths. The modern reader can only cringe when, in a piece called "The Epic of Wales," Morris starts out with the statement that Theosophy was the religion of the ancient Welsh.

Morris's Theosophical belief becomes as puzzling a critical problem as might result if, say, a sincere Scientologist started to produce real literature. Eventually, we are seduced by the quality of Morris's prose and imagination. The important thing, then, is to put aside all we know about Blavatsky, Sinnett, Olcott, Leadbeater—the whole shabby, sinister crowd, whose adventures are wittily related in de Camp & de Camp's *Spirits, Stars and Spells*—and concentrate on what Theosophy meant to Morris. Theosophical thought has, after all, influenced fantasy before, rather trivially in the case of Edgar Rice Burroughs, more seriously with Talbot Mundy, but mostly deeply of all with Morris. It was the most important fact in Morris's life, as integral to him as Christianity was to C. S. Lewis.

Morris's Theosophy then is a search for an inner light of the spirit, which is within all of us. There are echoes of Gnosticism and even Neo-Platonism. His characters seek, and usually find, enlightenment. There is much idealism, and very little genuine evil in his fiction. Beauty and truth predominate. It is a tribute to his artistry that he can prevent such a mixture from becoming either saccharine or merely dull.

"The Secret Mountain," the title story of Morris's first collection, is a key one. Here we meet one Varglon Fflamlas, who was a slave in Babylon. Varglon Fflamlas has three dreams. In the first, he has become a poet, inspired to chant a great song before the king. But in the middle of the performance, a stranger appears, whispers something to the poet, and his recital falters. He is no longer interested in the king's rewards, having received a hint of a higher truth. In a subsequent dream, he is a general leading troops into battle. The same thing happens. He leaves the battle, in search of the snow-capped Mountain of the Gods. And again, as a dream-king, he loses his place at the stranger's whisper and seeks the Gods.

Varglon Fflamlas, waking, then runs away, along the road that stretches from Babylon to Camelot (making clear, if it were not so already, but this is not set in the historical Babylon, but a never-never-land as fabulous as Dunsany's "East"). He achieves enlightenment in the wilderness, finding within himself memories of his former life among the gods on the mountain. He returns to Babylon, is arrested as a runaway slave and crucified. Dying, he beholds the snowy Secret Mountain of the Gods among the clouds. But he is not a deluded fool, dying for an illusion. Instead, he is a divine instrument, his purpose being to bring enlightenment to Babylon. ("In the night the city gates were opened from within, and the Gods entered Babylon; there to reign, it is said, for a thousand years or more."—p. 236.)

Several of Morris's stories deal with near-death or after-death experiences, in which enlightenment is achieved. More than one conclude with the beginning of a golden age. The mysterious stranger, who whispered to Varglon Fflamlas in the dreams, is a master, one of those "mahatmas" whom Madame Blavatsky imagined ruling the world by radiating cosmic wisdom from secret hideaways in the Himalayas. We meet several such persons in Morris. In "The Night of Al Kadr," a Spanish Christian warrior sneaks into a Moorish fortress, bent on slaughter, but instead ineffable peace prevails, because the aged Muslim lord of the place is also of that secret brotherhood which works for the betterment of mankind. Such masters are very much akin to the Taoist immortals, among whom the Chinese hero of "Red-Peach-Blossom Inlet" dwells for a time, but can never rediscover once he has departed their company. (Morris wrote three Chinese stories, all concerned with enlightenment and artistry; they are, incidentally, far, far superior to the much better-known pseudo-Chinese tales Frank Owen was publishing in *Weird Tales* about the same time.)

Morris's reputation as a writer of specifically Celtic fantasy depends more on *The Fates of the Princes of Dyfed* and *Book of the Three Dragons* than on his short stories, which range widely. There are Chinese stories. There are Greek stories. There is even an ironic tale of the afterlife which begins in a modern-day slum ("The Divina Commedia of Evan Leyshon"). "The Last Adventure of Don Quixote" is an utterly charming sequel to Cervantes, in which the aged knight rises from his death-bed (or seems to) and has one last, heroic adventure, which justifies his ideals. "The Lord of the Planet" evidences Morris's interest in pre-Columbian American myth; it is told, incidentally, from the viewpoint of a god. Certainly there are some Celtic stories too. "The Cauldron of Ceridwen" combines typical Morris motifs—failed artistry renewed by enlightenment, a spiritual journey at the threshold of death—with elements from *The Mabinogion*. "Sion Ap Siencyn" is about a man who hears the songbirds of Rhiannon, and listens for what seems a short time but turns out to be three hundred years. Then again, "The King and the Three Ascetics" is a Hindu fable.

All these settings and mythologies become, for Morris, aesthetic constructs, for the purpose of depicting an ideal, mystical world. The secret of Morris's success, what makes him a great fantasist, is that he never lost sight of his artistry. He didn't slip into banal preachments, taking his premises for granted as something every sensible person "knows." Instead, he built up his magical creations carefully, never losing lost his sense of the awe of supernatural wonders. These are beautifully-constructed stories, not sermons, from a writer who truly knew how to evoke those "mysterious silent Kings of Faerie" as surely as any druid could, in prose in which the "dark flame" that embodies the magical glooms more richly.

XXVII.

AN INTERVIEW WITH EDGAR ALLAN POE

(RECORDED BY DARRELL SCHWEITZER UNDER DUBIOUS CIRCUMSTANCES)

INTERVIEWER: It is a great honor to have with us this evening, Mr. Edgar Allan Poe. How are you, Mister Poe?

POE: More honored than you, Sir, and amazed, to be here at all. Having journeyed so unexpectedly into the *Mare Tenebrarum*, I, of all people, never imagined I would return to this Earth—and to such a century! I wrote of the future—half a fancy, half a speculation my tale called "Mellonta Tauta," setting the action *one thousand years* beyond my own era—and my imagined future was not half so fantastic as yours, of the year—what year did you say it was?

INTERVIEWER: 1993.

POE: Nineteen ninety-three. Such speed. Such noise. Such great machines hurtling through the air! I would have had you wafting gently from rooftops with hot-air balloons. And there is more. You are in thrall to that veritable God in a box, the *television*—

INTERVIEWER: It's one of our vices.

POE: I too, have my vices, and was undone by them once—in Baltimore, as I was on the threshold of such happiness... [Pauses in reflection. Returns to himself.] Ah, one of mine is talking about myself overmuch. That much I have learned while residing among the Shades.

INTERVIEWER: But Mister Poe, we *want* you to talk about yourself. That is why we've called you here—

POE: [Laughs.] A Mesmeric Revelation, yielding up Some Words with a Mummy?

INTERVIEWER: None of us would be here at the World Horror Convention without the work *you* did. Without "The Masque of the Red Death" and "The Fall of the House of Usher" and "The Cask of Amontillado," there wouldn't *be* a horror field.

POE: [Ironically. Faking his humility.] You flatter me, Sir. Am I not preceded by Mrs. Radcliffe and Monk Lewis?

INTERVIEWER: Few read *The Mysteries of Udolpho* these days. But your work, yes. Perhaps it is because you wrote with such passion about things that mattered to you so deeply.

POE: Perhaps, Sir, you are right. But I think not. For nothing written is a simple out-gushing of the soul. No, it is deliberate artifice. I prefer commencing with the consideration of an *effect*. Keeping originality *always* in view—for he is false to himself who ventures to dispense with so obvious and so easily attainable a source of interest—I say to myself, in the first place, "Of the innumerable effects, or impressions, of which the heart, the intellect, or (more generally) the soul is susceptible, what one shall I, on the present occasion, select?" Having chosen a novel, first, and secondly a vivid effect, I consider whether it can best be wrought by incident or tone—whether by ordinary incidents and peculiar tone, or, the converse, by peculiarity of both incident and tone—afterwards looking about me (or rather within) for such combinations of event, or tone, as shall best aid me in the construction of the effect.

INTERVIEWER: So all of it is as deliberate as taking a book down from the shelf.

POE: And opening that *specific volume* to *specific page* and reading a *specific line*, knowing, yes, that is the effect I desire.

INTERVIEWER: Most writers describe the creative process quite differently.

POE: Most writers, Sir, poets in especial, prefer having it understood that they compose by a species of fine frenzy—an ecstatic intuition—and would positively shudder at letting the public peep behind the scenes, at the elaborate and vacillating crudities of thought—at true purposes seized only at the last moment—at cautious selections and rejections—at painful erasures and interpolations. No, they would prefer to think that a tale springs like Athena, fully-wrought from the forehead of the author, Zeus. But it is not so. Those who believe it so have probably never composed so much as a grocery list of their own.

INTERVIEWER: I can't believe that a poem as beautiful as "To Helen" or a story as gut-wrenching as "The Pit and the Pendulum" is just a matter of mechanics.

POE: It is a matter of choice, for Beauty, the poem, for Terror, the tale.

INTERVIEWER: Which do you prefer writing?

POE: Whichever I choose. No, I do both as naturally as breathing. Do I prefer to inhale, or exhale? I must admit to, however, a certain point of superiority that the tale has over the poem. In fact, while the *rhythm* of the poem is an essential aid to the development of the poem's highest idea—the idea of the Beautiful—the artificialities of this rhythm are an inseparable bar to the development of all points of thought or expression which have their basis in *Truth*. But truth is often, to the greatest degree, the aim of the tale. The writer of the prose tale may bring to his theme a vast variety of modes or inflections of thought or expression—the ratiocinative, for example, the sarcastic or the humorous—which are not only antagonistical to the nature of the poem, but absolutely forbidden by one of its most peculiar and indispensable adjuncts. I allude, of course to rhythm.

INTERVIEWER: What about free verse?

POE: It is not verse. It is mere graffiti.

INTERVIEWER: For all the short story—the tale, as you say—has a wider range then, you seem to have specialized narrowly in horror—

POE: Hardly! Have you read all my works? Am I not witty in "Never Bet the Devil Your Head?" Clever in "Why the Frenchman Wears His Arm in a Sling?" And even such tales as "The Mystery of Marie Rogêt" and "The Murders in the Rue Morgue," for all their elements of mystery and dread, are primarily exercises in *pure intellect*, in, as I have often termed the activity, ratiocination. The scientific mind, applied to the darkness of human experience, brings, through diligence, the truth to light. But yes, yes, I have composed many tales of terror—and of horror, as Mrs. Radcliffe distinguished the two—I should call "The Pit and the Pendulum" one of horror, for the immediacy of the doom and suffering within it—for while a huge blade is swinging ever lower over a prostrate and restrained victim, nothing need be left to the imagination for long! "The Fall of the House of Usher," on the contrary, is a tale of terror, of the slow realization and then sudden and shattering revelation that we have for a long period of time been mistaking the sounds of *agony* for those of *mirth* or indifference.

Nevertheless, when I choose to write a tale of terror, I take down from the shelf, as you will, those aspects and elements which shall contribute to the *single and unified effect*, and include those *alone* in my composition, leaving out all which would distract from it. Again, this demonstrates the superiority of the *tale* over other literary forms, for the ordinary *novel* is objectionable in its length: as it cannot be read in one sitting, it deprives itself, of course, of the immense force derivable from *totality*. This totality is one of plot, which as I define it, is that in which nothing can be disarranged, or from which nothing can be removed, without ruin to the mass. It is that in which we are never able to determine whether any one point depends upon or sustains any other.

And what of the essence of *horror* itself, which is, to coin a phrase, the soul of the plot, let me say only that in horror there is *truth*, the inescapable *truth* which may not be denied by prettification of sentiment; for is not much of human existence melancholy and filled with tears? Does not all that is beautiful fade and die? Cannot the cruel and relentless conqueror worm snatch a man away from this life at the very moment of his achievement of happiness? Does not the grave yawn for us all?

If any species of literature—be it prose or poetry—is to have any worth, it must not deny, or evade, or mitigate *truth*, merely in the pretense of fulfilling those deepest-felt and dearest human wishes which cannot ever be fulfilled.

Tear aside the veil of petty conventionality, of trifling lies, and behold—in horror!—the cadaverous face of Truth!

INTERVIEWER: [Somewhat overwhelmed.] Thank you, Mister Poe.

XXVIII.

ONE FINE DAY IN THE STYGIAN HAUNTS OF HELL

BEING THE LORE AND LEGEND OF THE FABLED "EYE OF ARGON"

Dear typesetters, proofreaders, copyeditors, Noble Editor, everyone—the following passage is entirely *sic*. Please try to get it into print *exactly* as I've typed it:

> The weather beaten trail wound ahead into the dust racked climes of the baren land which dominates large portions of the Horogolian empire. Age worn hoof prints smothered by the sifting sands of time shone dully against the dust splattered crust of earth. The tireless sun cast its parching rays of incandescense from overhead, half way through its daily revolution. Small rodents scampered about, occupying themselves in the daily accomplishments of their dismal lives. Dust sprayed over three heaving mounts in blinding clouds, while they bore the burdonsome cargoes of their struggling overseers.
>
> "Prepare to embrace your creators in the stygian haunts of hell, barbarian, gasped the first soldier.
>
> "Only after you have kissed the fleeting stead of death, wretch!" returned Grignr.
>
> A sweeping blade of flashing steel riveted from the massive barbarians hide enameled shield as his rippling right arm thrust forth, sending a steel shod blade to the hilt into the soldiers vital organs. The disemboweled mercenary crumpled from his saddle and sank to the clouded sward, sprinkling the parched dust with crimson droplets of escaping life fluid.
>
> The enthused barbarian swilveled about, his shock of fiery red hair tossing robustly in the humid

air currents as he faced the attack of the defeated soldier's fellow in arms.

"Damn you,barbarian" Shrieked the soldier as he observed his comrade in death.

Okay, you can start preefrooding, er, I mean proofreading normally now. Whew! I don't think I could have taken much more of that, and I have this nagging fear that somehow my trusty Apple II GS computer will become infected and henceforth only be able to spew out... Argonese.

The above passage is the opening of one of the true underground classics of the fantasy field, "The Eye of Argon," by an otherwise unknown writer, Jim Theis. Formerly the secret, wicked pleasure of professionals, who gathered furtively to read aloud from Xeroxes of the manuscript until all broke down into hopeless convulsions of laughter, it has surfaced in the fan world and become almost a standard feature at science-fiction conventions. Already a large body of what can only be called legend has grown up about this fabled tale. And so, before things get out of hand, purely in the interests of Truth, I have decided to go public on the whole matter.

I first heard about what might have been "The Eye of Argon" shortly after I entered fandom in the late 1960s. I did not know its title then, only that "some kid once sent in a Barsoomian imitation and pros have been passing it around for laughs ever since." Whether that was even a rumor of the "Eye," or something else entirely, I'll never know, but over the years I continued to encounter vague references to a manuscript so badly written that it was, as Somtow Sucharitkul would put it, "totally awesome," which had, indeed, achieved such dubious immortality.

And then, in the early '80s, George Scithers got ahold of a copy. With typical, wicked humor, he put it in the "Must Read" basket of *Amazing* submissions, and everyone who had read it before me was careful to write only the vaguest comments on the attached card: "Unique," "Archetypal," etc.

And when I read it, I quickly realized that this *was* in all probability the fabled Flying Dutchman manuscript, which had been in circulation for nearly twenty years!

Some while later, at one of George's Last Friday parties, I participated in my first "Eye of Argon" reading, as fans and professionals sat around in a circle, giving dramatic readings of as much of the manuscript as possible before hysterical laughter made further progress impossible. It takes a strong mind to get beyond a few paragraphs. Diane Duane must be an exceptionally iron-willed lady, because, as I remember it, she was unusually good at "Argon"-reading. Either that, or she'd had practice.

It was our little secret then, but in the intervening years the secret has come out. At a Balticon a couple years later I attended my first "Eye of Argon" *contest* (although certainly not the first ever to be held), wherein people were challenged to read the thing aloud *perfectly*. Awards and ribbons were given out. I know there was a Purple Prose Award, and even a Cracked Egg (for the contestant who made the biggest fool of himself). Roger MacBride Allen read under a special challenge. He had agreed to read a whole page of "The Eye of Argon" in front of an audience. If he failed, he would then and there shave off his beard. He brought razor and shaving cream to prove his seriousness.

Roger escaped the event still bearded, but it was a near thing for a while there. He skipped a sentence, and the judges ruled that he had to go on with a further half-page, and, as a further handicap, that people from the audience should *act out* what he was reading. And so we did. I played a door at one point, while Roger loomed over us, striding from chair to chair to get where the action was (since he was obliged to *watch* this silliness without breaking up laughing). This was heroic stuff, worthy of the barbarian hero Grignr himself. And the beard survived.

The rest of the contest was less fun, because it was done by Strict Rules. I was eliminated quickly for skipping an adjective. Hell, I can't read my *own* work word-for-word perfectly, and always have to ad-lib a bit in my readings. The people who got the farthest read... very...slowly...and...carefully...and...not...very...dramatically.

The "Eye" readings at George's were much funnier because they were free-form: minor errors allowed, dramatization much easier, the sole disqualifying factor being the reader breaking down into uncontrollable laughter.

Now isn't it a tad cruel for all of us to be ridiculing some poor would-be scrivner's magnum opus and making a public, ongoing spectacle out of it?

No. Life ain't a bed of roses. You are responsible for what you write.

The facts, as I know them, are these: the Work was discovered by the late Thomas Scortia about 1970 in a fanzine, described to me second- or third-hand as "as badly illustrated and printed as it was written." Another noted SF writer carefully typed the text out, painstakingly preserving its unique spelling, punctuation, and syntax. Xeroxes have been circulating ever since. Over the years, the reputation of "the worst story ever written" has continued to grow, as the pro community, then the fans, like that curiously "swilvelling" barbarian, have become "enthused."

There may well be hundreds of copies in circulation by now. It has allegedly been circulated over the computer nets.

My own copy, made from George Scithers's, is twenty-two pages long, single-spaced, with spaces between the paragraphs. On page 20 there occurs a lacuna in the text, and a little note: PAGE MISSING. This is the classical, or California Manuscript of "The Eye of Argon."

But there seem to be others. At a "bad writing" panel at a Unicon one year someone whipped out a copy and we panelists did impromptu readings. *That* manuscript was slightly different, and did not have the PAGE MISSING notation. Whether some later copier had just closed the gap, or there actually was additional material, I could not tell just then. To date, no scholar has collated the variant texts.

The tale is, obviously enough, sword and sorcery of the classic sort. After sundry swordfights, a tavern scene with its inevitable wenches (and more swordfights), Grignr (pronounced, traditionally, "Grig-nir") is arrested, brought before a sneering, decadent ruler, and tossed into a dungeon. Subsequent adventures involve another wench, more swordfights, and an encounter with the hideous cult of Argon. The hero ends up with an all-devouring blob stuck on his arm. I suppose you could call it a cliffhanger of sorts:

> Grignr began to reel and stagger under the blob, his hcalk white face and faltering muscles attesting to the gigantic loss of blood. Carthena slipped from Grignr in a death-like faint, a morrow chilling scream upon her red rubish lips. In final desperation Grignr grasped the smoldering torch upon the ground and plunged it into the reeking maw of the travestry. A shudder passed through the thing. Grignr felt the blackness closing upon his eyes... He could feels its rip lessing as a hideous gurgling sound erupted from the writhing maw. The jelly like mass began to pubble like a vat of boiling tar...

As things progress, the prose gets even more convoluted and strange. There is a wonderful, very popular passage in which the aforesaid wench kicks an evil priest right in the "urinary gland." Grignr evades peril after peril. On page 14 we're told, "If not for his keep auditory organs and lightning steeled reflexed [sic], Grignr would have been groping through the shadowed hell-pits of the Grim Reaper." The fabled Eye itself is that rarest of jewels, "a dull red emerald" which serves as, you guessed it, the cyclopean eyeball of the dread Idol the aforementioned hideous cult of Argon. An actual description of this enormous statue strains our author's verbal skills to the utmost:

> The fantastic size of the idol in consideration of its being of pure ade [Sic—"ade" is perhaps a sub-

> stance unknown to minerological science, or maybe just a typo for "jade."—D.S.] was enough to cause the senses of any man to stagger and reel, yet thus was not the case for the behemoth. he had paid only casual notice to this incredible fact, while riveting the whole of his attention upon the jewel protruding from the idol's eye socket; its masterfully cut faucets [Yes! Sic! Faucets!!—D.S.] emitting blinding rays of hypnotising beauty. (p. 16)

I repeat, should we really be making fun of this?

I repeat, too, hell yes. I point out the *public* in publication. Were this a *submitted* manuscript, editors might save a few choice passages for their "funny file," but it would never go further, since a certain professional confidence exists between the editor and the author of an unpublished manuscript. However, Mr. Theis apparently *published* this thing in a fanzine, and put his name on it, so it belongs to the Ages now.

Well, not exactly. Legally, it still belongs to Mr. Theis, whoever he is. Many fans have expressed a desire to republish the "Eye" or sell cassettes of the readings, or otherwise exploit it, but they can't, because it is under the protection of Saint Copyright the Inviolate. First, to truly determine the history of this thing, someone will have to find and document the original publication. If the fanzine was in fact uncopyrighted and intended for general circulation rather than as a private letter-substitute (*i.e.*, there's a price on it), that would put the "Eye" in the public domain, but ripping it off would *still* be uncalled for. One does not pirate the work of living authors, copyrighted or not.

Now, I mentioned some of the legends that have grown up around the "Eye." The most persistent rumors are that it is actually the work of a famous pro, written as a parody, or that someone, somewhere has *found* the author and he still thinks the story is good.

As for the first rumor, don't believe it. No literate person could write something so unmitigated—twenty-two single-spaced pages of such prose! My own theory is that it's the work of a kid, about fifteen or so, who knew nothing about life, barbarians, or storytelling other than what he'd gleaned from comic books and sword & sorcery novels. Every single image in the story is utterly derivative and stereotyped. His overwriting, misspellings, and innocence of English usage are too relentless to be faked. I believe he wrote "The Eye of Argon" in all seriousness.

But what else is new? I wrote some stories nearly as bad when I was that age. So did a lot of people who are now widely-published, professional authors. On the plus side, this kid had a certain sense of structure, and an important writerly virtue—he *persisted*. He wrote a story in the neighborhood of 12,000 words. Before you completely dismiss him beyond the pale, stop and think how many people who say they "have wonderful ideas but no time to write them" will ever accomplish as much as Jim Theis did.

Now as for someone locating him, I am not convinced by that report either. It's something many people want to believe, or would like to claim, but there is no proof.

I imagine the real Jim Theis is now in his thirties or early forties. He may well have even turned out to be a writer in some other field. I doubt he has the vaguest inkling of the immortality his juvenile effusion has achieved.

But I wish he would come forward and identify himself, and, good-naturedly, have a laugh along with the rest of us.

Note: an earlier version of this article appeared in the final issue of *Fantasy Review*, which was sadly ironic because, of course, it never got any feedback, from the elusive Mr. Theis or anyone else.

1997 UPDATE

As this book goes to press, the mystery of "The Eye of Argon" remains unsolved. When the second version of this essay appeared in a fanzine, I still got no response. Mr. Theis remains as elusive as ever, and the subject of the equivalent of "urban legends," which tell how so-and-so contacted the author of "Eye," who then disappeared again, etc.

The most tantalizing clue to come into my hands is a xerox of what purports to be the *original pages* of the fanzine in which "Eye" first appeared. All I can tell you is that the illustrations are crude little sketches, and that there are no ads, running heads, or other incidentals which would reveal anything at all about the source. *Is* it the source at all, or perhaps a later, unauthorized republication?

There *do* seem to be textual variants. There is no "page missing" gap, and some of the most beloved malapropisms, such as the gelatinous mass that "pubbles" up Grignr's leg at the end, are not present. Alas, it merely "bubbles."

Quite possibly, then, the text has been "improved" in transmission, as part of what anthropologists would call "the folk process."

In the end, there is only the mystery...

XXIX.

CREATING FRIVOLOUS LITERARY THEORIES

In the January 1983 issue of *F&SF*, Algis Budrys descends from Mt. Sinai to smite the golden calf of academic criticism of science fiction. Most of his blows are well-aimed: at ignoramuses who chase the slightest nuance of thematic drift through pages upon pages of turgid, academic prose, but fail to do basic research, or even read a copyright page. The most spectacular example cited is the fellow who was teaching a course based on the idea that Orson Welles, who was responsible for the 1938 radio version of *The War of the Worlds*, was actually the son of H. G. Wells, and, further, the author of the radio script, which, in our space-time continuum, at least, was actually written by Howard Koch.

Budrys's subtext implies that the professor had the brain of a cucumber,[20] but that only applies if you assume that literary criticism has to adhere to some sort of scientific rigor and be *correct*. If you believe that, you believe literary scholars should read copyright pages and even call up authors and ask them questions about their work. But if you take literary criticism as *art*, as many people I knew during my years as an English graduate student did, then the whole perspective changes. Such investigative digging would merely spoil the fun.

Taken as a creative flight of fancy, the Welles/Wells idea rates about a B. It's pretty good. It explains a lot of things which have puzzled scholars over the decades. Further, we are now able to explain the hitherto inexplicable awfulness of the Orson Welles movie version of *Macbeth* in terms of the direction, casting, set-design, costuming, and much of the acting having been done by Martians. It's frightfully convenient and almost elegant.

What it is, in fact, is a prime specimen of an old, but only newly-recognized art form, the Frivolous Literary Theory (hereafter, F.L.T.).

The theory behind the Theory is simply this: it doesn't have to be true; it merely has to work. No matter of ridiculous, if the notion fits the seeming evidence and can't be disproven, your tenure may be assured. But, more than that, a really good F.L.T., like a good example of any art, should have a certain grandeur about it. It should be capable of giving aesthetic pleasure, and even have the power to change people's lives.

If we overlook such holdovers from antiquity as the old saw that the works of Homer were not written by Homer but by someone else of the same name, one of the earliest examples of the Frivolous Literary Theory is also one of the most super-colossal: the Shakespeare-Bacon controversy of the late nineteenth century. This is sort of the Arthurian Legend of the F.L.T. It inspired great writers to contribute to its growth. No less than Mark Twain wrote, "Is Shakespeare Dead?" (in *What Is Man? and Other Essays*). George Bernard Shaw got endless mileage out of it. Then there were the two prominent female Baconians who went to the site of the alleged Bard's alleged grave, having concealed shovels, picks, and perhaps a pneumatic drill under their copious Victorian skirts, petticoats, underskirts, underpetticoats, and whatever else women wore in those days. The plan was to hide until closing time, then dig the old faker up. Alas, they got scared away before they could even begin the excavation, but, benefiting from the experience, the two of them made handsome livings as shoplifters in hardware stores, filching numerous tools and supplies which they sold to the builders of the Capetown-to-Cairo railway for a tidy profit. They came to a patriotic, if Freudian end during World War I, when they tried to spirit away a top secret German cannon known as "Big Bertha." The German crew had left the safety off.

Certainly one of the joys of being an English major is that you don't need to wrestle with as many inconvenient facts as you would if you were a Chemistry major. For the most part, you can just wing it. I used to write B-plus quality term papers in one sitting, composed at the typewriter like fanzine articles. In fact, some of them later *were* fanzine articles. My favorite was the one in which I composed two "translations" of non-existent Anglo-Saxon elegies, then wrote a lengthy foreword explaining how they came to be found ("in the binding of an Arabic sorcery text once owned by the Elizabethan occultist, Dr. John Dee"), why they differed obviously from Anglo-Saxon poetic norms, where they fit into early medieval literature, and how they happened to contain wholly extraordinary references to King Arthur, Constantine the Great, and other people whose names I had inserted to make the alliteration work. So effectively was this done that when the result was published in *Ash Wing* a while later, many of the readers seemed to think it genuine, and were puzzled that a find of such literary significance would be appearing in a fanzine.

I was well on my way to becoming a practitioner of the Frivolous Literary Theory. My ruin soon followed.

I believe the potential for frivolous literary theorizing is in all of us, particularly in science fiction fans. It's so easy. You saw me doing it just a couple paragraphs ago, perhaps slightly embellishing the scene with the two lady Baconians with the pneumatic drills up their skirts. But just you try to disprove it? Was Shakespeare really in that grave after all? And whatever did happen to Big Bertha?

My friend and colleague, Lee Weinstein (who is best known for a splendid story, "The Box," published in *Whispers*, and for non-frivolous contributions to *Studies in Weird Fiction* and *Nyctalops*), is a natural, veritable gold mine of nonsense. Sometimes, when he is not trying to explain humor on the basis of words that are inherently funny at the syllabic level (a Frivolous Linguistic Theory, and a damned good one), he might attempt something like this:

> "Let's start a discussion on whether or not Edgar Allan Poe was black."
>
> "He wasn't," I say.
>
> "That wasn't much of a discussion."

This is to the more extended F.L.T. what the haiku is to the epic poem. But we can come up with more elaborate ones.

Lee is a fan of William Hope Hodgson, the British horror writer, whose *The House on the Borderland* is something of a classic, but whose *The Night Land* is a veritable monument to unreadability, and might be described as what would have result if E. E. "Doc" Smith had attempted to write a far-future epic in the language of Sir Thomas Malory after a plot by Fenimore Cooper. Hodgson also wrote a volume of vaguely Sherlockian psychic detective stories, *Carnacki the Ghost-Finder*.

My theory is that August Derleth wrote the last Carnacki story and slipped it into the Hodgsonian corpus without anybody noticing.

(I hasten to point out at this point that the modern State of the Art prefers that F.L.T.s be about esoteric subjects. They sound more impressive, as long as *someone* knows what you're talking about, sort of.)

The beauty and terror of the Derlethian Carnacki theory, which I made up off the cuff, is that it fits the following facts, which I have pointed out to Lee:

In 1918 Kaiser Wilhelm II made his biggest impact on fantastic literature by having Hodgson blown up by a German artillery shell, possibly in revenge for the fate of Big Bertha. This rendered Hodgson incapable of refuting the rest of this theory.

The final Carnacki story, "The Hog," appeared for the first time in *Weird Tales* in 1947, the same year it was collected in the definitive edition of *Carnacki the Ghost-Finder* under Derleth's mystery imprint, Mycroft & Moran.

Also in 1947, *Weird Tales* published "The Churchyard Yew," which purported to be a newly-discovered story by J. Sheridan Le Fanu (conveniently died, 1873), but which was later revealed to be a hoax perpetrated by August Derleth.

Just who do you imagine supplied *Weird Tales* with a copy of "The Hog?" Had anyone else ever seen the manuscript?

Further, the story seems to contain something resembling Cthulhu Mythos elements, which would have to post-date Hodgson's lifetime. In 1917 H. P. Lovecraft was little more than an eldritch recluse and a scribbler of bad verse.

Considering that Derleth had faked one "lost" story by a famous dead writer in 1947, why not two?

The strongest objection to all this is that "The Hog" is too good to be the work of August Derleth, who was a second-rater on his best days and seldom that when imitating other people. However, as my teachers kept reminding me politely during my grad-school career, the literary scholar cannot afford to consider quality. (In the sense of being bored because the text you are studying is rubbish.) *Titus Andronicus* is a worthy an object of scholarship as *Hamlet*. So there.

I guess those professors must have impressed some of their thinking on me, because I'm rather proud of this insidious theory of mine. It's like a sonnet that goes together with flawless ease. It may not say anything profound, but it's unquestionably a technically perfect sonnet. This is, again, the very essence of the F.L.T.

And my theory works terrifyingly well. For all its frivolity, Lee Weinstein became seriously intrigued or at least disquieted by the fiendish elegance of it. He wrote to a noted Hodgson expert, who replied that, indeed, there might be some merit in the idea, and referred him to a British expert who had allegedly seen the actual manuscript of "The Hog." The British scholar didn't know what the American was talking about, but suggested that if anyone could straighten this out, it would be the folks at Arkham House.

So, at a World Fantasy Convention, Lee and I confronted the then-editor of Arkham House, James Turner, with the idea. The two of them discussed it seriously for a while. Then Turner asked, "Where did you get this idea, anyway?"

"Oh," I piped up cheerfully. "I made it up."

There was a moment there when Turner, not a man to be trifled with, seemed about to permanently remove the possibility that I would ever one day become an Arkham House author. (Or go on Literary Theorizing, frivolously or otherwise.) I don't think he can see the *fun* in a good Frivolous Theory any more than Algis Budrys could, but Lee calmed him down by reassuring him that he *knew* I had made it up, but it seemed to fit the facts anyway.

And there it dangles, tantalizingly inviting further investigation, nothing disproven. The road to Ph.D. Perdition is paved with many less plausible *serious* literary theories.

If I designed swamps, I suppose I would get as much satisfaction out of a really effective patch of quicksand. Gloating is one of the rewards of the F.L.T.

I cannot, however, claim to be the leading twentieth-century practitioner of this art. The honor goes to my literary idol, Lord Dunsany. In the course of collecting material for a book I edited, *The Ghosts of the Heaviside Layer*, a volume of previously uncollected Dunsany stories and other pieces, I found a really classic specimen of the F.L.T. which His Lordship wrote for *Punch* in the '50s, "The Authorship of *Barrack Room Ballads*."

The alleged purpose of this article is to prove that Swinburne *didn't* write Kipling. First, Dunsany presents the evidence so often touted by the Swinburneans. Kipling was too young, too under-educated and inexperienced to have produced such masterpieces as the *Ballads* and *Plain Tales from the Hills* when he allegedly did, while they could have more plausibly be the work of an older, more established literary figure. It is true that Swinburne supposedly died in 1909, but he had become a virtual recluse for years before that and could well have continued to be one while composing the material which, to maintain his privacy, he ascribed to an obscure young journalist living in India.

To disprove this, Dunsany presents an overwhelming piece of evidence reminiscent of the Shakespearian ciphers so beloved of Baconians: a sonnet by Swinburne, in which the first letters of each line spell out "I DID NOT WRITE IF."

It follows that if Swinburne denied writing Kipling's most famous work, then he must not have written any of it.

However, for all that sonnet reads like Swinburne, and even fits into a sonnet-sequence Swinburne wrote, it does not appear in any edition of the poet's collected works. I know because I checked. It is in fact an extremely clever pastiche by Dunsany.

I am left speechless with admiration at the brilliance of this ploy. Dunsany created a compelling Frivolous Literary Theory, then *pretended* to lay it to rest, utilizing a crucial piece of evidence which a minimal amount of research will show to be a fake. It doesn't matter that he didn't apparently believe a word of what he wrote. These things take on a life of their own, like my Derleth-Hodgson theory. The seed has been planted. Someday, no doubt, academicians will owe their salaries to Lord Dunsany. I wonder how the Kipling-Swinburne Controversy will finally turn out.

I doubt I shall ever be able to do as well, but then Dunsany was a better writer than I am.

However, I can try. Here's my latest. It is like a vast clockwork, the gears furiously spinning, connected to nothing in particular. But they do spin prettily. So shut up and admire the design.

At the risk of seeming *passé*, we return to Edgar Allan Poe, a writer whose high reputation rests on few people having read the vast majority of what he wrote. If you go beyond the handful of famous stories, you'll find dry, synoptic little narratives, appalling attempts at humor, and a general ineptitude which will surprise you. You may come away with the impression that the few good stories are so different *that they seem the work of another writer*.

My theory is that they were written by M. G. Lewis.

Matthew Gregory Lewis (born 1775) was an Englishman, the author of *The Monk*, one of the most readable of the Gothic novels. After a brief burst of literary notoriety, he died in 1818 while on a ship in the Caribbean. His funeral had a suitably eldritch touch. The coffin did not sink. The wind caught the shroud like a sail, and off he went, out of sight over the horizon.

So much for history. Now we get creative. My theory is that in the course of a long and boring voyage, Lewis had a titanic outburst of inspiration and penned over a dozen first-rate tales and a dozen more great poems. But, when he knew his end was near, he was beset by a fit of niggardliness and insisted on taking the fruits of his labors with him. His coffin was lined with manuscripts. About twenty years later it washed up on the shore of Virginia, where it was discovered by an unhappy, unsuccessful, and rather morbid young man—you guessed it.

It has been noted that most of Poe's best tales have European settings and subject matter and hearken back to the Gothics more than they resemble anything in the American literature of the time.

Nevertheless, Poe was able to pass them off as how own work. He used them sparingly, interspersing his own, inferior writings with such masterpieces as "The Pit and the Pendulum," "The Masque of the Red Death," "The Black Cat," and all the rest. He gained some acclaim. He achieved modest financial success. But he kept ruining himself with his drinking. The drinking, of course, was brought on by the haunting realization that he could never, ever produce such high quality material himself, and on the day the found-manuscript supply ran out, he would be finished.

So, once upon a midnight dreary, as he pondered weak and weary over his dimming prospects, in from night's Plutonian shore flew a large black bird which had escaped from an Italian organ-grinder who couldn't afford a monkey.

"Oh when will I be able to equal such wonderful tales?" Poe moaned rhetorically, in despair. "When shall my pen ever put to paper something *worthy* of myself?"

Quoth the Raven, "Nevermore."

Go ahead. Try to disprove it.

NOTES

INTRODUCTION

[1]You can check the same way Galileo may well have. Study Venus through a small telescope. It has phases. The outer planets you can easily see, Mars, Jupiter, and Saturn do not. That means that we are moving around the Sun, between Venus and Mars. We can get around behind Venus, and see its night-side, but we can never get behind the outer planets, and thus only see their full, sunward sides.

CHAPTER XII

[2]*Selected Letters*, Volume III, p. 193.
[3]*Ibid.*, p. 192.
[4]*Selected Letters*, Volume V, p. 201.
[5]*Selected Letters*, Volume III, p. 136.
[6]*Ibid.*, p. 197.

CHAPTER XIV

[7]M. R. James, "Some Remarks on Ghost Stories." *M. R. James—Book of the Supernatural*, ed. by Peter Haining. London: W. Foulsham & Co., Ltd. 1979, p. 20.
[8]*Ibid.*, p. 27.
[9]M. R. James, "Introduction" to *Ghosts and Marvels*, ed. by Vere Henry Collins. Oxford: Oxford University Press, 1924, p. xii.
[10]"Some Remarks," p. 23-24.
[11]M. R. James, "Preface" to *More Ghost Stories of an Antiquary*. London: Edward Arnold, 1911, p. v.
[12]*Ibid.*, p. vi.
[13]M. R. James, "Some Remarks," p. 28.
[14]H. P. Lovecraft, *Supernatural Horror in Literature*. *Dagon and Other Macabre Tales*. Sauk City, WI: Arkham House, corrected 5th printing, 1987, p. 433.
[15]Included in *You'll Need a Night Light*, ed. by Christine Campbell Thompson. London: Selwyn & Blount, 1927. Lovecraft's next appearance in the series, with "The Rats in the Walls" and the ghost-written "The Curse of Yig," didn't occur until the 1931 volume, *Switch on the Light*.
[16]H. P. Lovecraft, "Notes on the Writing of Weird Fiction," in *Marginalia*. Sauk City, WI: Arkham House, 1944, p. 139.
[17]*Ibid.*, p. 139.
[18]As quoted in an interview, "Clive Barker: Spokesman for the Strange," by Stephen Haff. *Other Dimensions* #1 (Summer, 1993): 3.

CHAPTER XIX

19*Kipling's Science Fiction*, edited by John Brunner. New York: Tor Books, 1992.

CHAPTER XXIX

20One need not worry about hurt feelings from remarks like this, keeping in mind Somtow Sucharitkul's astute observation that every academic likes to hear academics insulted because he knows in his heart of hearts that he isn't one.

SELECTED BIBLIOGRAPHY

André-Drussi, Michael. *Lexicon Urthus*. San Francisco: Sirius Fiction, 1994, 280 p.

Balderston, John L. *Berkeley Square: A Play in Three Acts*. New York: Macmillan, 1929.

Dick, Philip K. *The Divine Invasion*. New York: Vintage Books, 1991, 238 p.

Dick, Philip K. *The Transmigration of Timothy Archer*. New York: Vintage Books, 1991, 255 p.

Dick, Philip K. *VALIS*. New York: Vintage Books, 1991, 241 p.

Haggard, H. Rider. *She: A History of Adventure*. London: Longmans, Green, 1887.

Joshi, S. T. *An Index to the Selected Letters of H. P. Lovecraft*. West Warwick, RI: Necronomicon Press, 1980.

Kipling, Rudyard. *Kipling's Science Fiction*, presented by John Brunner. New York: Tor Books, 1992, 178 p.

Le Guin, Ursula K. *A Fisherman of the Inland Sea*. New York: Harper Prism, 1994, 191 p.

Lovecraft, H. P. *Dagon and Other Macabre Tales*. Sauk City, WI: Arkham House (corrected 5th printing), 1987.

____. *Selected Letters II*. Sauk City, WI: Arkham House, 1968.

____. *Selected Letters IV*. Sauk City, WI: Arkham House, 1976.

Morris, Kenneth. *The Dragon Path: Collected Stories of Kenneth Morris*, edited by Douglas A. Anderson. New York: Tor Books, 1995, 382 p.

Skal, David J. *Hollywood Gothic: The Tangled Web of* Dracula *from Novel to Stage to Screen*. New York: W. W. Norton Co., 1990.

Stoker, Bram. *Dracula*. London: Constable, 1897. Limited Editions Club/The Heritage Press, 1965. Numerous other editions.

Turner, James, ed. *Cthulhu 2000*. Sauk City, WI: Arkham House, 1995, 413 p.

Weinbaum, Stanley G. *The Black Flame*. San Francisco: Tachyon Publications, 1995, 202 p.

Books by Richard Middleton

These five volumes were published by T. Fisher Unwin in Britain and Mitchell Kennerley in the United States:

The Ghost Ship and Other Stories (1912).
Poems and Songs, First Series (1912).
Poems and Songs, Second Series (1912).
The Day Before Yesterday (1912).
Monologues (1913).

The District Visitor. The Norman, Remington Co., 1924.
Richard Middleton's Letters to Henry Savage. The Mandrake Press, 1929.
The Pantomime Man. Rich and Cowan, 1933.

Works About Richard Middleton

Stephen Wayne Foster. "A Poet's Death: Richard Middleton," in *The Romanticist* No. 4-5 (1982).
Henry Savage. *Richard Middleton: The Man and His Work.* Cecil Palmer, 1922.
Vincent Starrett. "Two Suicides," in *Buried Caesars.* New York: Covici-McGee Co., 1923.

Media Works

Berkeley Square. A film directed by Frank Lloyd from the play by John Balderston. Starring Leslie Howard, Heather Angel, Alan Mowbray, and Irene Browne. Twentieth Century-Fox, 1933. 87 minutes.

ACKNOWLEDGMENTS

Some of the material in this book originally appeared as follows:

"Introduction." Original to this book.
"The Necessity of Skepticism" in *Science Fiction Review*, #2 and 3 (Summer and Autumn 1990). Copyright 1990 by SFR Publications.
"The Cost of Credulity" in somewhat different form as "The Question of Belief," as part of a column in *Aboriginal SF* (Spring 1994), Copyright 1994 by Aboriginal Science Fiction. This version appears here for the first time.
"The Layercake of History" in *Expanse* #1 (1993). Copyright 1993 by Steven E. Fick.
"My Career as a Hack Writer" in *Science Fiction Review* #4 (Summer 1991). Copyright 1991 by SFR Publications.
"The Lands That Clearly Pertain to Faery." Original to this book.
"The Return of the Factory System" in *Science Fiction Review* #8 (March 1992). Copyright 1992 by SFR Publications.
"Why Horror Fiction?" in *Marion Zimmer Bradley's Fantasy Magazine* #9 (Summer 1990). Copyright 1990 by Marion Zimmer Bradley Ltd.
"Intimate Horror" in *Necrofile* #10 (Fall 1993). Copyright 1993 by Necronomicon Press.
"Horror Beyond New Jersey" in *Necrofile* #18 (Fall 1995). Copyright 1995 by Necronomicon Press.
"The Limits of Craziness" in *Science Fiction Review* #5 (December 1991). Copyright 1991 by SFR Publications.
"Still Eldritch After All These Years" in *Amazing Stories* (March 1987). Copyright 1987 by TSR, Inc.
"About 'The Whisperer in Darkness'" in *Lovecraft Studies* #32 (Spring 1995). Copyright 1995 by Necronomicon Press.
"H. P. Lovecraft's Favorite Movie" in *Lovecraft Studies* #19/20 (Fall 1989). Copyright 1989 by Necronomicon Press.
"M. R. James and H. P. Lovecraft: The Ghostly and the Cosmic" in *Studies in Weird Fiction* #15 (Summer 1994). Copyright 1994 by Necronomicon Press.
"Richard Middleton: Beauty, Sadness, and Terror" in *Twilight Zone Magazine* (April 1986). Copyright 1986 by TZ Publications.
"How Much of Dunsany is Worth Reading?" in *Studies in Weird Fiction* #10 (Fall 1991). Copyright 1991 by Necronomicon Press.
"Count Dracula and His Adapters" in *Other Dimensions* #1 (1993). Copyright 1993 by Necronomicon Press.
"Philip K. Dick: Absurdist, Visionary" in *The Boston Phoenix* (1991). Copyright 1991 by The Boston Phoenix.
"*Kipling's Science Fiction*" in *Science Fiction Eye* #12 (Summer 1993). Copyright 1993 by Science Fiction Eye.
"*The Black Flame* by Stanley G. Weinbaum" in *The New York Review of SF* #91 (March 1996). Copyright 1996 by Dragon Press.

"On Brian Aldiss's *Barefoot in the Head*" in *Readercon 6 Souvenir Book* (1993). Copyright 1993 by Darrell Schweitzer.

"*A Fisherman of the Inland Sea* by Ursula K. Le Guin" in *The New York Review of Science Fiction* #77 (January 1995). Copyright 1995 by Dragon Press.

"*Lexicon Urthus* by Michael André-Drussi" in *The New York Review of SF* #87 (November 1995). Copyright 1995 by Dragon Press.

"Prospero's Dracula" in somewhat different form in *Pirate Writings* #7 (Summer 1995). Copyright 1995 by Pirate Writings Publishing.

"*Cthulhu 2000*, edited by James Turner" in *The New York Review of Science Fiction* #98 (October 1996). Copyright 1996 by Dragon Press.

"*The Dragon Path: Collected Stories of Kenneth Morris*" in *The New York Review of SF* #90 (February 1996). Copyright 1996 by Dragon Press.

"An Interview with Edgar Allan Poe" in *Crypt of Cthulhu* #84 (Lammas 1993). Copyright 1993 by Necronomicon Press.

"One Fine Day in the Stygian Haunts of Hell: Being, The Lore and Legend of the Fabled 'Eye of Argon'" in *Fantasy Review* #103 (July/August 1987). Copyright 1987 by Meckler Publishing Co.

"Creating Frivolous Literary Theories" in *Science Fiction Review* #55 (Summer 1985). Copyright 1985 by Richard E. Geis.

INDEX

Breinigsville, PA USA
13 December 2010
251324BV00001B/8/A

9 781880 448601